T0072450

"*A Big Life* is a must-read for any Madison Avenue executive or executive-wannabe. And it's a must-read for those curious about how advertising's postwar Golden Age ultimately decomposed."

—Bruce Horovitz, *USA Today*

"Anyone who doubts that advertising used to be a sexy, exhilarating business need only crack open Mary Wells Lawrence's memoir."

—*Forbes*

"[Lawrence's] unguarded emotions . . . give her autobiography the sort of energy and passion few books about business ever achieve."

—*Entertainment Weekly,* "Editor's Choice"

"[Lawrence] chronicles her career and her advertising so vividly, she's inspiring."

—Carlo Wolff, *The Boston Globe*

"Mary Wells in the late 60's . . . the stuff of dreams! Her idea of advertising was to 'create miracles'—and that's exactly what she did. . . . You fall for her energy, her single-minded drive, her ever-expanding appetite for life."

—Adam Begley, *The New York Observer*

"From jaunty opening words . . . we know we're in the presence of a smart, driven woman who rode the American zeitgeist with the zest of a ski jumper coasting on Alpine air."

—John Powers, *Vogue*

"[T]he first great personal history of the ad world's golden years . . . tells the author's own, riveting story: how an only child from a modest family in Poland, Ohio, shattered every glass ceiling and became a Madison Avenue legend."

—James Reginato, *W*

A Big Life
in Advertising

Mary Wells Lawrence

A TOUCHSTONE BOOK
Published by Simon & Schuster
New York   London   Toronto   Sydney   Singapore

Touchstone
Rockefeller Center
1230 Avenue of the Americas
New York, NY 10020

First Touchstone Edition 2003
Published by arrangement with Alfred A. Knopf,
a division of Random House, Inc.

TOUCHSTONE and colophon are registered trademarks
of Simon & Schuster, Inc.

For information regarding special discounts for bulk purchases, please contact
Simon & Schuster Special Sales at 1-800-456-6798
or business@simonandschuster.com

The Library of Congress has cataloged the Alfred A. Knopf edition as follows:
Lawrence, Mary Wells.
A big life in advertising / Mary Wells Lawrence.
p.   cm.
Includes index.
1. Lawrence, Mary Wells.   2. Advertising executives—United States—
Biography.   3. Women in advertising—United States—Biography.
4. Businesswomen—United States—Biography.   I. Title.
HF5810.L34 A3 2002
659.1'092—dc21
[B]   2001050402

Manufactured in the United States of America
1   3   5   7   9   10   8   6   4   2
ISBN 0-7432-4586-5

Grateful acknowledgment is made to Harcourt, Inc., and Faber and Faber Ltd. for
permission to reprint excerpts from "Burnt Norton" from *Four Quartets* by
T. S. Eliot. Copyright © 1942 by T. S. Eliot and renewed 1970 by
Esme Valerie Eliot. Rights outside the United States in *Four Quartets* from
Collected Poems, 1909–1962, administered by Faber and Faber Ltd., London.
Reprinted by permission of Harcourt, Inc., and Faber and Faber Ltd.

To Harding

ACKNOWLEDGMENTS

A heartfelt thank-you to my family, to Charlie and Stan and Moss/Dragoti Advertising, Kathie Durham and Catherine Lebow, Ken Olshan, Fred Jacobs, Philip Caldwell, Kate Ford, Ed and Sandy Acker, Roy and Billy Chapin, Bill Pickett, Ron Moore, Steve and Nancy Donovan, Linda Wachner, Joe Cullman and Jimmy Morgan, Phyllis Robinson and Ted Voss, Noel and Frank Duffy, Bill McGivney, Harold Singer, Paul Schulman, Andre van Stom, Eileen McKenna, Steve Karmen, Phyllis Wagner, Tom King, Jere Cox, Burt Manning, Bob Pliskin, Jo Foxworth, Walter Hayes, Bill Connell, Josh Levine, John Dyson, Paul Margulies, Lew Wechsler, Nancy Vaughan, Bill Luceno, Vic Olesen, Dick Hopple, Bert Neufeld, Murray Jacobs, Howie Cohen, Chuck Damon, Jane Maas, Murray Hysen and Dr. Larry LeShan. Thanks for the memories, the e-mails, the faxes, the telephone calls, the tapes and videos, the files and pictures and old magazines that conjured up the wonderful time we shared to help me write about it.

Thank you, Vicky Wilson at Knopf and Joni Evans at William Morris, for your caring, imaginative and profoundly intelligent collaboration. It has been one of the great treats of my life.

A Big Life in Advertising

I was working at McCann Erickson for the money, for little black dance dresses that showed off my Norwegian legs, for my baby daughters' smocked dresses from Saks and for an apartment larger than I could afford—but then I met Bill Bernbach and he made a serious woman out of me. In the fifties in New York if you talked about "Bill" you meant Bill Bernbach. He was the talk of the town because he was creating a revolution in the advertising business, which was a glamorous business at the time. He challenged all the big advertising agencies that had become important since World War II, saying they had killed advertising, ads had become dishonest, boring, insulting, even insane. Worse, they didn't sell anything to anybody. The big agencies defended themselves; they said they made advertising scientifically, with sophisticated research. But Bill said either they were liars or they were stupid; their pitiful research reduced advertising to, basically, one poor tired ad that was repeated over and over again. When he really got going he would say things like, "The big agencies are turning their creative people into mimeograph machines!" and all the frustrated creative people in town would stamp their feet and cheer, "Yea, Bill!"

The advertising business, like America itself after the war, had built up the fiction of safety with its hierarchies and armylike respect for the boss. In the big agencies the boss was a group of executives called the Creative Review Board. Their research told them that America hungered for happiness and peace, so they produced advertising that was happy and peaceful. Children were always clean and smiling. Dogs were clean and smiling. Firemen, police, farmers and coal miners were clean and smiling. Everybody waved to each other in the ads. Beautiful women stretched out on the roofs of cars in their gowns and jewels and furs to make the cars look prettier. Bottles of whiskey wore crowns and stood proudly on red velvet columns pretending they were the Duke of Windsor. Bill was right; advertising was the land of the insane. There was never any direct personal communication, never any tension or drama or interesting information in them, but those ads, based on spurious research, had been touted so long as scientific that Bill was seditious criticizing them.

He had galloped out of the Grey agency to set advertising free with a little gold mine of people: Ned Doyle, Mac Dane, Bob Gage and Phyllis Robinson. They opened an agency, Doyle Dane Bernbach, and set about changing the way advertising looked, what it said, how it sounded; they even felt free to change the product or the company that made the product if that was what it took to have a success. Bill gave lectures to the press. Radiating moral gravity, he would tell them that the big agencies had it all wrong: "Advertising is not a science, it is persuasion, and persuasion is an *art,* it is intuition that leads to discovery, to inspiration, it is the *artist* who is capable of making the consumer feel desire."

He utterly bewildered the big agencies. They asked each other, "Why is this guy making a ruckus and disturbing the peace? Who *is* this Bill Bernbach?" Pretty soon everybody knew who Bill was. It was as if he had cordoned off Madison Avenue and set up a stage where he called for advertising to be honest and candid, smarter and more interesting. He demanded bolder language, humor, wit and stylish design. He said, "All of us who professionally use the mass media are the shapers of society. We can vulgarize society or we can help lift it to a higher level." When Doyle Dane Bernbach's first ads began to appear, they were as effective as Bill promised they would be, and after that, in the advertising business, there was no turning back and Bill was the star.

Phyllis Robinson was his copy chief and when I went to my interview for a job with her I was not optimistic. I knew how the work I had done at the large, traditional McCann Erickson agency would look to Doyle Dane Bernbach. I was dying to work there, partly because everybody was dying to work there, it was the hot spot, the place to be, but also, although my mind was still a young and silly place, because I thought Bill's revolution was the most important event of my life. If he had been John the Baptist I could not have been more enraptured. I spent days creating pretend ads to suggest that I was more talented than what my portfolio of real samples had to show. I arrived much too early. When Phyllis finally came out to the waiting room to collect me I had become frail, I could have fallen to my knees. She, on the other hand, was like the lead angel in an opera, tall, handsome, strong, brimming with energy and humor and purpose, an honest-to-goodness adult, she swept me into her office and turned her intelligence on me like a beam from outer space. Seeing how overimpressed I was, she eased down into the role of a friend and did all she could to help me with the interview. "Oh, this is interesting," she said, "yes, mmmm, good, tell me all about this," and I melted into adoration.

From this moment on

A week later she hired me. She said she persuaded Bill to go along by showing him a campaign I had created for International Silver for its silverplate flatware, knives, forks and spoons. They had inserted a bit of sterling at the places where flatware gets the most wear but they never told anybody about it. I decided to call that reinforced silverplate DeepSilver and persuaded a lot of brides that it was as good as sterling and a lot better than ordinary silverplate. Phyllis liked my thinking. Bill wasn't sure but he said yes. When I met him he took my hand, looked soulfully into my eyes and baptized me, saying, "McCann Erickson is a terrible agency so you are a big gamble from my point of view but Phyllis sees something in you." I have never forgotten those exact words of his because it took me a few years to get over them, he was full of himself at the time and I wasn't, yet. Then he lit up as though he had thought of a great practical joke to play on me and said, "Now you have to meet Ned Doyle, he handles the Max Factor account and you will be working on it with him, let's see what he thinks of you!" and he led me next door to the man who was the head of account services.

Ned Doyle, as Irish as he could be, watched me cross his office without expression, but then I saw him think "Huzzah!" and I knew he was going to be a fan. He was a slender, older man with white-and-grey hair, cool eyes and a carved face. He was wildly flirtatious but in that safe, careful, old-fashioned way, and he liked everything about me except my nickname. "Where did you get the name Bunny? You can't work at Doyle Dane Bernbach with a name like Bunny. Get rid of it before you come here. Mary is a good name, I like Mary, from now on you're Mary." For a couple of hours we bantered, he wanted to see if I was tough enough to be any fun, and I learned a lot about the agency right away. Ned loved Bill, he said. Bill would not admit he loved— and needed—Ned. Bill was the genius but Ned was the businessman and Ned was also the gladiator in any fight for Bill's ideas.

Taken in pieces Bill Bernbach wasn't much. He was shorter than he sounded, he had a wary half-smile, cow's-milk eyes, pale skin, soft shoulders, he seemed to be boneless, but he communicated such a powerful inner presence he mowed everybody around him down and out of sight. In his peak years many people were afraid of him. I was; I didn't want to get too close. There was something volcanic, something unsettling going on; it was a little like being in the company of Mao or Che or the young Fidel. Many of us had hiding places at the agency where we could avoid him. One of his top talents, who worked for me later in my own agency, said he used to go to work at dawn to get his work done before Bill arrived in the morning and would be long gone before Bill put a foot into the place. It is true that even some of the surest men who were close to Bill drank more than they should have.

By the time I arrived the gods were firmly ensconced, the pantheon was established, the rituals, the sacred writings were already beloved. The Dei Majores were the originals, Bill, Ned, Mac, Phyllis and Bob Gage; they spoke a secret language. The Dei Minores were Helmut Krone and Julian Koenig, who were becoming famous for their Volkswagen advertising. There were talented others, the spirits and the elves, but the gods were the gods, everyone in the industry knew who was who.

Bill wrote few ads himself, but he had the great ideas and he had a sensibility that was rare in business in the fifties. Consider Avis, a car-rental company that barely existed before Bill got hold of it. Its stores were usually in places you wouldn't take your mother. There was really only Hertz at the time. But Bill told the world that Avis was Number Two, making a mountain out of a molehill to say the least. He also told the world that because Avis was Number Two, it tried harder. Almost overnight Avis became perceived as a threat to Hertz—an awesome act of magic—and people began going to Avis because Avis tried harder than Hertz.

I once attended a meeting with some Avis dealers. Nobody was more surprised than they were to discover they were Number Two and trying harder than Hertz. Some of them flew into a rage because all the new customers they got from the new advertising were so *expectant,* they would march into Avis offices with the dirty ashtrays they found in their cars, dump the ashes on the managers' desks and demand their money back. It was nip-and-tuck for a while whether the dealers would go along with the new image and the expectations. "I couldn't even get a job at Hertz," one of them told me. "Now you people tell me I am better than Hertz? That I try harder than Hertz? Are you crazy?" But in the end they did go along, and the wonders never ceased.

When Bill looked at a product he saw it in its most successful metamorphosis. He saw the advantage in a disadvantage and could turn things around. When Volkswagen first appeared in the United States nobody would buy it. It was small. It was ugly. It was seen as a German car, a Nazi car, too soon after the war. Bill looked at the car and saw an opportunity to break all the rules in the automobile book. In the fifties God lived in Detroit and every advertisement for an automobile had His blessing; you could tell that by the religiosity, the weight of the advertising. America took its cars seriously, cars *mattered,* they weren't equipment, they weren't toys. Your choice of car revealed everything about you, your position in society, your dreams for the future, your secret self, even your sexual longings, and success meant, literally, being able to trade in your car for a new model every year, a concept that was kept humming by the Detroit automakers.

One of the Volkswagen ads put down that idea by saying, "The '51, '52, '53, '54, '55, '56, '57, '58, '59, '60, '61 Volkswagen," along with a simple picture of the unchanged, original Volkswagen. From the first ad Volkswagen advertising was as entertaining as it was respectful of the reader. It communicated in the simplest way; there was just the Volkswagen itself and a plain, sans serif headline and a few easy-to-read blocks of inviting, informative copy. The headlines were self-deprecating, irreverent, funny, even a pun. But they were smart, each was memorable. One of the early ones said "Think Small" at a time when Detroit cars were big and getting bigger. My favorite ad confessed to an occasional mistake. "Lemon," the headline said. The story goes that Bill sold the ad to a German executive who did not want to admit he did not understand English very well. He didn't get the double meaning of the word "lemon." By the time it was explained to him it was too late to object; the ad was winning every award in advertising.

Detroit didn't understand those saucy headlines, those simple ads in the beginning. But it understood the effect they had. Automobile buyers loved the advertising, and in short order the beetle became the beloved icon for the intelligent man's car. Being small was seen as an advantage, modern, young, when that was the age to be. The advertising was contagious, it took off like a viral epidemic, everybody wanted to create ads like Volkswagen ads.

I was not Bill's kind of writer; I wasn't good at clever puns, I couldn't be cute and cool at the same time. My strong suit, theatricalizing life with dreams, irritated him. He was forever lecturing me about my moral responsibilities in advertising. When I tried to suggest that his way of turning disadvantage into advantage, as he did with Avis and Volkswagen, was just a different way of creating dreams, he would go crazy and I would go hide. I was lucky to work on accounts for women because when his ideas for Max Factor cosmetics didn't fly he gave up and decided that women had different psyches than men and he stayed out of most of my ads. After a while I got my arms around a lot of the agency's advertising for women because Phyllis was so engaged in the Polaroid account. The client was Dr. Edwin Land, the brilliant inventor of the instant camera, the sort of man who chooses work over life and has to be dragged from his laboratory to sleep nights or to have Christmas dinner with his family. He operated to a different beat than most clients. The first time he met with the agency he said, "My rule is that first you must have inspiration, then you experiment with it, but if you succeed you must never imitate yourself. It is OK to experiment, OK to fail, nobody has a 1000 batting average, but when you do succeed, *move on,* do not waste a second of your life imitating your own successes!"

There was an imaginative, adventurous man who translated ordinary life to Dr. Land and Dr. Land to ordinary life, Ted Voss, and he adored Bill and Bob Gage and Phyllis, so working in that atmosphere with no fear of failure was duck soup for them. To explain the camera when it first appeared and no one knew what a Polaroid camera was or did, Bill and Bob created a black-and-white bleed spread for *Life* magazine— one mammoth two-page picture that presented the camera with the film in the back and the picture coming out. That ad didn't need a word. Polaroid advertising was never about words. It was about images that keep you enthralled with the miracle of a camera that could develop a picture *instantly.* In the early days Phyllis and Bob produced live commercials for the *Today* show and the *Tonight!* show. Steve Allen was their darling. He was a master ad-libber, he loved to ham it up with the camera, and one night his Polaroid went berserk and kept gushing out yards and yards of film. Steve kept talking as if everything was normal while the film fell all over his lap and then all over his feet. He kept a perfectly straight face but let his eyes go wild and the audience went crazy with that silly joy that funny accidents give you. It was terrific theatre; the audience gave Steve and his camera a standing ovation and the following day sales of the camera doubled. Booboos often sell better than perfection, perhaps because they humanize products and make people care about them.

When the high-tech SX-70 Polaroid was ready for introduction, Phyllis says, she wrote the words describing the marvels of the camera and then she and Bob looked at each other and said, "Who can say these words without sounding like a horse's ass?" They decided Richard Burton or Laurence Olivier could say them. As I recall, Richard Burton was out because his dogs had once messed up the carpeting in Dr. Land's house, so Laurence Olivier was the choice. Luckily, he needed money at the time and agreed to make the commercials, and they were a great success. They became classics and he used to say, "After all the Shakespeare I've done, it will be Richardson [Ralph] who will be remembered for his Shakespeare, I'll be remembered for my Polaroid commercials." After those Olivier commercials appeared, actors who had thought it was beneath them to appear in commercials felt free to work in them.

In that blooming season at Doyle Dane Bernbach nobody cared about the French tourist account. Nobody at the agency wanted to waste precious time in France when the thrills were in the New York office. So I grabbed the account. I wanted to go to France, to India, to Istanbul, to the moon. I am and have always been an experience collector. In the fifties, before 747s and mass travel, Americans traveling to France went only to Paris. The French tourist bureau was eager to lure them into the countryside so they would spend more of their money in France instead of Italy or England. We were told to head for the countryside to see what it had to offer. One of my traveling companions from the agency, Bill Taubman, was a superb art director but he was one of those people who are terrified to leave home. He spent hours on the telephone in towns he couldn't pronounce moaning and groaning to his wife. He became paranoid, certain we were giving him the worst room in every hotel until, in desperation, we would all line up at the hotel entrances and allow him to select his rooms first, then we would stash our stuff. The administrator of French tourism would shake his head; finally he gave up traveling with us.

But our photographer was savvy. Elliott Erwitt, a Magnum photographer, is one of the worldly supershooters who win prizes for pictures taken in impossible situations, hanging out of planes or running from terrorists. He has laughing eyes and even laughing hair, so much joie de vivre that it shows up in his most serious photographs. He sees little smiles in life that most people miss. In his camera dogs grin and cats giggle and little old ladies flirt slyly with young, muscled hunks. He shrugged off the discomfort of our tours, but behind his easy manner he was always at attention, and watching him, I learned how to work in uncertain circumstances. Elliott is the one who took the signature photograph of the Frenchman and his son, both in berets, bicycling down a lane of platane trees, the boy clutching a big baguette, for our first ad. That picture is still France's symbol of its countryside.

Elliott Erwitt's iconic photograph of a French father and son was shot for the introductory ad of our campaign for the French tourist bureau.

We toured in a big dusty black car up and down France's hills and dales, sampling the very best the country had to offer tourists. When Bill Bernbach heard about those trips and that I was planning one to the caves of Dordogne, where I had been invited to photograph the prehistoric Cro-Magnon rock paintings in the precious caves of Lascaux before they were closed to the public, his eyes turned to crystal with envy. He decided that he and his wife, Evelyn, would make the trip with us to see the caves. I smelled disaster. My French tourist bureau advertising group had a necessary bohemian side that cheerfully braved some of the worst hotels and plumbing; it took a while after the war for Europe to spruce up its countryside hotels with American bathrooms. I didn't know what the Bernbachs expected in the way of creature comforts, but I was certain it was more than we experienced in the small villages of France.

Keeping Bill Taubman happy roughing it was enough for me. So I tried to warn Bill and Evelyn that the trip would have its lean and mean moments. The blacker I painted the facilities, the surer they got that I was trying to keep the jewels of France for myself and that they must certainly go.

Our group left Paris in high spirits. We got through the Loire Valley and its chateaus smoothly, and with the Bernbachs around even Bill Taubman tried to be debonair. The paintings of Lascaux were so impressive I thought we were home free; in fact, in the Hall of Bulls Bill and Evelyn were so blissful I toyed with the idea I might get a raise out of the trip. But as we left Lascaux, Bill suggested that we change our plans and go straight to Cannes. He said he'd had enough country plumbing and antique mattresses. We were scheduled to photograph Le Puy-en-Velay, a spectacular sight. I longed to see it, so I lied and said the French tourist administrator insisted that we shoot Le Puy.

The trouble was that there were no good cafés and no real hotels in Le Puy then. The town did have a whorehouse, which wasn't all that bad, so we bribed the owner to rent us all the rooms, a fact we swore on blood oath to keep a secret from the Bernbachs and Bill Taubman. Evelyn Bernbach was a highly intelligent woman, but I had a hunch she would not be happy sleeping in a whore's bed.

We had dinner in a café that served only the unmentionable parts of a cow. I was so busy with Bill Taubman, who could not look at his plate—"What is it? Oh no. I can't eat *that*"—that I lost track of Bill Bernbach. In the morning he appeared looking wan and begged us to leave right away to find a clean service station. We made quick work of photographing the marvels of Le Puy. They, too, are volcanic. It is one of those places you have to see to believe, cradled by three towering peaks, each with a church or a chapel or a statue on top. We didn't dawdle, and soon Bill and Evelyn took a train for Paris. It was another week before I returned to Paris and saw Bill again. I met him by chance in front of the Ritz Hotel. He stared at me as if he'd seen a viper and began to tremble with fury. It seemed he had been brooding about Le Puy. He had a fit, he yelled "You are a very willful woman!" and stamped away.

All or nothing at all

Even today I can feel the chill that slipped up my legs and down my back as I watched him disappear. "My God," I thought, my heart was racing, "I've lost my job." As if I was watching a movie, I saw how young I was. Even though I had daughters I was still fundamentally somebody else's daughter, I wasn't an adult by a long shot, and I was living like a free spirit, everything was a game. I thought writing copy was fun and a lovely way to make a living and I was proud to be at Doyle Dane Bernbach but I wasn't a serious person. I'd never worshipped a god before or stretched to meet one's standards. I had not understood how very important Bill Bernbach and his agency were to me. I stood there staring into the years ahead of me realizing that what I was gambling was not just a job or a career but my life. I had the first inkling, then, of just how big or how small my life could be.

I was getting light-headed so when I finally lost any sight of Bill I went into the Ritz and sat in one of those big chairs in the long hall off the lobby. From some point so deep inside that I have no idea where came the word "focus." I said it to myself, "focus," and I thought about it for a long time. I thought about focusing my energy and my intelligence and my desire on goals and I left the Ritz clutching that word, that idea. It took a while but I did learn how to focus, how to bring everything that mattered to bear on whatever I wanted to accomplish and eliminate everything else. My ability to focus may have finally become my strongest suit. People have been known to say to me, "Please, don't focus on me, Mary, focus on somebody else," in recognition of the power coming from a focused person. I tell every young career person who will listen, "Learn to focus, life will be a lot easier."

He didn't fire me and nothing was ever said again about Le Puy. Only the gorgeous memories of Lascaux came up from time to time. But my relationship with Bill Bernbach changed because I focused on it. About a year later I was made an associate copy chief and vice-president in charge of a group of writers and, to celebrate, I had a Caribbean orange vinyl floor installed in my office. As the pinnacle of advertising talent Doyle Dane Bernbach enjoyed looking plain. The agency had the right values, it didn't need decorating, that was the idea. Mac Dane kept a tight fist around expenses and managed to persuade us that our cheap rented furniture created an atmosphere of sublime confidence. But I was tired of spending so many hours every day in an ugly office, so I bought my own provincial desk, a big palm tree, matchstick blinds and a pair of exotic rattan chairs for clients. My orange floor was a scandal and everyone found excuses to visit it, but Bill just smiled and trooped new clients around to see it, reciprocating my new, heartfelt devotion. He began introducing me as "the agency's dream merchant."

One of my clients needed a big dream. General Mills had found a way to dehydrate ingredients so that with a little water, they would fluff up into delicious Betty Crocker casserole dinners. They were tasty, but when you looked into the boxes the dry ingredients looked like dust and wood shavings, it was hard to imagine eating them. I was thrilled with them, though, because Betty Crocker casserole dinners would have to be sold on television and at last I would have a television account of my own. Ordinarily an instant dinner casserole would require a demonstration to show how quick and easy it was to make, but the ingredients in those boxes defied visualizing. I decided to give women a dream inside each box instead, a dream so big they wouldn't see the dust and wood shavings. I researched the ethnic origins of each casserole, England for macaroni and cheddar, France for pasta provençal, Spain for

Spanish rice, and created commercials that made you see England and France and Spain when you looked into those boxes. General Mills thought it was in the travel business for a while, everybody there wanted to go to Europe with me to shoot those dream commercials. In a small town in England we found a handsome old pub where we filmed macaroni and cheddar oozing and bubbling while the locals drank and sang uproariously. In a villa in Cap Ferrat we heaped the kitchen high with fat red tomatoes and French cheeses and boiling pasta. That kitchen was so close to the sea people told us they could smell the soft Mediterranean air in the commercial.

But it was in Spain that we won our prize. In my research for the campaign I discovered a fiesta in Valencia called Las Fallas. Every March the town is filled with huge papier-mâché monuments that lampoon all the evil acts that occur in Valencia during the year. The monuments cost a fortune and it takes a year to build them in hidden little squares all over town. As the evil acts are re-created up to 100 times life size—in excruciating personal detail—if you were portrayed in one of them as committing adultery you would have to leave town immediately and forever. The night of the fiesta, as the church bells ring, at the moment of midnight, men in masks scurry around with their torches setting fire to all the hideous, embarrassing, evil monuments and for a while all of Valencia seems to be burning to the skies. Fireworks take off to the moon, bands play triumphantly, the people of Valencia cheer the destruction of evil and when it is all over and done, when the embers of evil have stopped crackling, the town begins a new year with a clean slate.

When I read about the fiesta I became so determined to see it I named the Spanish rice casserole Rice Valenciana and flew to Valencia with a television crew. Our film of the festival was amazing, perhaps a bit over the top for a Betty Crocker casserole, but we also shot authentic paella being made in one of Valencia's inns that was famous for making it exactly as they did in the good old days. This mighty dish, created with enormous effort and pride, contained 1,001 small creatures from the sea I had never heard of. They were sprinkled, live, at the last minute onto the paellas as the great pans were shoved into huge roaring fireplaces. To our horror some of the ingredients shrieked and suddenly all the paellas were screaming. No one in Valencia was at all surprised, but Bill Taubman fainted dead away into a lump on the floor and none of us could eat the paellas when they came out of the fires. We remade the soundtrack, the commercial won the top awards and General Mills sold a lot of rice—but to this day I can't eat paella; I identify with the ingredients.

Barbara Baxley, an actress with a delicious, crackly voice, was the voice-over I chose for the casserole commercials. One afternoon I presented the next batch of commercials, which I was going to shoot in Greece and Rome, to Bill Bernbach. After kidding me about seeing the world on Betty Crocker's nickel, he assured me that he admired the campaign and that he was mad about Barbara Baxley's voice. Then it turned very quiet in the room, Bill and I were standing together staring down at the storyboards piled on my desk, I started to become nervous about the silence when he reached over and very gently stroked my hair. It was such a delicate gesture, it was just a breath of wistfulness, but there was trust in it, trust that I would not misunderstand, and we smiled at each other, with feeling, for the first time. Any fear I had left of Bill Bernbach was replaced, after that, with sweet loyalty.

While I was in Rome shooting my Betty Crocker risotto commercial I had a recording session with Orson Welles, who was desperately raising money for his productions. Bernie Endelman, one of my pals at the agency, had arranged it for cash. Orson arrived wearing a tent; he was huge and could only get into tents. During a break in the recording he ushered in a man lugging a case of tent fabrics. Orson studied the samples carefully and chose a few, all of them black, all exactly the same as far as I could see. He looked at me out of the corner of his eye and said, "It's in the details." Then he turned to the man with the samples, "Chelli, tell her what I wear under the tent." I imagined vast white cotton megashorts. I looked at him, at that slight smile of his, those eyes from purgatory, and then he laughed and he laughed, and nobody laughs the way Orson laughed, that digital, operatic voice, when he laughed in Rome he made music in Cleveland, and the samples man laughed, too, and we all began to laugh, and then I understood why we were laughing, because, of course, Orson wore nothing under the tent. It is a thought I carry with me for when I need a smile, especially when I am in Rome and it is cold, I see Orson sailing down the Via Condotti, as he did, naked under his tent.

Just one of those things

That night when I called the office in New York, my secretary told me that a Mr. Marion Harper was trying to find me, he would call me at my hotel, "It's important, he says." I had never met Marion Harper but I knew he was building the world's first advertising agency conglomerate, Interpublic. In the advertising business clients do not usually give their accounts to agencies who are already working for their competitors. Conflicts—two car accounts or two cosmetic accounts— are traditionally not allowed. Marion was trying to circumvent that tradition, as it limited an agency's opportunities for growth; he was trying to build a loose corporate connection between autonomous agencies. This seems an obvious idea now that it has been refined into what we call global networks of agencies, although if you examine those networks today you still won't find many of the mightiest competitors living under one corporate roof. The idea was so shocking in the late fifties, early sixties, that Madison Avenue viewed Marion as either unethical or frivolous. One of Marion's agencies at Interpublic was McCann Erickson, so he knew something about me. "I've had my eye on you, I've been following you," he said. "When are you returning from Rome? I want to make a date to see you—I am going to make you an offer you won't be able to refuse."

I was renting a small house near the sea in Quogue that spring. I took my mother and father and my daughters, Katy and Pam, there weekends. My marriage was a headache and it was a relief to leave the city because I knew that my husband, Bert, would say he couldn't leave, he had to work. Marion sent his Interpublic plane (proof of his immoral ways) to fly me to lunch with him on a Saturday. We met at one of his clubs, where he was graceful about being fussed over by the staff and he was warm welcoming me. I had accepted the invitation with a narrow view of what he would be like and was a little surprised to see he had such an attractive, educated manner. Mid-lunch, when he suspected that it was not going to be easy to convince me of his plans, he was fun to watch because he stoked up a fire in his eyes and concentrated on seducing me with an irresistible dream.

He told me that he had created something like a think tank around Jack Tinker, whom I had worked for at McCann Erickson. Marion's idea was to have one, unstructured, highly talented group that would remain independent but would provide a never-ending stream of fresh ideas and superlative creative work for all the other, larger, more mundane agencies in the Interpublic network. Thanks to Doyle Dane Bernbach's success, most of the big agencies were slowly taking steps to produce more creative advertising. Such a major sea change takes time, and there was a lot of trial and error as the giants lifted their legs to try to shimmy and shake in those days. Marion wanted to speed things up. He figured it would be easier and faster to create one small group of brilliant alchemists who could turn dross into gold when it was called for than it would be to reshape big traditional agencies.

Jack Tinker had happily moved, with a few partners, into a grand duplex suite in the Dorset Hotel, next to the Museum of Modern Art, and they were working on projects for Interpublic agencies. It was an agile, efficient concept. Jack Tinker & Partners could draw on all of Interpublic's resources, the large research and media departments, for example, and did not need to reproduce them. But after a couple of years Marion was starting to worry about the concept and about Jack Tinker & Partners. It was looking expensive to him. It had no income of its own and the Interpublic agencies were not at all happy paying for creative work from Jack that they preferred to do themselves.

Eyes glowing, his energies firmly aimed at my mind, determined to pull me in that day at lunch, Marion said that he thought it was time to turn Jack Tinker & Partners, the think tank, into an advertising agency with clients of its own. He wanted me to join Jack and take my experience at Doyle Dane Bernbach with me to build a new-wave agency that would set the standard for the industry. "The agency will be your dream, whatever you think an agency should be in this era. I will back you every step of the way. Jack agrees completely, you are as much his choice to run this agency as mine. We know you can create the agency for the new world, a television agency, an agency that will be as much about the theatre as it is about advertising." He must have seen something in me he was looking for, because at that point he became more forceful and began discussing terms, what my salary could be and what contract he had in mind. I don't know whether Marion had researched me well or was something of a mind reader, because he was right, it was an offer I had to consider. I did dream of creating an agency that would be based on the theatrical television advertising I imagined for the future. I agreed to meet Jack in his suite at the Dorset and I left Marion with sangfroid—although, in fact, I was shocked to discover that it was in me, that it was *possible* for me, to consider leaving Doyle Dane Bernbach, my salvation, the home of my Gods, my Heaven on earth. There was absolutely no one I could talk to about the possibility. My husband and I weren't talking about anything important, I didn't want to frighten my mother and father, my daughters were babies, my friends would have hooted me out of Manhattan: "Leave Doyle Dane Bernbach for Jack Tinker & Partners, the think tank? You have to be kidding!"

When I went to the Dorset Hotel for our meeting Jack opened the door of the suite. I hadn't seen him for five years but he was still the earnest, charming man I remembered. He had great style, he smoked a pipe and had leather elbows on all his jackets. He could lean against the fireplace of the suite with aristocratic élan, grin at you and make you feel you were a special treat for him. That suite! The reception room was three stories tall with a circular stairway designed for Fred Astaire and Ginger Rogers. There were valuable antique rugs scattered around, a grand, grand piano, even a Hollywood bar with leather stools.

Jack appeared to be happy to see me. Yes, he said, the agency would be my dream. We would have Interpublic's money and Marion's power at our beck and call. We would be a great team, he did not doubt that we could pull off a great agency, together, and there was no question, he repeated, that the agency would be my dream, no one else's. By the time I left him that day I was convinced that I had to accept the offer. There are many ways of dying; to have refused that offer would have been, for me, a kind of suicide. Ready or not, I could not refuse to run with that dream.

But how in the world would I tell Bill Bernbach that I was leaving his religious order to go to work in a think tank? He would have me committed. In fact, I never did really resign. I told Bill and Ned that I needed a year or two of a sabbatical, out on my own. I was too dependent on them, I had to experience the dangerous world without them. It was time for me to grow up. I promised to return to Doyle Dane Bernbach a far better and mature advertising executive. They were thunderstruck; "Ohhhhhhh, Mary," Bill whispered. They thought so little of Marion Harper and Interpublic they never doubted for an instant that I would return. I was not a threatening loss to them. Doyle Dane was booming and talent was hanging out the windows, my own group of writers was superb. Still, I was family and they were seriously worried about me. They warned me of all the dangers "out there" in the advertising world. Later, I heard that Bill sometimes wondered about me as if I was a daughter who had left home for her own apartment and he wondered what I was really doing there. But whatever they may have thought or said as the years rolled on, the tough rope of that idea that we were family took a very long time to break.

With a little help from my friends

My first impression of Jack Tinker & Partners was that nothing at all was going on there. There had been big projects in the past but the place was idling, in neutral, waiting for somebody like me to come along and do something. I had been given a key and when I opened the door my first morning I may have been the first one to arrive; the grand reception room felt like a chateau that had been given its white linen covers and shuttered for the season, as if nobody at all was expected. There wasn't a sound of any kind, an eerie sound in itself in New York, where even padded rooms don't conceal murmurs from the streets and subways. The sofas were spotless and plumped, the liquor bottles at the bar were full; nobody'd had fun there last night, I guessed. "This is a tomb," I thought, I felt like a poacher, it was hard not to tiptoe. I had a second of being completely baffled by how I had come to be working in this dead place. It begged for loud and live music and laughs and creative people posturing and spouting with ideas, some kind of society that was vibrant and doing something to marvel at. I hadn't heard him but Jack had come in behind me and was standing in the doorway. When I turned and saw him he had a face full of sympathy and understanding and without saying one word about our thoughts we became fast friends and in tune about what we were going to do with Jack Tinker & Partners.

I had calls from old friends at McCann who warned me that Jack and his partners, Herta Herzog and Myron McDonald, had really been put out to pasture at the Dorset Hotel. They were expensive people who had been bypassed for one reason or another at McCann and Marion didn't know what to do with them but he respected them too much to retire them early. They had not chosen each other, I was warned, they weren't mad about each other, there were squabbles, it was a pretentious, old-world-agency mess. I told them all that they were nuts. I told them it was a dynamic place. I told them they would have to excuse me, I had so many interviews, we were hiring the cream of New York, we were rockets.

Herta and I had never met in my McCann days. When we met at Tinker she looked like an Austrian movie star. She struck me as very smart and politically tuned. She had been told that I was from the new young world of advertising and was a revolutionary, so she was wary. But she was game; she wanted something exciting to happen there. I loved talking to her. She had a magnificent Viennese accent that did not sound make-believe, she sounded like Freud or maybe Moses, like she had all the answers. Myron McDonald was an enigma. I never did understand what his role was. He was introduced to me as the business partner but he was always on the fringe of groups, on the outside, with what looked like a frustrated flush. He had a curious habit of tossing his tie over his shoulder, a small gesture that gave me the willies, it was so tense.

Jack Tinker & Partners had developed a statement of their philosophy they had been giving to the press. They said they had been too busy supervising others at McCann Erickson to devote themselves to the important business of making advertising, so they had created Jack Tinker & Partners, where they had finally become free to do the work themselves. The work atmosphere was unhierarchical, they said. Everybody at Tinker worked on everything together, and from that chaos, that wonderful democracy, came great breakthrough concepts. It sounded OK, in tune with the times. But they had so little to show. It didn't worry me much, because Marion had told me about a couple of good account possibilities hovering in the wings. All that really mattered was the work we would do for them, that's what would build our reputation, so I immediately started hiring the best creative people I could persuade to work there.

Tinker had a good art director when I got there, Stewart Greene, but his style was a little soft so I hired Dick Rich to work with him. Dick had been at Doyle Dane Bernbach for a while but Bill had not understood him, he was a little too much like Woody Allen for Bill's taste, in fact Bill called me and told me that hiring Dick was my first mistake and it was a doozy. But I thought Dick's edgy, contemporary humor would sharpen up Stew Greene, who was too much like that guy you saw in the movie *Pleasantville,* always calm and encouraging no matter what was falling down around him. I expected Dick's style to help me sharpen up Jack Tinker & Partners' style as well, and it did. By the end of the year we'd hired an exceptional group of writers and art directors: Gene Case, Bob Wilvers, Herb Green, George D'Amato, Phil Parker, Charlie Moss. They took a chance on working at Tinker because I overpaid them so much they assumed I knew something about the place that they didn't know. Right away, as though he had just been waiting for me to hire a few creatures from Mars and Jupiter to prove we were a new-wave agency, Marion brought Walter Beardsley and Walter Compton of Miles Laboratories in to meet us. They made Alka-Seltzer and they were looking for a new agency. They wanted something modern with a little magic, so they had been considering Doyle Dane Bernbach, but they liked the sound of our new place and figured that if we failed we were backed up by Interpublic's other agencies.

My newly hired creative crew thought like creatures from outer space but they looked perfectly normal so they were a bit of a disappointment at first to Marion as well as to Walter Compton. Starting in the mid-sixties, for about ten years a lot of businessmen hoped to find something eye-boggling when they visited the new, younger agencies; they were inexplicably moved by the idea of having Mick Jagger or Led Zeppelin doing their advertising. I found myself promising Walter that my creative talents were harbingers of a world as hip and successful as the Beatles'. Walter said to me (earnestly), "Does Herb Green always wear a jacket and tie? Tell him he doesn't have to wear them for me. I want him to be his true self!" Walter Compton was a great client but he couldn't get over his disappointment in the wardrobe at Tinker and sometimes, just to keep him feeling that he was in a nest of flower power, I used to vaguely allude to peyote problems in the backrooms.

Those backrooms were a cubist's dream, they were bare squares. After a while the walls took on that arty littered crust that advertising creative people used to give to walls before computers cleaned things up; Charles Saatchi would pay anything to have them in his "Sensation" collection. Before I arrived Jack Tinker & Partners had needed very little office space beyond the grand reception room, one other comfortable meeting room with a big table and leather chairs and the pleasant offices Jack and Herta and Mac had made for themselves. The few worker bees were in what the Dorset Hotel called "single rooms." They weren't fancy but, as they were hotel rooms, each had a private bath. As soon as I started hiring people we added a whole floor at the Dorset, emptied all the rooms of furniture and rugs and installed a typewriter or an art director's drafting table, two chairs and a very large wastebasket, advertising's most important accessory. It was a grand lark that nobody had real furniture but everybody had a private bathroom. Creative work meetings were apt to happen with one person stretched out in a tub, somebody sitting in the sink and somebody else on a covered loo.

But as mad, bad and dangerous as those offices appeared, the writers and art directors who moved into them were respectable, sincere, even sweet. Bob Wilvers was tall and handsome with a loving smile, he loped around like a friendly Labrador retriever surprising everyone with how brilliant he was. Gene Case wore long, blond, Aryan bangs, he was movie-star material, but he was a man of few words, his solemnity could be heavy going, he made people uncomfortable, but he was a wonderful print writer and that was all I cared about. Herb Green was the best-dressed one, with a country house and prize horses that were always in magazines. He was the uptown one with a great sense of humor, and George D'Amato was an Italian teddy bear who took his own work reverently. They were the odd couple, devoted to each other but, as Walter Compton observed to me, a bit prim. You could have mistaken Charlie Moss for a high-school teenager, he looked so innocent and he was so nervous. He was the only one in a shirt with short sleeves, all the others wore long-sleeve white shirts and ties while hanging around waiting for clients. Disappointingly, there was no orange hair in the group, no face paint, no raspberry T-shirts. There may have been some marijuana in a few jackets, and in later years one or two may have become, temporarily, psychedelic, but the only thing that was anti-establishment at Jack Tinker & Partners was the work we did, and that work put us on the map in no time.

Makin' whoopee

We all believed in the fresh results we got from breaking rules, in deliberately cutting through expectations based on tradition. We started right out ignoring all the old ideas that had gone into Alka-Seltzer advertising when we got the account. For far too long it had been represented by Speedy, a cartoon disk with a squeaky voice and pop eyes. Speedy had done a good job of communicating the speed of relief you get from Alka-Seltzer, but by the sixties Speedy may have been the corniest symbol around. Alka-Seltzer was in big trouble when the men from Miles came to see us. Its loyal users were getting old and they were people with little education. Even among that shrinking group Alka-Seltzer had become the symbol of people who drank too much and ate too much, it had become the unforgivable symbol of a slob, a hangover cure. It was so déclassé to be seen taking Alka-Seltzer that people sneaked into their bathrooms to take it. "I take it in the dark," one woman told us in a study we did of the upset-stomach market.

Young people didn't admit to getting heartburn or indigestion, they would die before belching or burping, they told us they "coughed" instead. What could Alka-Seltzer do for a market that craved higher volume, harder pounding, motorcycle jackets, chemicals and transcendence? They said they thought Alka-Seltzer was for their great-grandparents.

But I thought that anybody who was anybody in the sixties would have to have indigestion or heartburn. It was, after all, a stressful time, and it is stress that causes most head and stomach upsets. If you were over 30 you were working, traveling and even relaxing stressfully. If you were in college you were playing stressfully or had stressful causes. The new young world was ambitious, educated, stimulated by so many choices and always exhausted. There was never enough time, never enough money, television had put the world's problems on everybody's lap and everybody felt pursued by one thing or another. Even if you got a cold you thought you had to keep going. Everyone of every age we talked to had head and stomach upsets regularly from their stressful lifestyles. We learned that indigestion and heartburn are not symptoms of age, they are lifestyle accessories and you get them from overindulgence, not only of food and alcohol but also of life.

Well, God made Alka-Seltzer so that you can survive life in the world—for the upset stomachs, the headaches, the heavy downer feelings, the indigestion and burning gut you get from anger, frustration, overwork, underappreciation and being exploited. You may smoke pot to relax but you still get heartburn. If you don't get heartburn you are a nobody. That became my overall thesis for Alka-Seltzer: You're nobody if you don't have heartburn.

To top it off, in the sixties there were all those new, spicy, ethnic foods on our tables and all the fast foods, all the pizzas and all the wine, the good stuff, we thought at the time. "Ye gods," I said in a presentation to the Miles executives in Elkhart, Indiana, "if we were going to create a perfect market from scratch for Alka-Seltzer, we would have to create *this* market and *these* years. Alka-Seltzer itself is not old-fashioned, it is Alka-Seltzer's image that is old-fashioned, and that is something we at Tinker know how to fix better than anybody."

It says something about the convincing persuasion of the youth culture that the executives in Elkhart believed in us as we turned their world upside down because we were *young*. Traditionally, pain-relief products had been advertised in gruesome commercials filled with horrors that would have given you pain if you didn't already have it. People ran around groaning, clutching their heads and stomachs, men and women crawled into corners and shrieked "Pain! Pain! Pain!" at television viewers who immediately turned off their sets. In one Frankensteinian commercial an ugly Neanderthal man went through a series of tortures, hammers dropped from the skies to pound his head, hoses appeared like snakes to whip him with water, straitjackets tied him up, you wanted to scream at him to "get off my telly!" People did not watch proprietary drug advertising unless they already had a headache or stomach problem and were looking for a quick fix, so most of the time, from the advertiser's point of view, advertising was like throwing money into a black hole.

At Tinker we plotted and schemed to develop advertising that would seduce every man, woman and child of every age into watching Alka-Seltzer advertising—in fact, to make them look forward to watching it. We did it by being *entertaining*. Certainly, the only way we could get young people to watch the commercials would be to make them entertaining. By getting and holding people's attention we would vastly increase their awareness of Alka-Seltzer. But it would take more than entertainment and attention to save Alka-Seltzer, we had to make television viewers see it as a modern product and that it was the smart thing to take for a wide variety of life's aches and pains.

The Tinker bunch used to sit around that grand reception room, draped all over those big white sofas, all over the floor, old, cold coffee and half-eaten sandwiches producing heartburn left and right, thinking of all the times you should take Alka-Seltzer to survive life. We would slouch there or get up and prance about the room describing to one another the dregs and pits of life that made Alka-Seltzer so necessary, so marvelous, so smart to have on you at all times. For example, after the presentation to the client from hell who hates you, you eat a greasy cheeseburger running to catch your plane, it's canceled, there isn't another flight, your head throbs and your stomach crawls up into your throat and suicide is the only solution, you gotta have Alka-Seltzer. When your wife nags about your mother who has moved in with you and the baby screams all night and the Beatles never stop singing that same damn song and you want to kill your wife, your mother, the baby and maybe even the Beatles, you gotta have Alka-Seltzer. The Blahs was the malaise of the sixties, everybody had it, Alka-Seltzer was made to order for it. We kept acting out scenes of The Blahs. We antiqued the antique rugs with coffee stains and smashed peanuts; I don't think we ever got rid of the smell of old food in that room. For a couple of weeks we barely left it and the hotel maids kept as far away from us crazies as they could.

Jack watched us in awe. He said he thought I had created a madhouse, not an agency. But by improvising, exaggerating and laughing at each other we broke through all the old ideas that had straitlaced Alka-Seltzer. Such shared creation freed us to have the courage to do a completely new kind of advertising for a pain-relief product. And it gave us the unusual idea of a campaign with a series of completely different commercials, different reasons to take Alka-Seltzer, a noncampaign campaign, which turned out to be a vitally important way to motivate people to use Alka-Seltzer more often for more kinds of upsets.

We were very careful to do our homework professionally and we experimented. We learned that Alka-Seltzer works fine with only a lit-

tle bit of water—good news for people who can't swallow a lot of liq-
uid. Then I tried it on the rocks, ice cold, on a scorching hot day. "Hey,"
I said to the troops, "try it on ice, it tastes a lot better, it's really good on
ice!" We took ideas like those to the labs at Miles and they tested them
for the claims we hoped to make. We tried Alka-Seltzer with everything, in everything, and with every imaginable chaser. Herb came to
work with a cold, we doused him with Alka-Seltzer and took his tem-
perature and his pulse so often that he hid. If anybody came to work
with anything that resembled a hangover he was in big trouble, we
force-fed him so much Alka-Seltzer he hiccuped all day.

Dick and Stew created the kickoff commercial that set the style for
all the variety of commercials that followed. It was a truly wonderful,
iconic commercial, an ovation to stomachs, a sweet-natured montage of
big ones, little ones, slim ones, fat ones, all filmed at stomach level.
There was a street digger's jackhammer stomach, a young chick's bare
midriff, two men talking, facing each other, one with a flat stomach and
one with a big round one, an array of stomachs presented with self-
deprecating humor and sweet humanness to a happy, bouncy tune. "No
matter what shape your stomach's in" was its opening phrase. Self-
deprecating humor was new and popular in the sixties and unheard-of
in drug commercials, when it appeared it was news.

It was followed by 16 completely different commercials, each entertaining and stylish, each giving you a different reason to take Alka-
Seltzer. People started talking to each other about the campaign and
about Alka-Seltzer. They came out of the closet and started taking it in
public, at the table, at the bar, at the desk. It became smart to be seen
taking Alka-Seltzer and sales did an abrupt about-face and increased
sharply. One very hot night when I returned to New York from Elkhart
I saw our new outdoor poster for "Alka-Seltzer On The Rocks" as I was
coming over the bridge into Manhattan. It looked so refreshing, so
right, that I went straight home and had one.

And then we hit gold. We met an attractive doctor at Miles, Dorothy
Carter, who demonstrated to us that in order for aspirin to break
through the pain barrier it often required two aspirins, not one, to do
the job. As aspirin is one of the ingredients that make Alka-Seltzer

effective, we asked her if two Alka-Seltzers would work better than one. Yes, two would work better than one.

But the directions on the packages said to take only one. And all the old Speedy commercials demonstrated only one fizzing in water. Dick and Herta and Jack and I did a little dance with Dorothy Carter in the laboratory. What a stroke of good fortune that was! We changed the directions on the packages and began showing two Alka-Seltzers dropping into a glass of water in every commercial. Plop Plop Fizz Fizz. Miles created portable foil packs that held two Alka-Seltzers each and sold them in new places, magazine stands, bars, fast-food restaurants, powder rooms—they became ubiquitous—and, naturally, Miles began selling twice as much Alka-Seltzer.

The advertising business is about good fortune like that, good and bad luck. It's about timing, who happens to come along at a particular moment. It is about talent. It is about relationships inside the advertising agency and relationships with clients. Clients always have a wide choice of agencies that would love to handle their business; clients get love letters from agencies every day. Most agencies are capable of putting together teams of talented people who will do good work. If a client fires you and leaves, the traditional agency-client contract calls for them to pay only three months of advertising revenues to you, the agency they fired. Yet expenses—the rent, for example—can't be limited to only three months. If a client fires you and leaves, your agency has to keep paying that rent and all the other expenses incurred for that client until you get new business that will absorb those costs. So how do you keep a client in love with you, how do you keep his eye from wandering, how do you persuade all of his executives who have friends in agencies galore to sit still, how do you become such an important part of a client's marketing equation that you feel secure enough to let go of his hand nights and go home to sleep? How in the world do you manage to sleep at all if you are responsible for the life of an agency?

Experience counts a lot with some clients; they stay married to agencies, not out of loyalty or love, but because of the experience those agencies have built up with them that translates into priceless wisdom. Other clients, however, always have an eye out for something new that may be better. So an agency must have at least one person who has the gift of providing clients with something they believe is unique and valuable enough to offset the occasional calamity.

After we got the Alka-Seltzer account at Jack Tinker & Partners and were well on our way to becoming an agency, I inherited the responsibility for keeping the account like a second skin. Not only had I been anointed by Marion; Walter Compton chose me as the place to put his trust, and no one thought for a minute I would not deliver the goods, least of all me. That is the issue that defines who will lead an organization. You can be extremely gifted in a specific way but not be talented at accepting responsibility for the whole, for keeping everybody safe and blooming.

I sensed that Walter Compton would not only count on me to see to it he received outstanding advertising for Alka-Seltzer, he would pray that I would have the same passion for his product, for his business, for his own personal success. That's what all clients pray for. If I could demonstrate those passions to Walter, I would become too valuable to lose, I would become a true friend and could weather what fate had in store. Walter Compton began to care about me when he saw how beautiful Alka-Seltzer was to my eyes, when he listened to me talk about it, when he absorbed my thoughts about it. He knew he had found a soul mate, someone, finally, who understood what an extraordinary product he had to offer. "No one else has ever understood Alka-Seltzer in the same way, with such ambition for it, as you have," he told me years later when he gave me the account a second time, at another agency—my own.

There is an element of self-hypnotism required in a service business that is as personal as advertising. Everything that interested Walter Compton interested me enough to make me learn about it so that we could have interests in common in order to understand each other better. He loved Japanese culture and collected rare and fine Japanese swords and their accessories. He had a climatically perfect room built in his home where he could protect and display his collection. I knew nothing, zero, zilch, about Japanese swords—to be honest, I found them daunting—but I used to go to auction houses and buy catalogues when Japanese swords were to be sold. I read those catalogues and stared at those swords until I got a glimmer and then illumination. I was obsessive. In my opinion, if you are not obsessive in the advertising business you will always work for someone else. For a time I was conversational, even *interesting,* about Japanese swords and tried to have something—a clipping, some news about swords—for Walter when I went to Elkhart, because I could see the enormous pleasure he got from my interest. Walter's wife, Phoebe, included me in dinners and special ceremonies celebrating rare swords. In between the chicken and the speeches by Japanese experts, Walter and I talked about ourselves and our dreams; that's how our friendship grew into trust. It wasn't counterfeit, it was real, and it turned out to be irreplaceable.

You would laugh if you knew all I learned in order to talk to clients who were mostly men. I learned to talk horses with Jack Landry at Philip Morris, who had a lot to do with the Marlboro Cup race that Philip Morris sponsored; he thought it was hilarious that I knew anything about horses, but horse talk helped forge our friendship. Once I had a client who was a big elk hunter and he always looked into the eyes of the men at the lunch table, not into mine, when he talked elks. I didn't know what an elk was, so I went to the library and found out all about elks and elk hunting. It didn't take long for me to know more about hunting elks than anybody else on Madison Avenue, and he started looking into *my* eyes when he talked about his elks. I learned about African big-game hunting and salmon fishing. I was an expert on government regulations from A to Z and that was a hit with every client I ever had. I learned about California wines, antique cars, Swiss cantons, mountain walking boots, what makes a good suit good, rare fish, western six-guns, the Boy Scouts, the best hotels and where a man could take his kids to have fun in almost every city in the Western world. When I didn't need it, I lost it. All those elks and government regulations just faded away.

The Alka-Seltzer advertising gave us status as an agency of young revolutionaries, nobody called us a think tank anymore. Jack said, "It's as if we had a face-lift, we're young and beautiful again." He was tickled when we got so many inquiries from companies looking for new agencies that we could afford to be choosy. When some of his old gang at McCann, who had poked fun at the Dorset operation, called him to suggest moving over to work with us, he was euphoric. Once he hopped like a rabbit into my office shouting, "Vengeance! Vengeance! Vengeance is so sweet!" Marion loved to pop in and just absorb the ambiance of swarms of young people coming and going at all hours, producers, musicians, editors. I caught him once listening intently to "I Wanna Be Your Man" playing over the din, he was trying to get the words from Paul McCartney, trying to memorize them. I wondered who he was hoping to sing that song to. Like in a fairy tale, Jack Tinker & Partners changed into a handsome prince.

Come fly with me

And a handsome prince changed my life. Bob Six and Harding Lawrence came to see us about Continental Airlines. Bob Six was the chairman, he looked like a tall, black-haired, grinning pirate. Harding was the president, and he looked as if central casting had sent him over to play the president of an airline. It was not exactly love at first sight when Harding and I met, although it was one of those meetings when you look into another person's eyes and, unexpectedly, feel something you would rather not feel right at that moment, so you look away, steel your mind to forget it, and then look back coolly—but you don't forget. I had read about him, admiring stories, the press liked him. Continental was considered a smart, profitable, forward-thinking airline in the sixties. It was giving fits to its larger competitors, its Chicago–Los Angeles run made the competition look shabby and it had a reputation for understanding what made the business flier tick. Harding was given much of the credit and there were rumors in all the papers that other airlines were trying to kidnap him.

They came to see us looking for something special to help them launch the supersonics they had ordered. Many airlines were placing orders for supersonics. The Concorde was a thrilling idea; getting to your destination faster seemed like something that would naturally happen in the airline industry. Bob and Harding wanted to promote supersonic technology ahead of the arrival of the planes to stir up excitement for them and to rub that sophisticated imagery onto Continental's regular fleet. Together, the two men had enough charisma to shatter glass and enough energy to accomplish anything they set out to do, they knew their industry as if they had been the authors. I could imagine the effect they had on their competition. They stirred us up, too, and we agreed to fly to their offices in Los Angeles to learn more.

Bob Six was married to Audrey Meadows, who played the role of Alice in Jackie Gleason's *Honeymooners* series; earlier he had been married to Ethel Merman. He was the kind of man who looked at life as a superlative meal and could digest anything, he would never need Alka-Seltzer. I knew nothing about Harding Lawrence's personal life. When we made our trip to Continental in Los Angeles I learned a lot about supersonics but nothing much about him; he seemed distracted. At lunch he murmured, "Something has come up that may interest you. I'll call you about it as soon as I know more." When he called he told me that Troy Post and his insurance group had bought controlling interest in Braniff Airways, an airline based in Dallas. Troy wanted Harding to turn that small airline into an important carrier with a new fleet of jets and an ambitious program. Harding said that he had been receiving offers to run other airlines but the opportunity at Braniff was such a rare and challenging one he couldn't refuse it. He planned to resign from Continental and join Braniff in the spring.

"I want to hire you people at Tinker to help me reintroduce Braniff to America. Actually, I want you to introduce Braniff to the world. You'll need to make a presentation to the executive group I'm going to hire," he said. "Listen, Mary, I need a very big idea for this airline, something so big it will make Braniff important news, overnight. I'm going to buy a large fleet of jets and they'll cost plenty. Braniff has a great route structure, you'll be amazed at the routes it's got, but the airline is virtually unknown, we have to become hot news from coast to coast. I don't want to fly a lot of empty seats around. You people will have to play a big role in this makeover. It's going to take me a while to hire everybody I'll need and I don't have time to wait. I want to turn the airline inside out and make it the best in the industry. What do you think? Can you help me do that?"

So even before we were officially hired to work for Braniff, Jack and Stew and I started to visit airports in New York, Washington, Chicago, Denver, Dallas and other cities on Braniff's system. We hiked through miles of terminals, I was getting claustrophobic in them, depressed. Then one morning, standing by a check-in gate in Chicago, I turned around and I saw a jail, the army, a prison camp, a ghastly desert and a lot of grey people. I'm having a nightmare, I thought, but it was just the terminal. Airlines had developed out of the military and modern marketing hadn't discovered them yet. Planes were metallic or white with a stripe painted down the middle to make them look as if they could get up and fly. The terminals were greige. They had off-white walls, cheap stone or linoleum floors, grey metal benches, there were tacky signs stuck onto walls any place at all. Even the doors to the first-class clubs were hidden behind stairways, those doors never had a frame, they looked like cupboard doors for mops. Stewardesses, as they were called, were dressed to look like nurses or like pilots who could fly the planes in case the real pilot had a heart attack. There were no interesting ideas, no place for your eyes to rest, nothing smart anywhere.

And there was no color. This was the sixties, mind you, when color was a hot marketing tool. I started talking about color to Jack and everybody at Tinker and then to Harding when he would call. He liked thinking about color; he reminded me that Braniff would be flying to places associated with brilliant color, Mexico and South America.

I saw the opportunity in color the way Flo Ziegfeld must have seen an empty stage. I saw Braniff in a wash of beautiful color. I tore up a hundred magazines collecting pictures of automobiles in color, colorful interiors, colorful clothes. Jack and Stew began exploring ways to make the planes colorful. Jo Hughes, the fashion expert at Bergdorf Goodman, set up a meeting for me with Emilio Pucci, who stood for color in women's clothes more than anyone else in the world. He and I met, he understood me before I opened my mouth. Emilio was phenomenally prescient and I got a clue to his energy at that meeting. He seemed to me to be on the ceiling most of the time, although I knew that was not possible; still, in the months to come he often seemed to me to be on the ceiling. But then we were doing everything possible to turn Braniff upside down. We searched for Alexander Girard, the designer of La Fonda del Sol, a restaurant in the Time-Life Building where my mother and I used to take my daughters. It was a high-octane color montage of Mexican and modern, he worked with Herman Miller designers and was a colleague of Ray and Charles Eames and Eero Saarinen, the people who had created my wedding furniture. He lived in New Mexico and Stew and I flew out to see him in his vivid New Mexican house with its art gallery, a riot of folk art. We saw a thousand ideas for Braniff's terminals, check-in counters and clubs in his house and he had a thousand more when we signed him on as the project designer. I thought it was a good omen when he said he had been brought up in Florence and knew Emilio; it all came together as if preordained.

Jack sketched possible ways to give the planes color. We spread them out over the floor of the reception room and walked around them for a few days, just *feeling* them. There was something very right but also very wrong about each design. Stew simplified one design until the plane was basically one color, green. I asked him to make the same design in different colors because I didn't like green. We walked around those different colors for a few days and we sketched airport fields filled with all-green or all-blue planes. Then I asked him to do one with all different-colored planes. When that sketch hit the floor of the reception room it was a thunderbolt, there wasn't a doubt in my mind or Stew's or Jack's, the sketch of the solid-colored planes in seven different colors was the hit show. A field of planes that were all the same color looked ho-hum. Seven colors looked like a big idea and wow and friendly and it would be big news. People would go out of their way to see them.

Before we made a full-scale presentation of our color program to the new Braniff executives, I wanted to give Harding a preview of the idea of planes in seven different colors. He never stopped telling me that he wanted an idea so big it would fill up his new jets overnight because, as he said a few hundred times, "an empty seat from Dallas to New York is revenue lost forever." When he studied the sketches of his planes in seven different solid colors he was quiet for a minute. I don't think I breathed. Then he laughed. He said, and I will never ever forget it, "That will do it!" That had to be the moment I fell in love with him.

I stood at the door to his office with the sketches packed up, ready to leave for the airport. I knew I looked perfectly calm, he told me later I was discouragingly professional, but I was keeping a lid on emotions that seemed extremely dangerous to me. I felt powerful undercurrents zinging back and forth between us that could mess up my life, his life, a lot of lives. Neither of us had marriages that could last through any stress, mine was falling apart hour by hour, there was a red light blinking in my mind, I didn't want trouble, I wanted to build the best advertising agency in the world, I didn't have time for life-altering love, when I looked at him to say goodbye he was looking away, talking to someone on the phone. I ran.

Alexander Girard created the final design for the solid-colored planes and their interiors. He designed the terminal waiting areas and the check-in accessories, then he and, later, Phil George designed Braniff club rooms, filling them with sunshine colors and Mexican art. City by city Braniff became the beautiful one, and for a little while, before all the airlines in the world got the picture and redesigned themselves, Braniff made most other airlines look sad.

Emilio Pucci's mind raced at dangerous speeds and we were always chasing after him to slow him down. Somehow he got the idea that Braniff routes always took people from cold places to warm places. He designed outfits for the stewardesses—who had become "hostesses"—that allowed them to take off a little bit of their chic uniforms one piece at a time as Braniff planes flew to warm destinations. We called this antic process "The Air Strip" and made a commercial of it that shocked a few people, but when we ran it on the Super Bowl it was a sensational hit. After the Super Bowl everyone knew that Emilio Pucci had made the Braniff hostesses the most exciting ones in the world and business-men went out of their way to fly Braniff to see them. Emilio thought women were delicious creatures and that he was freeing the Braniff hostesses from looking like jailers. He even made teeny-weeny bikinis for them, an inch of cloth, and although they did not wear them on the planes, Emilio saw to it the bikinis were photographed so often for the press that the business community expected to see hostesses in them on the planes and was disappointed—but amused. It was wonderful to watch Braniff's hostesses feel so beautiful and begin to walk like models, one foot in front of the other, tra la la, on the planes.

We thought we should test one or two of the colors we were planning to paint the planes, so we painted a grounded DC-6, an old cargo plane that looked as if it was sitting down and couldn't possibly get up, it was dented all over, it looked like it had pimples, and it was turning into tin. Braniff painted it yellow on one side and orange on the other out on the field at the Braniff base. Jack and I flew to Dallas to join Harding, Ed Acker, Tom King, Glenn Geddis and Jere Cox to take a look. It was a scorching Texas day. We drove out onto the field in a large black car, we were all in dark suits, we got out of the car and walked around the half yellow, half orange plane meditating on it as if we were in Mecca. Back at the base hundreds of workers grouped at the windows and doors to watch us. The word was that we planned to paint every plane in the fleet half yellow and half orange. The faces of the men at those windows showed what they thought of that idea.

When I saw that plane painted yellow and orange I felt a sharp stab of panic. "Well," I consoled myself, "we can paint them all beige." But Harding was cool, Ed gave the plane a sympathetic little pat, Jere and Tom didn't even blink, Glenn smiled beatifically, Jack puffed his pipe—he said later he would have given anything to disappear into thin air, he didn't know *what* to think. We got back into the black car, no one said a word, we drove back to the base, had a coffee and planned the painting of the fleet.

The first jet, which was a very different animal than that old DC-6 cargo plane, was painted a stunning cobalt blue. It looked like a fast blue arrow, like a rocket to Mars, it was the most glamorous plane anyone had ever seen. I got up at dawn to see it. There it was, all by itself at the terminal, standing in a Dallas drizzle with a grey sky that turned its cobalt blue paint into a thrilling high-tech lavender. I watched as all the early-morning businessmen shuffled out to the gate clutching their Styrofoam cups of coffee. I expected at least a couple of expressions of surprise, confusion or, who knows, even outrage from those dismal early travelers, but one by one they climbed the plane's steps and not one of them even noticed that their plane was purple. I went back to bed secure that even the orange plane would not cause a riot.

America cheered. Braniff held a press conference on the base when the first five 707s were painted blue, green, yellow, red and a shimmering turquoise. Press arrived from all over the world to see the planes stage a "fly-by," each plane flew very low and slow and close to the grandstands in smart formation. The French, English, Italian, Greek and Chinese reporters stood up and yelled their heads off. I can't imagine what it would take to get 300 reporters and photographers from around the world to yell their heads off today.

"The advertising has to live up to the planes," I told Charlie Moss, who was chosen to be the writer for Braniff. "Go ahead, be as sensational as you've always wanted to be," I said. I should have kept my mouth shut. Charlie was so impressed with the painted planes, the Pucci hostesses, the sexy Air Strip, Alexander Girard's interiors and clubs and dishes—it was too much for him, he got writer's block. Every day I would visit him and his art director, Phil Parker, in their big empty room to see what advertising was coming forth. Nothing. I tried exciting them. I tried threatening them. I tried love, hypnotism, charades. Charlie turned blue. Phil, who lived in a fedora and was so talented he could always make an ad look better than it was, became bleary and vacant and he couldn't talk, he couldn't utter a syllable and he began drinking martinis at lunch. "What's the matter with you?" I asked them. "There's nothing to say!" Charlie cried. "You've lost your mind!" I told him and he agreed with me. I walked over to their big wastebasket, "What's this?" I asked, pulling out the most wonderful ad for Braniff I could imagine. Phil had drawn a big orange plane across two pages. On one of the wings he had put the entire Braniff crew in their Pucci uniforms, Alexander Girard's multicolored seats and a ten-piece Mexican band. Charlie had written the headline "The end of the plain plane. We don't get you there any faster. It just seems that way."

It *was* the end of the plain plane. Airline advertising and marketing and design would never ever be the same. There were groans from other airlines. They complained that the paint made the planes heavy—every airline that told that silly story is now flying fleets of painted planes. Paint gives a plane a smoother surface that makes up in speed for the slight difference in weight but, more important, it is a lot easier to steam-clean a painted plane with detergent than it is to clean metal surfaces with machine polishers. As time is money in the airline industry, paint wins the prize.

In 1966 if you hadn't heard about Braniff you had to be in solitary confinement. In less than a year we received more publicity in newspapers and magazines than we paid for advertising in over ten years. Jack Tinker & Partners was growing at such a rate we took another floor at the Dorset; I shared an elevator one morning with 50 shiny new wastebaskets and felt a flush of success, I just beamed at them. I was feeling free, light, even euphoric. Bert and I had agreed to divorce. He had come to the agency the evening before, we sat in the reception room talking like polite strangers without tossing any blame around, we had the sort of friendliness that was possible because neither of us wanted to hang on to a marriage that was nothing more than platonic. He told me he was falling in love with a woman who loved him the way he needed to be loved. He wanted to be free to be with her, he wasn't worried about our daughters, they were so young and he was certain we were above doing anything that could hurt them. Relief was the only feeling I remember, the rush of relief. I would get a divorce, one of those quickies in Mexico.

He did remarry; but not many years later, while he was still in his early forties, he died of a massive heart attack. I thought I saw the ghost of him once when I was ill, I thought he appeared one evening, friendly, but anxious to tell me something. I've wondered about that and I keep expecting him to reappear in some way, as if he left something unsaid, unfinished.

But in that elevator with all the new wastebaskets, a free woman, I had excess energy for my meeting with Marion, who was coming to have coffee with me to discuss Nelson Rockefeller and his campaign for

Braniff launches its big color program in 1965 with this ad, "The end of the plain plane."

airline collection along with his regular designs in Florence, the airline clothing stole the show.)

At the same time, Girard was busy redesigning our airplanes.

Tearing them apart would be a more accurate description.

He didn't just lay in new carpeting, or replace a set of dishes.

He threw out nearly everything we had, and started from scratch.

Where airplanes had always looked like huge aluminum cigars with stripes down their sides, Girard selected 7 colors and painted the entire fuselage.

(You can fly with our airline 7 times and never fly the same color airplane twice.)

Where airplane seats were always covered with tasteless upholstery, Girard covered the interiors of our planes with Herman Miller fabrics.

(These are some of the most expensive fabrics in the world, but remember, Girard was spending our money, not his.)

Again, 7 different interior designs. Seven different color schemes.

Nothing was left untouched.

Tickets and ticket offices were redesigned.

Dishes and flatware.

Inflight stationery.

Our passenger lounges.

The packages that hold the sugar for the coffee.

Even the tissues in the lavatory.

In little more than six months, Girard and Pucci initiated 17,543 changes.

We have the most beautiful airline in the world.

Braniff International
United States Mexico South America

reelection as governor. Nelson had troubles, it was unfair, he had built so many new roads that, end to end, they could have run from New York to Hawaii, and those roads had given a jump start to the state's economics that had lasted a long time. But if you talked to people around the state nobody remembered Nelson's roads. He had overhauled the state's education program, too; in fact, he'd probably saved it from collapse. He'd forced through money for new campuses, new buildings, new teachers. Nobody remembered any of that either. All people remembered was his divorce and his new marriage to Happy.

I had been recruited to research and understand the situation, so I had spent days on people's front porches and back porches and in their kitchens in upper New York, drinking watery coffee with bad cookies, holding babies "just for a minute" while Mom did the dishes. A group of us canvassed the state and then we held sessions in the upper Bronx as well as on Wall Street. We knew our stuff, we weren't guessing when we decided that Nelson should stay off the television screen, that his campaign had to dramatize what he had accomplished for each and every New Yorker, that Nelson had to give them hard cold reasons for voting for him again. Bob Wilvers and Gene Case created the campaign for Nelson and it drove right through all the cheap gossip and knocked it flat, it was riveting, just what Nelson needed.

It is hard to tell a charming, forceful politician who loves to meet people, loves to feel them, to shake their hands and who loves to talk and be on stage, that he should not appear in the television commercials he is paying for, himself, at a crucial time in his career. It was hard to persuade Marion and his political advisors at Interpublic that we would be more successful presenting the truth to Nelson than to flatter him with advertising that would not reelect him. It was also hard to find anyone at Interpublic or Tinker who wanted to be the messenger with the news for Nelson. That was why Marion had come to have coffee and a chat, he thought that the gift of gab was one of my strong suits and I should make the agency's presentation. I tried to persuade him to allow Bob and Gene to present their own stuff, they were a powerfully persuasive dual act, but Marion wanted me to do the job and he wouldn't hear of anyone else.

It wasn't exactly a smoke-filled room—it was the sixties, not the forties. Nelson Rockefeller arrived with a covey of advisors and his primary strategist, William Ronan, an astute fellow who went on to become the head of the Port Authority. Marion and Jack and the partners stood around the walls of the Tinker meeting room that looked over the Museum of Modern Art garden. Nelson greeted me warmly and said he'd heard about my meetings around the state, then he told me a few stories about the sculpture in the museum garden. He was all smiles and twinkles and openmindedness. Everyone else in the room was twitching.

The only woman in the room and the only actress, I walked to Nelson and stood directly in front of him, as if we were alone. I let the room become quiet for a few seconds to give everyone time to appreciate that there I was, all alone, brave and blond, Joan of Arc. I said, "Governor Rockefeller, I know what a success you have had on television, how moving you are in person, what a deep impression you make when you talk intimately to voters." Then I told him that in this campaign we were going to keep him off the screen and instead use the screen to dramatize all that he had done for the voters of New York State because they had forgotten all that he had done. I almost whispered to him about the cold moral gravity we had found in the high awareness of his divorce and the low awareness of his achievements. I said that if we put him on television personally, people would see nothing but his divorce, it was so darkly entrenched in their minds; that to reelect him it was essential to impress the voters in a way they could not forget of how much he had improved their lives.

I believed what I was saying to him and I wanted him to trust me, so I was simple. We just looked into each other's eyes and into each other's minds for a bit. Gene and Bob presented the strong campaign they had created that I was sure could bridge the gap between Nelson's private life and public accomplishments and then I told Nelson how vital it was to get that campaign on the air to get him reelected.

No one said anything when I finished. Nelson sat staring at me, and then Bill Ronan nodded yes and Nelson stood up and applauded. A few pit-pats, enough to turn everyone in the room into believers. It all went nicely from there, the campaign was successful and, despite a press attempt to massacre him, Nelson was reelected.

Ain't no way to treat a lady

The next morning Marion called to say he was coming by to talk to me about something important. I assumed he had decided it was time to make good on his promise to make me the president of Jack Tinker & Partners. Instead, when we met he offered to pay me as if I was the president, to give me the authority of the president, but he said he could not give me the title of president because he was certain that would limit the exciting growth of Jack Tinker & Partners. "It is not my fault, Mary, the world is not ready for women presidents. You have worked so hard to make Jack Tinker & Partners what it is, so many people are dependent on you for what the agency can become, you wouldn't want to limit the agency's future just for a title." He was shocked at the blazing fury that came over me, the war he saw in my eyes. I resigned. I left him sitting in my office talking to himself.

He called the following morning and pleaded with me to come to his office. Ever hopeful, I thought he might have changed his mind. He was solicitous, Marion was always respectful with me, he offered me $1 million paid over ten years if I would sign a new contract. In 1966 that was a lot of money. Carl Spielvogel was with him, he once told the press Marion offered me $2 million and he referred to my steely blue eyes. My eyes are limpid, sexy brown and if Marion had offered me $2 million I would have accepted: I had two daughters to support, my parents needed help, my marriage was over, I couldn't have turned away from $2 million.

I called Harding and told him about Marion's offer. Harding asked me why I didn't open my own agency where I could be the president as well as the chairman. He didn't promise anything, but it would have been confusing for Braniff at that time if the airline did not go with me to a new agency: I had every swatch of fabric, every Pucci sketch, every sample cup and saucer and every plan for the big Braniff color program in my hands. For a brief moment in time I was important to Braniff.

Jack and I talked about the idea for hours late one evening. We sat in the meeting room looking down on the museum garden until dusk turned into a jet-black starry night. There had been times in our years together when I knew Jack had wished he could bridle me or lock me up, I was fueled by such strong intuition that there were moments when he saw me as a tank without a driver. He was a careful, cautious man; while he was looking for alternatives I would be galloping on. He veered between deep affection, respect, frustration and amused disbelief. But we had come to care a lot about each other, we believed in one another. That night he told me to go. He knew that some of the others would want to go with me but he assured me he could continue enriching the agency's success. He said he had made a terrible mistake years before when a similar opportunity came his way and he had let it pass and it would drive him crazy to watch me make the same mistake. His only worry, he said, was that I was so young and so goddamned determined, but "Go do it," he said. When we locked the door of Jack Tinker & Partners that night we were exhausted, we could imagine missing each other.

Still, in some beating hopeful place, I knew it was make-or-break time. I spoke to Dick and to Stew and I found Charlie Moss as he was going down the elevator to catch a plane for Peru to shoot a Braniff commercial. I told him not to be afraid of anything he heard while he was away, he would have a wonderful choice on his return. He got off the elevator white as a sheet. I called Walter Compton and we vowed to stay good friends.

Chemical Bank gave me operating money. Dick and Stew and I took eight rooms at the Gotham Hotel for offices, my mother answered the phones and Wells Rich Greene, Inc., opened its doors in April 1966. I was the president.

My own peculiar way

So I let loose the bear. When I had my chance, everything that I was and everything I'd learned came together in Wells Rich Greene and made theatre out of the advertising business. My way of running an agency was as if it was a motion-picture company with a lot of productions happening at one time. I was the director, sometimes the star. The people I hired were the cast of characters and I was Elia Kazan, Mike Nichols, Francis Ford Coppola or Robert Altman—whatever it took to make them as good as they could possibly be. I gave each of them parts to play and then whispered in their ears, cajoled them, hypnotized them, overpaid them, cradled them, tickled them, soothed them or terrified them into turning out exceptional work. I wanted a heroic agency, I dared everybody to be bold, to be thrilling and I dared our clients to be bold and thrilling. I kept saying that our goal was to have big, breakthrough ideas, not just to do good advertising. I wanted to create miracles.

All of that is true but first there was bedlam. For a few months newspapers from all over the country called us morning, noon and night to see what new business we had been given in the last 24 hours because from the very start an impressive group of businesses called to make dates to talk to us about their advertising accounts. My mother and the hotel telephone operator never got past ten o'clock in the morning without screaming at one another and my mother finally got fed up so we hired a professional operator. We couldn't work in the rooms the first few days, we had to get rid of all the beds, a dozen swearing men jostled mattresses and headboards out the doors while we rented desks and art director's drawing boards and typewriters. We kept one twin bed and I pushed it against a wall and piled it high with pillows thinking it would make a temporary sofa for a reception room where we could meet the men from Philip Morris, Bristol-Myers, Smith Kline &

French, Seagram's, General Mills, Hunt Foods, Alcoa, Utica Club Beer, Western Union, American Safety Razor and Clark Candy who made dates to see us.

The first explorer to come and take a look at us was Jack Landry from Philip Morris. We got all spiffed up for his arrival and tried to look like the advertising stars New York believed we were, but he started laughing before he even got through the door, he thought the setup at the hotel was hysterical and when he sat on the twin bed we'd turned into a sofa he kept sinking so he pulled up his legs and reclined like Cleopatra. "Tell me all about yourselves," he said, and then I thought he would die laughing. Jack was in charge of advertising and marketing for all Philip Morris brands and his reputation for leading his agencies to great victories was legendary. He was a nice-looking Irishman with a gleeful expression when he smiled and he smiled at us a lot that day. He had made a big star out of Julie London with Marlboro commercials in which she sang about flip-top boxes in the same sultry voice she used for "Cry Me a River." He lay on our hotel bed telling us funny stories about new Marlboro ads he had been shooting out West and the reactions of real cowboys in Montana to the photographers and models from New York who couldn't get up on a horse because their painted-on, crotchless jeans were too tight.

His boss was Joe Cullman, the chairman of Philip Morris. Joe had a new cigarette that was longer than king-size, it was the era of the miniskirt and long legs and Joe thought there might be a fashion connection to be made for his cigarette, Benson & Hedges 100s. He told the press that he liked my style and thought I would know what to do with a cigarette for women. Cigarette accounts were prize accounts, everybody smoked in the sixties, cigarettes were considered safe compared to the sudden, shocking drug culture that was sending freaked-out kids to places like Bellevue. We were delighted with the opportunity, as every agency would have been. Jack told me later that he hadn't thought there was a "chance in hell" that we could pull off a campaign for Benson & Hedges, but he respected Joe Cullman's instincts so he gave us the challenge, and anyway, he said, "I really like that sofa in your offices."

Braniff gave Wells Rich Greene its first account and the big Braniff color program moved into high gear shortly after we opened our doors. *Fortune* magazine photographed everybody at Wells Rich Greene sitting on the blue wing of a Braniff 707. I sat in a peacock chair. That Technicolor spread of Wells Rich Greene in *Fortune* says it all, Blessed Bunch. By the time Braniff's colorful planes got into service and were flying around America the country knew all about the airline and the planes and Emilio and Wells Rich Greene. Many of the businessmen who visited us in our first months said they wanted "a Braniff," meaning an idea so big it would become the talk of the time.

We had a fine account executive in Bill McGivney, who flew to Dallas and moved in with Tom King and Glenn Geddis to help with the thousands of details that kept coming at us in waves. Harding said to us all, one very tired Friday, "We're creating a completely new airline, you know, from scratch, from zero, from nowhere. I never said it would be easy." "It *looks* easy," I said. It did, it looked like fun and fliers thought it was fun, they jammed the planes, drove out to airports with their kids on Sundays to see them. They reserved seats months in advance and said amazing things to the people in reservations, like, "I've flown on a blue one and a green one, I want to fly on a red one, can you tell me where I can fly to on a red one?"

Dick and Stew and I agreed that the potential in Benson & Hedges had nothing whatever to do with miniskirts. It was in the extra puffs you got from a cigarette that was longer *at no extra cost*. You got more cigarette for no more money. There was one other longer cigarette around at the time, Pall Mall Gold, but it wasn't featuring its extra length, so the window was wide open.

Dick started clowning around imagining all the troubles people would have to go through to smoke Benson & Hedges, all the little accidents that would happen if you weren't used to smoking a longer cigarette. In a couple of days he and Stew had improvised one of those campaigns that change the entire history of a brand, people's cigarettes got caught in elevator doors and in other people's beards and they broke in kitschy little accidents because they were so long. No one had ever mutilated, let alone broken, a cigarette in advertising before. It was

America's favorite cigarette break.

Benson & Hedges 100's Regular or Menthol

Cigarettes in Benson & Hedges commercials get into trouble because they're longer than people are used to.

unthinkable. And the commercials were sweetly hilarious. Cigarette commercials had never been funny before either. Yet, amusing as the B&H commercials were, they were hard-selling; the voice-over crooned, "Benson & Hedges are a lot longer than king-size—maybe three puffs, four puffs, even five puffs longer—at the same price as king-size. And you never have to worry about lighting your nose." Every time a Benson & Hedges cigarette got into trouble it reminded the viewer of the extra puffs you got at no extra cost.

It certainly wasn't the campaign Joe Cullman was expecting. When we took it to him and Jack they were shocked and astonished and amazed but they loved it. I've heard stories that Jack had to convince Joe but that's not true. The two of them understood the campaign completely. It is true they had to convince a few others at Philip Morris, it wasn't as elegant as most Philip Morris advertising. But it was the stuff of myths, because it was irreverent and entertaining, it broke through tradition and it made the people who smoked Benson & Hedges look and feel totally hip. In 1967 so many people wanted to look and feel totally hip that Benson & Hedges became the fastest-growing brand in the country.

One giddy night we staged a public-relations reception at the Four Seasons Restaurant in the room that used to have a small movie theatre. We had completed only three commercials by then but we looped them so they played endlessly. Beautiful models in glittering miniskirts served champagne and perhaps a little stardust because people jammed into the movie theatre and wouldn't come out, they just watched those three commercials over and over again, laughing and applauding each turn of the loop. We had invited press from everywhere and Manhattan's trendiest crowd. They pumped Joe's hand, congratulating him, women kissed him on both cheeks. "I don't believe this," he kept saying to me. "I don't believe this."

Charlie Moss had returned from Peru and come straight to Wells Rich Greene to continue working on the Braniff campaign. Phil Parker came with him as well as Herb Green and George D'Amato. We were hiring the brightest and the best, in those halcyon days we struck gold with everyone we hired, we had a wand. Noel Duffy, who was our receptionist, became Charlie's secretary and then his right and left hand until we forced him to allow her to head up creative hiring and she became known as the best in the business. She was typical, she was so good at anything she decided to do. That's what Wells Rich Greene was made of, talent from top to bottom, and the reason we were able to accept so much business so fast. No other agency in history ever grew as we did in our first five years.

Years later it was pointed out to us that we were at the forefront of the swift ethnic changeover on Madison Avenue in the sixties. What had been primarily an old-school, WASP advertising society with only the occasional Jewish agency became an ethnic shake of everything from everywhere, often people from art schools and trendy trade schools. We weren't trying to breed a new social culture at Wells Rich Greene, we didn't harbor any lofty motives, we were looking for men or women who had a gift for cinematic use of television combined with a nose for selling, people capable of outsized ideas and industry revolutions. Such talent was rare and it wasn't packaged uniformly, we took it as it came. Sometimes clients complained about our "New York" humor. They meant ethnic humor, but in fact the talent we found was as often Southern from the Carolinas and Georgia as it was Irish from Belfast, Italian from Brooklyn or Jewish from Manhattan.

We were falling out the windows of the Gotham; they probably wanted us gone because they refused to give us more rooms, so after a few months we found office space on Madison Avenue, nothing much, they were modest offices, we were pretty tight, but I had an office of my own. We didn't have time for decorating, although we did plaster the walls with Love posters and tossed psychedelic pillows around and we allowed Mick Jagger to sing "Have You Seen Your Mother, Baby?" in the waiting room.

My life has resonated with music, in the late sixties and early seventies it was rock, it identified the players. Idealistic in those days, all about hope and love, it helped paint us the way our clients wanted us to be, the way we were when we were young. I filled the offices with Elton's song and his tiny dancer and Jimi's purple haze hung suspended in the air. The Beatles and Janis Joplin preached to us from every corner and we added a little spice, Mick, Led Zeppelin, David Bowie, always Joni Mitchell. *Rolling Stone* appeared about the same time we did and we sent issues along with hot albums to clients who, even if uncool, relished the thought.

Peter Godfrey came to see me, the president of Menley & James, he had just come off a success with Contac time-release capsules, he was one of the bright lights of a company that was chockablock full of elegant WASPs, every one of them had pink cheeks in winter and a perfect Massachusetts tan in summer, they were the only clients I ever had that blushed, but maybe it was something about us. Probably. Peter came with two partners, Bill Howe and Sam Rulan Miller. Sam blushed no matter what we said. They were very correct, from Philadelphia. They wanted me to help them break into the steaming youth market with a cosmetics line designed specifically for younger women. When we knew they were coming we made sure an exotic menagerie of young creatures floated about the agency. Styles flit, who knows what would feel right tomorrow or even tonight?

Peter's problem was that he didn't have a department of cosmetics experts to create a new cosmetics line. To afford such a staff he needed the approval of Smith Kline & French, the parent company, and it was ultra-conservative, used to making big money on sales of prescription drugs. He didn't think they had a clue about rebellious youth and how big a market it was for them. He wanted us to put together a convincing plan and presentation for Smith Kline's board of directors. I knew from hunting in drugstores that there was very little out there for young women, young skin, young attitudes, just a scattering of Mary Quant here and there. We thought that the potential in a young cosmetics line was worth the gamble of our time and Peter did offer us a reasonable fee to cover expenses. He and I started out creating the basics ourselves. My one luxury, a tiny powder room off my office, became our product-development lab and that's where we began our search for a signature fragrance. We smelled everything Peter's lab had to offer. We talked fragrance to young women at the agency and in department stores, we stopped them on the streets. Finally we agreed that the only fragrance that smelled like the young sixties was lemon. It had zing, it was heady, it was happy, it felt free, it was so simple and obvious that it hadn't been overused in products for older, more sophisticated women. Lemon topped the popularity charts when we put it into fragrance tests so Peter and his group experimented with it and pretty soon Wells Rich Greene smelled like a lemon grove, everybody was wearing something lemony as part of a test.

We had a role model for the makeup products—Elaine in *The Graduate,* played by Katharine Ross. Dustin Hoffman had been pounding on church doors screaming "Elaine!!!" and she was who we had in mind when we created our cosmetics line. We made the first foundation that was so sheer it was merely a touch of color, just enough to even out the natural color of young skin, and we made a see-through lipstick and gloss. We listened obsessively to young women babbling about what they wanted in cosmetics and couldn't find. We made a body lotion after girls told us they hated to put anything oily or greasy on their bodies, they wanted something light, fast-drying, something that would give them a smooth slick, much like today's hydrating lotions.

The name for the line came easily, the Beatles were saying that love was in the air and I thought that was as good a reason as any to call it "Love Cosmetics." Packaging was a challenge. I called Murray Jacobs and Cay Gibson, who had been the promotion whiz kids at Doyle Dane, and hired them by phone. They came because I said, "Listen, Murray, Cay, I want to revolutionize cosmetics packaging but you will have to do the impossible, we don't have time to make models, we don't have investment money, not one red cent, we have to pull this one out of thin air, overnight, maybe it really is impossible, even for you, what do you think?" They had always loved doing the impossible, I knew they would come. Murray took existing production bottles and made them look young with some abandoned dome tops he found. They gave the bottles a sensual look, and the lipsticks were almost scandalous— we called them Lovesticks. After Dick Rich saw them he told Murray he should circumcise them.

Peter was calm about those phallic-shaped bottles but by the time he saw them he had met Cay Gibson and nothing ever shocked him again. Cay was a recognizable genius, wonderful to talk to, but she did look unnervingly like a large squaw with brilliant black metal eyes aimed at you, glittering, ready, waiting to catch you being ordinary, boring, over the hill. She was brutally candid, her sense of humor was raunchy, even scary, but because she smoked too much, she had a turbulent, gurgling smoker's hack that screened most of her extreme remarks. Clients treasured her, and, sooner or later, they loved her dearly.

Until our "Love" campaign, Revlon's Fire & Ice promotion had set the record for an expensive cosmetics launch. Bill McGivney and I planned the massive launch for Love because Peter intended to give the line to his loyal drugstores as a payback for making Contac a success. Department stores would want it but they wouldn't get it, at least not at first, so advertising would have to make up for Love's limited distribution. I didn't agree with Peter's strategy and fought to give Love to department stores, but you can't win them all so I insisted on a $10 million budget, a vast sum for a cosmetics introduction in the sixties, but I knew we needed to flood the country with enough advertising for Love cosmetics to induce young women to get up and go find them if they were only going to appear in better drugstores.

In all the world Bob Schulman was the last writer you would imagine for cosmetics advertising, at the time he was a brilliant, mischievous, overstimulated dropout. I would have preferred somebody like Warren Beatty but Charlie was sure that if we put Bob Schulman together with advertising's prince of beautiful art direction, Tom Heck, and prayed a little, we would get what we hoped for. Tom was out of a Fitzgerald novel, Bob played the bad boy. He would wander in at strange hours and drop crumpled pieces of paper on Tom's lap and mumble something like "I did this—not very good—you won't like it—it's really shit" and then disappear. Tom would howl. Charlie or I would soothe him. But the crumpled pieces of paper had the right words in the revolutionary but innocent and very young sixties. For Love's Basic Moisture, for example:

I'm a skin man myself.
I guess I come by it naturally.
My father's a dermatologist.
My mother's an exotic dancer.

I've been exposed to skin all my life.
Which brings me to my girl.
Sensitive.
Pretty.
Rich.
But her skin didn't come up to my high standards.
Then she started using something different on her skin.
She used so many things I didn't pay any notice.
But this stuff really worked.
It's done wonders for her whole mental outlook.
And our relationship has improved 100%.

One evening about nine, just as I was leaving, he handed me this poem for the Lemon fragrance commercial:

> *The first time I saw her*
> *She was standing over there.*
> *There was something different about her.*
> *Something that made her*
> *Stand out from the rest.*
> *I thought at first it was her skin.*
> *So soft, so fresh, so clean.*
> *But there was more.*
> *As I stood next to her*
> *I detected the subtle odor of lemon.*
> *I became obsessed with lemons.*
> *I developed an insatiable thirst for lemonade.*
> *At night I dreamed of lemon groves.*
> *Of all the women I have ever known*
> *I chose her,*
> *I picked a lemon in the garden of love.*

We set these Schulmanesques against Donovan's song "Wear Your Love Like Heaven." In only three months we were able to go to Smith Kline & French with a position, a plan, a budget, products, packages and merchandising units plus a complete television and print media schedule. Smith Kline & French approved our ambitious program, we had a public-relations launch in a hip young hangout in Paris, the basement of Le Drugstore, where we had Donovan and Liza Minnelli and Régine perform for the glamorama of Paris, including the Duke and Duchess of Windsor. Six months later Love was viewed as the most successful cosmetics launch in history. Lemon sold out *overnight,* Peter's drugstores were delirious. Gallup & Robinson's "recall" measurement told us that more people recalled Love Cosmetics than the Statue of Liberty.

Everything we touched in those first years of Wells Rich Greene set some kind of record. We never fell into the trap of believing our fortunes couldn't change, though; we ran scared a lot of the time, we used to describe those days as living in a tank full of jellyfish, we kept expecting the sting. It was too good to be true, too good to last.

Come rain or come shine

Charlie and I took all the new advertising that followed the introduction of the new Braniff International to Dallas, by that time Braniff was thoroughly mythologized and needed to move on and announce its promotions and schedules and its increasing number of destinations. In our meeting with Harding it seemed to me that he had become a dozen executives in one, I had never seen anyone address so many different issues all at one time; people stood in line to get an opinion or an approval. His meetings tended to last three minutes. He had a clear and roaring-fast mind and he needed it those months, those years, building that airline. He was fearless, too, up to necessary confrontations, and there were a lot of confrontations in an industry that was competing for routes in Washington.

He was good-looking in a romantic way, sexy. I saw the libidinous glints in the eyes of the women who hung around him. I used to wonder who all those women were but thought it would be a leading question for me to ask. And I also observed the soft sweet ways the thousand and one Braniff hostesses had when they were near him. I tried not to think about him personally but that was just a little game I played. When we finished our advertising meeting with him Charlie took the five o'clock flight back to New York with all the adapted advertising and the new plans we'd made. I pulled the last bits and pieces together, said my goodbyes to Tom and Glenn and left for the airport to catch the seven o'clock flight. I checked in and when I looked up I saw Harding standing there watching me, tossing the keys to his car from one hand to the other. We looked at each other and connected in some crucial way—if this was a gothic novel I would use the word "primordial," it's the word for that connection. I don't remember leaving the terminal with him; everything stripped away from me except that awareness of connecting, and after that night in Dallas that connection never let up, never loosened, even though after we married he worked in Dallas, I worked in New York, we both spent more time traveling around the world on airplanes than we did with each other and we lived together only on weekends. It didn't matter, it simply didn't matter where we were, it still doesn't and it won't. Somewhere in both of us where there are no boundaries and no end there is an infinite connection.

We married in Paris at the *mairie* of the eighth arrondissement. We loved France and thought we could have a romantic and reasonably private ceremony there. Halston had been making hats at Bergdorf Goodman, nobody had ever heard of him, but I had seen his sketches and I asked him to make me a green velvet wedding dress. It was the first dress he ever sold to anyone. He made little versions in green velvet for my daughters, too. Hubert de Givenchy made a black ruffled and flounced organza creation for me to wear the evening before the wedding and, what with all the fittings and fuss, became a dearly beloved, forever friend, important to my life. I was something to see in that glorious dress; Alexandre had given me a head full of vampy curls. We led our wedding party to the Tour d'Argent with its walls of windows on the Seine where we created a dance floor and danced all night with Paris shimmering at our feet.

Harding and I announce our engagement in Washington, D.C., in 1967.

We bought a big lovely family house in a garden of pink azaleas in Dallas and Billy Baldwin decorated it for us. Katy and Pam went to a school that sat on a green park half the size of Manhattan. It was the fairy-story period in our lives. There wasn't time to take a honeymoon but later that year Harding and I spent a sleepy week alone in St. Tropez while my mother vacationed in East Hampton with the girls. Grace Feldman, my assistant, had been looking for the perfect secretary for me. She had pretty much settled on a beauty, a sunny blonde, Kathie Durham, because she had excessive energy and her handwriting was like mine. But she wanted to put Kathie to the ultimate test, she told her she had to go to East Hampton to baby-sit my mother, Katy and Pam. Kathie didn't like children, had never read a bedtime story, she put up a struggle but she went, she says, to get the $20-a-week raise Grace promised. She became not only an aunt to Katy and Pam, but my lifelong buddy and secret sharer and a pillar of the agency at a time when we needed pillars.

As months passed and I was expected to be in more and more places at the same time we discovered that Kathie had the gift of being me, first as a stand-in at special events, but later as a class act of her own appreciated by clients, society and the press, making it possible for me to become Houdini and appear to be in more than one place at one time.

In 1967 when Harding and I married it never entered his mind or mine that I would leave Wells Rich Greene, that we would have a traditional marriage living and working in the same town. Betty Friedan established NOW in 1966 and although she was already focusing on the ERA and the right of women to control their reproductive lives, the psychological shift that the women's movement brought to society had not yet changed it. Long-distance marriage was major news and we were forever being interviewed about the details of ours. There was just enough awareness about what Betty Friedan called "the problem that has no name," the growing sense that motherhood and housework were not enough for some women, that our marriage was examined with respect, if not awe. Harding and I are both naturally nomadic and our timing was good, the jet was cutting the world in half, in fact the world was fast becoming small as his interests became increasingly international and mine were breaking out all over.

I'm stepping out

The compliments we were getting from the press attracted businesses that had sagging brands, the kind that were number two or number three in sales and were sliding. They read about our dramatic turnarounds and brought us their emergencies and they all had great expectations and total faith. God knows we were sincere in our ambitions for them—we were ready to do just about anything to keep our reputation growing. I welcomed them as if I were the Mother Superior of Lourdes and persuaded my fellow workers that we had been given divine insights—all we had to do was work overtime. We worked endless hours and I looked upon anyone who left the agency before eight or nine p.m. as a traitor—an attitude that was nurturing and animating at Wells Rich Greene but didn't help me in my long-distance life with my family in Dallas.

By then Wells Rich Greene looked more like a rock group than a reliable business. We all had long hair, peacock clothes, amazing, irreverent offices (the art directors' offices were filled with talismans like Judy Garland's red feather fan and Abbie Hoffman handbills and purple silhouettes of David Bowie), we had New York humor, untrammeled optimism and we talked hip talk.

On the other hand, we were expected to provide all the traditional advertising services—marketing, media, research, sales promotion—as though we had been in business for centuries. In those early days, when we needed an executive with experience that we didn't have, I tried to find the best. For example, the big companies that came to us had important television interests. We needed to demonstrate that we had media sophistication in order to become agency of record for them and handle whatever TV programming they did. I thought of Pat Weaver, telephoned him and invited him to lunch.

Sylvester "Pat" Weaver was the very spirit of television. When he was the chairman of NBC he created the *Today* show with Dave Garroway and the *Tonight!* show with Steve Allen. He conceived the idea of "Spectacular" television shows, big enough to allow multiple sponsorship, and he produced them with the most talented people of the time. One of them, *Your Show of Shows,* with Sid Caesar and Imogene Coca and Carl Reiner, was written by people like Mel Brooks, Neil Simon and even Woody Allen before they were names. Somebody once said that Pat originated every big idea that has been done on television.

He was a legend when the Sarnoffs pushed him out of NBC so that General Sarnoff's son, Bobby, could run it. Pat resigned and then spent a little time with Marion Harper as chairman of McCann International, and more recently he'd been wrestling with the first pay-television operation. He was too early with that idea, it was attacked by the television industry and some Californians who saw it as the beginning of the end of the civilized world, so it went into Chapter 11 and he was at loose ends. I thought just maybe he would consider a relationship with us that would give us an aura of distinguished television know-how and time to build an impressive TV department.

Pat suggested lunch at "21," the hangout for television people. I'd heard about his taste for high living and his extravagant expense accounts and I made a mental note to discuss all that. I reserved a table in the backroom that had the red checked tablecloths and hamburgers so expensive they must have been salted with diamonds and where everybody who was anybody waved at each other throughout lunch. I'd never seen Pat in person before. He was very tall and wore expensive clothes that hung on him in a way that reminded me of those old Hollywood photographs of stars in tennis sweaters and white flannels. He had a lanky, casual kind of walk and he flung his arms around some of the people in the restaurant. Just the way that he greeted them told me that he wasn't an operator, he wasn't a smoothie, I guessed that he was even gallant.

"Hello, Mary Wells," he said with a nice smile. He ordered a drink and took a long and careful look at me. "I know all about the advertising business," he said, "some of my best years were at Young & Rubicam. I should've stayed there, too, I'd be getting rich now." He sighed a sincere sigh. Pat never got rich and he would have loved being rich. I discovered why he didn't in the weeks to come—he was a visionary poet, not a down-to-earth businessman. "Did you know that I worked for a time with a friend of yours, Marion Harper? He's still trying to figure out how to get back into business with you," he laughed. "But you want to talk to me about television, don't you. Because I am television." He could see that I agreed with that so he eased into his drink and said that of everything he'd produced at NBC he thought *Producers' Showcase* set the standard. We talked about the night when *Producers' Showcase* presented *The Petrified Forest* with Humphrey Bogart and

Henry Fonda and Lauren Bacall. Nobody talked about anything else that week. It took television up a notch in class.

He ordered another drink and told me about his pay-television venture in California. The people had been brainwashed to vote against it in a referendum, he said; the California Supreme Court ruled the vote illegal and he won all the appeals but the cost of the defense put him out of business. He must have had three or four drinks before he nibbled the edges of his hamburger and then he pulled out a small stack of papers with charts and red pencil notes. I realized with a sinking heart that the reason he was lunching with me was to propose that Wells Rich Greene go into the pay-television business with him. I tried to think of a way to bring him down from that dream to Wells Rich Greene's piddling media needs. He wasn't drunk, but almost. I wanted to interrupt him but he had prepared a lovingly detailed presentation so I listened to him for a long time. Finally, when he took a breath, I told him that we were not interested in pay television, that we needed a television executive as exciting as Wells Rich Greene itself to lead us into the future, and before he could refuse I started negotiating an impressive salary with him plus a hefty expense account. He was getting older and he needed money so he put on a good face and we struck a deal. But I revered him and I hated disappointing him. For a few minutes I devoutly wished I was interested in pay television.

We were the last to leave "21" and people stopped by to pay their respects to Pat on their way out of the restaurant. Bill Paley leaned over and whispered something in Pat's ear about NBC that made Pat wince and then noticed me. He came on to me in the most practiced way. I was surprised. He was so confident that I would be attracted to him. I've never equated power with sexiness and I didn't find Bill Paley at all appealing. I ignored him. He remembered, I think he kept score of the conquests he didn't make, and years later, when we were friendlier, he reminded me that I snubbed him when we met that day with Pat. Leland Hayward came over to Pat to say a warm hello and he was gracious and charming so he went on my good-guy list. We left "21" and Pat Weaver joined Wells Rich Greene in the fanciest office we could provide then and oh my, his expense account did upset me as time went on. He paid for his "21" lunches, though, right away, because he brought Roy Chapin in to see us.

Roy Chapin was the new chairman of American Motors. AMC had been put on the map by George Romney, who gave America the Rambler, an economical little box on wheels. George was born in Chihuahua, Mexico, where his parents and other Mormons moved to avoid U.S. laws against, of all things, polygamy, and he became a Mormon missionary in England. Later, he became a missionary in Detroit, too, as he was determined to spread the joys of owning a small economical car at a time when America was driving bigger and bigger cars. In Detroit they said that Romney was such a rousing, persuasive speaker he could swing a crowd, and his little Rambler compact that sold for a pittance got to be popular enough to force the Big Three car makers into designing small cars.

But when George left American Motors to become the governor of Michigan, AMC lost its focus as the small-car leader. It started copying the bigger cars at Ford and General Motors and Chrysler just about the time that America changed its mind and turned instead to smaller, sportier, sexier models. Then the youthquake hit and American Motors became totally confused, it didn't know what in the world to do. The company started to look endangered. Older people stopped buying the cars, share of market slipped to less than 3 percent, most young people said they had never even seen an American Motors car. The Detroit press claimed American Motors was slipping into a red hole, the company lost $60 million (a lot to lose in the sixties), and the summer that Roy Chapin came to see us it faced a December due date of another $66 million in short-term loans. "Bankruptcy!" screeched the press. One by one, nervous dealers said adios and moved to Ford and General Motors. It felt like the plague had struck American Motors. There was nothing but bad news and depression, and every time the phone rang it was a threatening banker. Executives started coming in late and going home early because they were looking for jobs someplace else.

The board of directors met and probably had bankruptcy in mind when they chose the treasurer to become the new chairman and chief executive officer. Roy Chapin was the treasurer. He'd grown up in automobile land, his father had founded the Hudson Motor Company, and Roy knew all the dos and don'ts in Detroit. But he turned out to be a genetic surprise to everybody. He didn't care a scrap about Detroit's dos and don'ts when the boat began to sink. He had strong faith in his own convictions. Not long before he became chairman, he and beautiful Sis Chapin shocked conventional, clubby Detroit by falling in love, getting divorces and marrying each other with obvious relish. I thought that was a good sign he was not easily intimidated.

In the weeks before he came to see us at Wells Rich Greene, Roy sold off assets to reduce debt, sweet-talked his bankers into renewing his loans, chopped prices of cars and lifted two new sporty cars out of the design studios to attract the new young world he knew he had to reach. He and his president, Bill Luneberg, ran all over the country replacing the 400 dealers that had defected and did everything they could think to do to assure car buyers that American Motors was going to be just fine. After all, nobody wants to buy a car from a company that's about to disappear. When he saw the advertising that his agency presented, he thought it was "the same old bland, boring advertising that wouldn't change a thing." He wanted a different kind of advertising that could make a real difference and that talked clearly to the new young world. That's when Pat called him. Pat was friendly with Roy's father, they belonged to the same clubs, and he learned that Roy might be looking for a new agency. He told Roy about Wells Rich Greene and sent him press clippings that raved about our miraculous powers and cool ways with the youth market.

We were still at 575 Madison Avenue with our psychedelic pillows and posters and John Lennon singing about love when Roy Chapin, Bill Luneberg and Bill McNealy, AMC's marketing chief, visited us. I spent the day before they arrived hiding our most colorful people and pictures because I thought Detroit executives might be the last ones on earth who still had an ultra-conservative view of youth. Well, if we unnerved them, they didn't show it. They were looking for the most contemporary agency in the business and we were the Now agency, so they were prepared for anything. Nobody at Wells Rich Greene knew much about the automobile business except what some of us had witnessed at Volkswagen. But they weren't looking for automobile experience, either. They knew all about Braniff, Alka-Seltzer and Benson & Hedges and they wanted that kind of thinking and advertising and that kind of success.

Roy had been the chief executive officer of American Motors just a few months when he walked into my small yellow office. He was lean and agile, like a tennis champ, wearing a narrow suit with a vest. He had the misleading, shy smile that Mel Gibson has and I wondered about him as a leader until he looked straight into me with Mel Gibson's laser-beam eyes.

We bunched into my office, Roy, Bill Luneberg, Bill McNealy, Pat, Dick, Stew, me. Roy put on his glasses, took them off, put them on again—something I learned he did whenever he was nervous—and very slowly, very quietly he spelled out his problems as if he were sitting around a campfire telling horror stories. For a couple of hours he told us about the deep purple gloom taking over the company, the depressed executives, the frightened dealers who wouldn't take his calls and the loyal owners of American Motors cars who seemed to have gone up in smoke, they had just disappeared. He spoke candidly about his dangerous financial situation; then Bill Luneberg and Bill McNealy told us about the current fleet, describing it in detail, car by car. We could tell there wasn't anything special about any of those cars, but they had to be sold and Roy did have his two smart, sporty cars coming down the line, the Javelin and the AMX. Survival was the immediate issue and confidence was the key. That, Roy said, was why he had come to Wells Rich Greene. He wanted theatrical, legendary advertising and he wanted it to be surefooted — sure-wheeled, he corrected himself with a grin—in other words he wanted it to be so conspicuously self-confident that the advertising's confidence in itself would rub off on American Motors and make it appear certain to be around for a long time. And he wanted advertising for his stunning new Javelin and his AMX so evangelistic it would be transcendent for the company. He stood up and paced my little rug. "We're in trouble for the moment. But we can get out of this if you're as good an agency as you say."

Yes. Sure. Dick and Stew and I sat there trying to wind up our enthusiasm and our nerve. Dick was always telling the press, "If we were modest we'd be perfect." Conceit was part of our zeitgeist. But we were *carefully* conceited. We weren't crazy. We understood Roy and we saw the dangers. I could see we were making Pat Weaver nervous, he was so pleased with himself for bringing in that account. He wanted us to jump up and shout hosanna and sign a contract. My office had been getting warmer and warmer. We were all damp when we finally stood up. The early-evening sun was reflecting off the floating dust in the air and the place felt explosive. I was feeling big-time pressure, not hosanna. I knew they would offer us the account and I knew that helping to save American Motors would cement our reputation. But what if they did go bankrupt? And they certainly could. Agencies are usually liable for the media purchases they make for clients. If Wells Rich Greene committed to television time and magazine space and American Motors couldn't pay, we would have to pay. And we could not possibly pay bills of that magnitude at that early stage of our business. We would go bankrupt right along with them. I had looked into insurance before they came to see us but it was even more expensive than bankruptcy.

They left us, it was late and dark. As the elevator door closed on them I saw a lot of creases shoot across Roy's face for the first time that day. He was a lot more worried than he was letting on. He had been impressively controlled with us. I was taken with his acting ability, and for some reason it gave me the courage of an insane person. I turned to Dick and Stew and gave them a big jackpot smile. "This is our cup of tea," I said brightly. They looked at me and saw a lunatic and went home, shaking their heads, leaving the elevator hall in silence and me musing on the pathetic eagerness advertising agencies show in accepting new accounts.

In ad biz, during an agency-and-client courtship, there is not enough time for the intimate research it would take to prepare an agency for the truth about the products the client makes or the services it sells—or its marketplace—or its competition. No prenuptial sleuthing reveals the client's soul, either. No bank or accounting firm will give out the kind of between-the-lines information an agency would do well to have before signing a contract that makes it responsible for media payments and for hiring expensive talent. Advertising executives, like most sales-men, are so responsive to fantasy they assume they will find a life with the client that will make everybody happy, famous and maybe even rich. They eagerly tie on blinders and open their arms to new accounts. (The more the merrier!) Then, after the contract signing, after the press announcements and after the agency self-congratulations the truth slowly but surely reveals itself. Agencies and clients learn to live with each other, sometimes with enormous success, until, over time, one or the other loses interest or there is a disaster. It is a lot like getting married.

Gambling on American Motors gave me a primal motivation to move heaven and earth to make them successful enough to pay their media bills. Roy Chapin understood that in spades. From the moment he called to offer us the account, Roy went into business with Wells Rich Greene as partners, creating a relationship with us that was unusual in royal, powerful Detroit at that time.

He held a news conference in Detroit's Statler Hilton Hotel to announce that Wells Rich Greene was American Motors' new advertis-ing agency and to introduce me to the Detroit press. He bounced down a red-carpeted ramp, grinning his confident grin. "I told Mary," he said to the large group, "just remember, we can't paint all our cars purple." We had agreed that I should exude confidence, too. It was no day for shrinking violets. I told the press that just as we had caused a stampede for extra-long cigarettes, painted planes and revolutionized Alka-Seltzer, we were going to electrify the market for American Motors cars. I said I thought the cars were terrific and just needed smarter marketing and that the new cars coming down the line were so good they would change the face of American Motors and probably Detroit. I said we had thrilling plans. Roy and I pulled flowers and rabbits out of the air that morning. The truth was that I hadn't seen the cars yet and it would be a week before I even had a glimmering of what we had to do.

After Roy disappeared down the elevator that evening at Wells Rich Greene we quickly reached out and hired some surefire, expensive talent to focus on the challenge with us. For $100,000 a year (a prince's ransom then) and the promise of becoming our creative director, Ron Rosenfeld left Doyle Dane Bernbach, where he was a star and had worked on Volkswagen. Stan Dragoti had been at Young & Rubicam winning art director's medals all over the world for his elegant Eastern Airlines advertising. We won him by promising him Ron Rosenfeld would be his partner and that he, too, would receive the same record-setting salary. We also hired the merchandising chief of Lincoln Mercury, Herb Fisher, to head up the account group. He looked like a young Lincoln and at that perilous time we needed Lincoln with us in Detroit to reassure everybody. He was an enormous help to us because he knew all about cars and marketing them. At Roy Chapin's press conference I introduced these advertising stars to the press as if they were astronauts about to leave for the moon. All the American Motors executives in the room were swept up in the confidence and enthusiasm of the moment. Bill Pickett, the sales chief, waved thumbs-up to everybody and looked as if he had just won the lottery. Wells Rich Greene's newly famous commercials were singing and dancing on the walls. Every beautiful girl that worked for us was there smiling, laughing, flirting. Happiness was so palpable at that press conference it must have been catching, because there was a melodramatic mood change. You could hear it in the laughs and in the delighted applause. And you could see it in all the upbeat stories we got in the following days. *Life* magazine was so excited by all the new optimism at American Motors that the editor followed Roy back to his office and arranged to photograph Wells Rich Greene during the important weeks ahead as we created the new advertising. He promised Roy a four-page story featuring the new Javelin, something American Motors needed badly.

As press conferences go, on a scale of one to ten, that one was a ten. I've played a part in many press conferences much more carefully orchestrated, based on unimpeachable facts, that didn't come off nearly as well. That American Motors press conference was all hype and theatrics but it was based on hope and prayers and desperation and sometimes that is a powerful combination.

Flying back to New York, Stan Dragoti noticed that Ron Rosenfeld was wringing his hands. "What's the matter, Ron, you're not feeling well?" Stan asked him. Ron was moaning quietly. He said something like, "You work all your life, think you're getting somewhere, then you find yourself right back in the arena." Next day, he didn't show up at Wells Rich Greene. "He said *what?*" I asked in disbelief. Stan and Dick and Stew and I were absorbing this setback. "Well," Stan said, "he could see what was expected of him and I guess he just wanted to be a creative director, not a magician."

Dick and I considered other possibilities but each would take too much time to negotiate. We decided to ask Charlie Moss to kill himself and handle both Braniff and American Motors. Dick called Charlie at home that night. Dick called everybody Bubby. "Bubby, you say you want to be rich? Well, here's your chance!" he schmoozed. Yes, Charlie wanted to be rich, he would kill himself to be rich, so he and Stan became the star team for American Motors. Stan was a little disconcerted that he had left Young & Rubicam to work with the great Ron Rosenfeld and was now going to work with Charlie Moss, a kid with an Afro haircut. Stan Dragoti has always looked like Mr. Hollywood, a tall, dark matinee idol in natty clothes. He and Jack Nicholson and Warren Beatty must have their white suits and blue shirts made by the same tailor. It took Charlie Moss a little while to start wearing Armani and then he became a clotheshorse. But when Stan first met him he was a skinny kid wearing Levi's and an alligator shirt. Charlie always wore a sober suit at meetings with Harding at Braniff but as far as I know that was the only suit he had. And he did indeed have a large Afro hairdo. One of my dearest memories of Roy Chapin is the expression on his face when he first saw Charlie Moss with his Afro, the writer who was going to save American Motors.

Charlie Moss and Stan Dragoti would turn out to be the Rodgers and Hart of the advertising business, but they didn't bond for a while. On their first working trip to Detroit they argued so fiercely about how to make great advertising they paid no attention to where they were going and got lost for hours, missing the first important meeting we had at American Motors. I would have had a fit but there wasn't time to be angry. Bill McNealy, the marketing chief, came into our offices the next day to give us an intensive education, everything we needed to know about American Motors cars and the competition to get us going.

Great advertising, the kind that works, almost always comes out of the product you are going to advertise or the product's world. You need to have an open mind, the nosiness of a detective, and to assimilate all the information you can get from every imaginable source when you start to create advertising. It is knowledge that stimulates great advertising ideas and your own intuition. If you find that the product is factually superior to its competitors in any important way, you are in clover. For example, if you have fluoride in a toothpaste called Crest and the ADA approves your claim of its superior effectiveness against cavities, it is no time to be coy. Go for it. There is nothing better than a fact if you have a great one. If, on the other hand, your product appears to be inferior to its competitors, maybe it is and maybe it isn't, but don't be naïve; it is always possible that the competitors' advantage is really just a way of looking at the product, a dream that some other advertising wizard had and presented in advertising so good it has been accepted as a vital truth. You yourself have to *know* before you can spin. You have to gather up information, positive and negative, take it apart and analyze it coolly, shrewdly and with imagination. Unique products and clear cases of superiority don't come along every five minutes—a lot of products are similar to other products—so with knowledge to guide you, that is the moment that your imagination kicks in and you become a storyteller. Advertising, in any form, is about telling stories that captivate readers or viewers and persuade them to buy products. "I love you" is a sales story—a very persuasive story, too. Doyle Dane Bernbach told very talented stories and turned an ugly little car into a beloved icon. Talented storytelling has turned Nike running shoes into one of the hippest and snobbiest symbols of all time. You can tell stories in many ways, with or without words. But knowledge is the fuel that ignites your talent in the advertising business.

Bill McNealy came and made it clear he was gung ho. He was totally on board with Roy's plan to bring American Motors back to health, wealth and youth. He pored over statistics and specifications with us trying to clarify the different models and show us where they stood in the overall Detroit picture. American Motors cars were me-too cars, copies of the other automobile companies' cars. But they weren't as sexy, they had no va-voom. I'd never been a car buff, all the statistics made me dizzy and sleepy, so I asked for an emergency demonstration at an airport where we could see and drive every American Motors car and its competition and begin to feel the cars in our imaginations, and hopefully love them for some reason, any reason at all.

Rounding up those American Motors cars and some of the competitive cars and getting them to a side field at the airport was like organizing Barnum & Bailey and sending its elephants and lions and tigers from Los Angeles to New York on a superhighway. But we moved that mountain in a couple of days and Charlie, Stan, Herb Fisher and Vic Olesen, a smart fellow we hired to head our new Detroit office, met me at the airport, where we inspected every car and some of us drove them all.

That is where I got the strategy for the first campaign we would create for American Motors. Charlie and I were driving side by side, Charlie in American Motors' new Javelin and me in Ford's Mustang, waving at each other, pretending we were racing at the Grand Prix in Monte Carlo, when it hit me that only 3 percent of Americans owned American Motors cars, which meant that 97 percent of Americans knew as little about them as we did. So American Motors cars were a big zero in America. We had to position those cars in automobile buyers' minds just as we were positioning them in our own minds by driving them and the competitive cars out there at the airport. The only way to do that was to compare each American Motors car, side by side, with a competitive car that was a star, a famous car that everybody knew and admired and was similar to the American Motors car. Such a direct comparison would tell prospective buyers what sort of animal the American Motors car was and, if we were clever, get across the idea that the American Motors car was superior to the other, well-known car. For example, comparing the Javelin to the Mustang would tell you instantly what sort of car the Javelin was, and if we played our cards right, we would persuade you that the Javelin was the better high-performance car of the two.

The problem was that Detroit automakers had an unspoken agreement cast in virtual bronze that they would never compare their cars with rival cars. Competitive advertising among Detroit cars was considered derogatory to automobile business in general and, in particular, to the aristocratic gentlemen of Detroit. This may sound quaint today but in 1967 Detroit protected itself by playing with white-gloved gentlemen's rules endemic to a town that felt it bred a superior breed.

We can't afford to wear white gloves, I thought behind the wheel of that car that day at the airport. I was sure that presumptuousness, even intelligent impertinence, was expected of us by American Motors. Roy had come to Wells Rich Greene in search of the unorthodox and he understood that ideas big enough to change people's minds usually break rules.

We learned our lessons at the airport, each of us made notes about the cars using the specification sheets as guides. We noted everything from the space in the baggage compartments to the carpeting on the station-wagon floor to the size of every window to the strength of the bumpers to overall quality and style. We were scheduled to present a marketing plan complete with advertising to the board of directors in only three weeks. We took rooms in a hotel near the agency to get away from day-to-day agency pressures and we pored over mountains of statistics and all of our notes looking for inspiration. Hunting for anything that could make a difference to car buyers, with the clock ticking, three weeks to go, built up an atmosphere of siege. Passing each other going in and out of the hotel rooms or the agency, we slipped each other notes and passed on interesting discoveries in stage whispers. At times like these it is absolutely impossible to sleep. You don't want to sleep, you are afraid you will lose the thread that is leading you to a great answer.

We had discovered that American Motors cars were made just a little bit better in small ways than many competitive cars. We had a collection of examples that could suggest American Motors made its cars more lovingly, that they were more in tune with the consumer. They put carpeting on the rear deck of the station wagons, they put their ashtrays on ball bearings, they made the gas tanks a little bigger, the trunks a little roomier, the batteries a little more powerful and added a few inches of hip room to backseats. The cars had an aura of a little more strength, a little less tin. There were plenty of nice extras to use in comparison advertising, but nothing was earthshaking.

What was earthshaking was the Javelin. It turned out to be a really hot high-performance car that we thought beat the Mustang in many ways, and the Mustang was America's most adored car. The Javelin gave us the excitement we needed for the company and was the linchpin for all the selling stories we were pulling together for the entire fleet of cars. "Well," Bill McNealy said uncomfortably, "I don't know how soon you can have the Javelin for the campaign. We're a little behind there." He shuffled his papers, wouldn't look at me. Everybody else in the room looked at me. My startling comparison strategy for American Motors depended heavily on the Javelin-Mustang comparison.

"Wait a minute," I said, "what time frame are you talking about? What do you mean you're a little behind?" I remember standing up and glaring down at Bill McNealy. "Nine months is what they're saying," he said. "WE DON'T HAVE NINE MONTHS," I said. "Pardon me?" he asked. "We don't have nine months. We'll be dead in nine months. We have to have the Javelin on schedule." I repeated myself: "We have to have the Javelin on schedule. Bill, please leave right now, get the next plane out, tell Roy Chapin that either we have the Javelin on schedule or we will not be able to make a presentation to the board of directors in two weeks. It'll be all over. We are out of time. We were promised the Javelin and this campaign has to have it to make any sense. WE MUST HAVE THE JAVELIN IN THIS CAMPAIGN." Well, there was no doubt about that and Bill McNealy agreed, so he left for Detroit and called in the next day to report that the Javelin was back on schedule.

We were having trouble with the Ambassador, American Motors' most expensive big car. It was a lot like the largest Chevys and Fords and it was in a price category where an image of luxury and style was half of what you paid for. American Motors was known for its sturdy Ramblers and Rebels but not for luxury or style. The Ambassador was a good-looking, comfortable car but we had to give it a new image so it could compete with the Chevys and Fords on their territory in people's minds.

I've never inspected anything as closely as I inspected that Ambassador. Charlie and I measured the roof and the windows and I actually crawled into the trunk to see if there was a good story in there and then one of our little group that was going autocrazy said, "What if it had air-conditioning standard? Would that do it?" Yes, we thought, that would do it. Air-conditioning standard was unheard of in that class of car in the sixties and would say more about the Ambassador's luxury and quality than all the clever advertising in the world. I told our group to just assume the Ambassador would have air-conditioning standard. Automobile companies are not in the habit of taking advice on product changes from ad agencies, but I was willing to gamble that Roy would buy the idea because it was such a good one.

By that time I was certain we needed a parallel-runway type of campaign. We needed my comparison advertising in print—impertinent, anti-establishment double-page magazine spreads that compared each American Motors car with its most famous rival, beginning with the Mustang and the Javelin. (I could just see them side by side, two bright-red sporty cars, the Mustang icon and the new contender for the throne, the Javelin SST.) This print campaign would position the cars so that America could understand and admire them. However, to change the image of the company, the creator of the cars, American Motors, from dull to glittering, to display the sublime self-confidence Roy had asked for, to thrill America and to wake up and seduce the disinterested youth market, we needed something much more presumptuous than double-page comparison spreads in magazines. We needed chutzpah television, brazen commercials that could not be ignored and would be talked about from Maine to California.

It was show-business time. Charlie and Stan went to the Commodore Hotel and hung the Do Not Disturb sign on the door. They looked at each other; they talked about marriage, wives, children, old girlfriends; they talked about why they got into the advertising business; they talked about Charlie's terrible clothes and where he should buy his suits; they told jokes; they revealed secrets. They smoked their lungs out and drank pots of coffee. They had dozens of ideas but they were paralyzed with fear and didn't trust them, they didn't trust each other yet, either, they were so newly wed. This is a traditional occupational hazard in the advertising business. Writer's block, art director's block, idea block, shyness between the writer and the art director, inferiority complex, depression—it can happen to any creative team when the stakes are so high.

They kept piling tissues of scribbles and words into stacks in corners of the room. When nothing came forth I should have remembered the writer's block Charlie had when he started working on the Braniff account and done something to bring down the stress. I had such confidence in them and I thought the solution was so clear that I turned away from them for a couple of days to deal with other clients who were pounding on my door complaining "Where did you go?????" as they do when you are out of sight more than five minutes. Charlie and Stan felt, they said, as if they were locked inside a cage that had been lowered into a sea swarming with great white whales and killer sharks. Finally, Charlie went home and hid.

He went home to his six-month-old baby boy, Robbie, took him out of his crib and rocked him for a while in the baby's dark room and whispered, "I'm sorry, Rob, your dad's a failure, God knows what is going to become of us, I just can't do it, I don't have it in me, big opportunity like this and I've let them all down." He telephoned Dick Rich at home and told him that he and Stan were not getting anywhere. "I don't know why," he said, "we just haven't connected, we're a fizzle—it's my fault—take me off the business and give Stan another writer." Dick called me and said Charlie had told him to "fire me, not Stan." I told Dick to tell Charlie to cut it out, he knew perfectly well what a scintillating talent he was, he must return to the hotel immediately. They had a date to show me commercials in two days and I couldn't wait to see them. Tell Charlie, I said, to remember Braniff.

Charlie returned to the Commodore and told Stan that they better have something great on paper for our meeting or I would very likely murder them. Stan asked if it wouldn't be enough to just verbally outline ideas and Charlie said, "You don't know her, after an expensive week at the Commodore Hotel we have to give her scripts and storyboards to introduce the campaign or all hell is going to break loose."

(Charlie, inexplicably, always pretended that he feared my wrath if his work was not superb. In fact, for 35 years I was his most adoring fan—probably because he always came through with great advertising solutions, albeit frequently at the last possible second. It's true that I have been known to exercise my dramatic abilities with other creative teams when they brought me terrible work. There was a myth that I could sell anything, but that was not true—I could not sell bad advertising, it made me physically sick. When it was presented to me I would overreact to ensure I would get great new stuff right away. But I was always adorable to Charlie.)

Just after midnight the morning we were scheduled to meet, Charlie and Stan created storyboards and a script for an amazing commercial in which workers happily beat a Ford Mustang to pieces with sledgehammers and built a gorgeous new Javelin in its place. It was a jarring, antiauthoritarian, brave and hypnotizing way of introducing a new car using the theatrical powers of television.

I arrived very early to see what they had and they presented this commercial to me. Charlie says that, as he could always tell whether I was bored or interested, he knew right away I was interested, and when they got to the part where they blew up the Mustang's trunk I looked really ecstatic. When they finished I beamed at them and said, "Nifty!" That was my Pulitzer word for creative work I thought extraordinary. I had developed an assortment of silly expressions to use at times when we were all frightened and couldn't show it. It helped to overcome the fact that, whether they admitted it or not, the men at Wells Rich Greene had a vein of nervousness about being led by a woman. I could see that my silly talk (or, sometimes, macho tough-guy talk full of daring and pride) had a tranquilizing effect. I suppose it made me look breezily confident. The commercial *was* nifty, and I knew then we were safe, they were on the right road.

Encouraged, Charlie and Stan went back to the hotel and developed the ideas that had been piling up in the corner as well as their faith in each other as partners. As each commercial was finished they would bring it back and I would say, again and again, "Nifty!" and in one week they completed all the television commercials and all the

The way it was for years and years, meeting with Charlie Moss in my office.

magazine and newspaper ads we would need and would produce for the coming year.

Alchemy plays a big role in creative businesses. In the advertising business a writer and an art director are assigned to one another by agency management and they have to toss ideas at one another until they establish an intimacy and a trust, at which point a psychic marriage of their talents takes place and they are magically able to produce advertising that sings. Sometimes. Sometimes alchemy doesn't happen and you have to find them different partners. It is a mysterious process.

"An unfair comparison between the Mustang and the Javelin." That was the headline for the first comparison ad created for magazines. The two cars, side by side, looked like big red rubies. The copy was direct:

An unfair comparison between

We asked a professional photographer to take a picture of both cars under identical conditions.

Thereby putting the Mustang at a disadvantage.

Our Javelin is equipped with massive contour bumpers.

Unfair to Mustang, because thin blade bumpers don't photograph as well.

Our Javelin is endowed with yards of costly glass. Side windows are all one piece, without vents to break up the line.

Unfair, because Mustang isn't nearly so generous.

Our Javelin has a richer, more polished look. Roof joints are hand-finished.

Unfair, because it is cheaper to make roof joints by machine.

Our Javelin has a bigger displacement and more horsepower in its standard 6-cylinder engine, bigger displacement in its standard V-8.

Unfair.

Our Javelin has more leg room, more

The 1967 Mustang

We declare war on Ford with this American Motors ad comparing the Javelin with the Mustang.

the Mustang and the Javelin.

head room, the backseat is a good 5 inches wider.

Unfair.

Our Javelin has a bigger gas tank, a roomier trunk, a more powerful battery.

Unfair.

Our Javelin comes with a sophisticated (flow-through) ventilation system, wheel discs, reclining bucket seats and a woodgrain steering wheel.

And, unfairest of all, our Javelin lists for no more than the Mustang.

The preceding comparison was made between a 1968 Javelin SST and a 1967 Mustang Hardtop, only because this year's model was not available from the manufacturer in time for this printing.

We really tried to get one.

American Motors
Ambassador · Rebel · American · And the new Javelin

The 1968 Javelin SST

Price comparison based on 1968 list prices. Vinyl tops and whitewall tires optional on both cars.

We asked a professional photographer to take a picture of both cars under identical conditions.

Thereby putting the Mustang at a disadvantage.

Our Javelin is equipped with massive contour bumpers.

Unfair to Mustang, because thin blade bumpers don't photograph as well.

Our Javelin is endowed with yards of costly glass. Side windows are all one piece, without vents to break up the line.

Unfair, because the Mustang isn't nearly so generous.

Our Javelin has a bigger displacement and more horsepower in its standard 6-cylinder engine, bigger displacement in its standard V-8.

Unfair.

Our Javelin has more leg room, more head room, the backseat is a good 5 inches wider.

Unfair.

Our Javelin has a bigger gas tank, a roomier trunk, a more powerful battery.

Unfair.

Our Javelin comes with a sophisticated (flow-through) ventilation system, wheel discs, reclining bucket seats and a woodgrain steering wheel.

And, unfairest of all, our Javelin lists for no more than the Mustang.

The preceding comparison was made between a 1968 Javelin SST and a 1967 Mustang Hardtop only because this year's model was not available from the manufacturer in time for this printing.

We really tried to get one.

We made a magazine ad that compared every American Motors car with its rival. We exaggerated a tad with the Ambassador—we placed it in the center of a double-page spread with a Cadillac on one side and a Rolls-Royce on the other. After all, those two cars had air-conditioning standard, too (at a steeper price). That ad wowed the dealers and tradi-

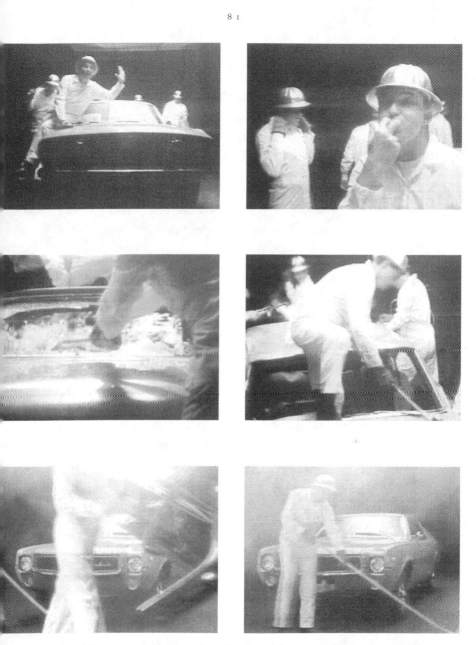

American Motors attracted the youth market for the first time with commercials like this one in which workers dismantled a Mustang and turned it into a Javelin.

tional Ambassador owners. One wrote a letter to us thanking us for making his wife "finally appreciate my intelligence and good taste after twenty-five years of marriage."

The television campaign began with Charlie and Stan's audacious destruction of the Mustang and its reconstruction as a Javelin. That commercial was intended to awaken the world to American Motors as well as to introduce the Javelin. Almost everybody who wrote an advertising or marketing column wrote about the originality and power of that commercial. A few people worried about showing violence on television but most viewers marveled and its Gallup & Robinson research scores for awareness and impact soared with every age group, particularly young men.

In that era of anti-authority American Motors was transformed into the young man's sporty automobile company because we dared. Sledgehammering an icon seemed a wondrous thing to young people. We almost didn't get the commercial on the air, though, not because of the violence issue, but because the networks were so concerned about angering Ford, one of their biggest spenders. Pat Weaver and Lew Wechsler, our director of network television, used their considerable weight with the chiefs of television, took them to long lunches and persuaded them to run the commercial by promising we would beat up a dummy car instead of an actual Mustang. No one could tell the difference between the dummy and the real Mustang in the commercial except the networks and the people at Ford, and it ran, successfully, for many months.

It was easy to make great commercials for the Javelin. One that became a classic and was remembered years after it went off the air featured the actor Herb Edelman driving it. First he attracts a group of flirtatious, beautiful blondes in another car who shout "Hey, Javelin!" at him and he smiles back politely. When he stops at a red light, a long-haired motorcycle cowboy pulls up to him and says, "Wanna drag? Come on!" When Edelman nods no the cowboy zooms off and an Italian pulls up in a fancy car, jerking his head to indicate he wants to race. Edelman tries to be polite and explains, "I've got a bowl of goldfish on the seat." Next it's a Frenchman in a convertible, who says, "Allo, mon ami, you want to race wiz me?" "No . . . merci," says Edelman. The announcer, the voice-over, says: "We at American Motors never had the reputation for building hot sporty cars. Then we built the Javelin." Edelman has now given his Javelin to a young, hotshot parking attendant, who races it up into the garage with a loud screech. Edelman closes his eyes and grimaces with pain as the voice-over continues: "It can go from 0 to 60 in 7.86 seconds. Now we have the reputation for building hot sporty cars."

The commercial was directed by Howard Zieff, one of advertising's premier directors. Howard is famous for giving television advertising tremendous visual style and a unique look but he isn't famous for his sense of humor. Stan picked up the line about the bowl of goldfish when an actor accidentally ad-libbed it at an audition. "You hear that, Howard? Isn't that funny?" Stan was so excited. But Howard never thought anything was funny. Stan told Charlie about the line, Charlie thought it was funny, I thought it was funny and America thought it was funny. "I've got a bowl of goldfish on the seat" became a household expression in the U.S. for years.

Those first American Motors television commercials starred a number of seriously good actors. In one that we called our *West Side Story* commercial, a young Richard Dreyfuss is a member of a gang of hoods who go crazy when they see a Javelin parked on the street because it's got such great parts to steal. And in another, young Robert De Niro brings his new Ambassador back to his old neighborhood to give his mother a ride and she does a take on the old "my son the doctor" line—she proudly brags to all the neighbors crowding around the car, "This is my son Joey, the one with air-conditioning standard."

The Rebel was a harder sale, but the commercial that won the most awards and love letters and sold a lot more Rebels than anyone ever expected was about a driving-school instructor. We discovered in our research that driving schools bought more Rebels than any other car because they held up so well. We filmed a series of vignettes in which a driving-school instructor goes through a series of funny tortures with his student drivers, pointing out that the Rebel was probably going to outlast the teachers.

American Motors predicts that the Rebel is going to outlast the
embattled driving school teachers in this commercial.

Life magazine's writer and photographer had been following us around, their cameras prowling from office to office all day long. There was no escaping them. When they first appeared we were concerned about what they would see or hear us say but after a while, with time ticking away, we forgot about them completely and they became wall-paper to us. Still, it was a little nervous-making to find them already seated in the board of directors room at American Motors the morning we were to present the new advertising. There they were, all set up to click the meeting for their story.

Detroit boardrooms, like the boardrooms of all of America's largest, most powerful businesses, have a solemn atmosphere that can be intimidating or even stupefying if you are not confident. They are usually a large oblong room with an enormous table made out of a seamless piece of wood from some majestic tree. This was a special meeting that was to include all the top executives of the company as well as board members, as Roy wanted everyone concerned to preview a program that could seriously affect American Motors' destiny. A small army of men came into the room, looking especially natty, as though each man had dressed up a little bit to greet a pivotal day. They were psyched for a big change in their advertising approach, ready to be young, ready to be cool.

Roy introduced us, explained our credentials, and relaxed everyone with his elegant, cheerful certainty that Wells Rich Greene was about to present the strategy, the advertising and the attitude American Motors needed so badly. He turned the meeting over to me and I talked about automobile advertising for a few minutes and the need to be human and to reach out and touch readers and viewers so that they would feel the automobiles and be moved by them. I talked about love in advertising, a word I always felt I had to decipher because business-men acted as if love were an erotic Russian word they did not under-stand. (Love? What's love got to do with it?) I said that if we did not communicate that we loved our cars, nobody else would love them, either. I explained that love in advertising is an attitude toward the product and also toward the reader and the viewer. In some subtle way, every ad, every commercial should produce a feeling of love between the product and the potential buyer.

After my love-in-advertising opening I gave a detailed report on the research we had done on each car and the competitive cars and I said that, except for the magnificent new Javelin, we felt their cars were not any sexier than the competition, so if people were going to buy on the basis of sheet metal alone they were going to go for the other guys' cars. The executives looked crestfallen. But they perked up when I told them that we had found extra values in the cars that no one else had and we were about to show them ways to make those extra values so exciting in ads and commercials that they would attract many thousands of new buyers into the dealers. Not only that, I guaranteed that a large percentage of those buyers would be under 30 years old.

Roy was happy. He smiled left and right. But then I told them about the Comparison Strategy, and before anyone could remind me of Detroit's unspoken law against comparison advertising I introduced Charlie and Stan, who were in great theatrical form and presented first the comparison print ads and then the television campaign.

The men in that room were so stunned to see a Ford Mustang appear in their expensive double-page announcement ad for the new Javelin, then to learn for the first time that their Ambassador had air-conditioning *standard* and see it sitting confidently between a *Rolls-Royce* and a *Cadillac*—and then, ye gods, to see their friend Henry Ford's Mustang beat up with sledgehammers in an American Motors television commercial, they lost their tongues and sat there staring at me, blinking.

Roy said, "You mean you want me to spend a couple of million dollars advertising the Mustang?" We had expected Roy to say something like that and had decided that we would pretend we hadn't heard him and Charlie and Stan would move quickly on to the other commercials that were equally startling but a little lighter, a little easier to swallow. They presented them smartly and everybody liked those commercials so much that the hearts beating in that room stopped fibrillating and returned to a normal rate.

Roy was not weak of heart and he had resolved to buy an advertising campaign that was different enough to make a very big splash. He would have been terribly disappointed if we had given him something journeyman and formulaic—so he gulped, but he was with us. He said

Charlie performs as we present our first campaign to Roy Chapin and the board of directors of American Motors. He cut off his Afro for the meeting.

that his only worry was that some of the comparisons were derogatory. I promised we would never attack a loser, we would always compare ourselves with a winner and we would never insult a winner, we would always say it was good, it sets the standard, but ours is a little better. "All right," he said, "just as long as we're positive, not negative."

Roy had such a mandate, he was such a Detroit insider versed in the bylaws of the community, that all his executives followed his lead. They gave us a vote of confidence and we left with approvals for every ad and commercial we presented. The only problem we ever had about the introduction advertising came up a few days later. Vic Olesen flew in from our Detroit office to tell me that Roy had ordered a new American Motors symbol, a circle with an AM inside it, used on everything everywhere, including the advertising. I flew to Detroit immediately and met with Roy to discuss logos. I told him I thought the ads and commercials with the greatest impact almost always felt as if they had been made for one and only one viewer, that quality is what makes them so believable. A designy logo disrupts that intimacy, that sincerity, that you-and-me mood. It reminds you that the advertiser is a big corporation advertising, not just to you, but to a million other people, thereby killing much of the personal selling impact. Roy struggled with himself for a minute or two. "We've spent a year developing that logo, Mary," he said, still thinking it over. "Well, you can order us to use it, Roy," I told him, "but I guarantee you that it will destroy something personal and precious in the campaign. Automobile advertising is traditionally cold stuff—our new advertising is human and warm and intensely personal—that is one of the reasons it will be so widely noticed, it is so different from other automobile advertising. Just a simple, personal-looking American Motors signature is the right signature."

Why did Roy go along with me? Why did American Motors allow a group of Young Turks to tell them what to do? Clients who came to us at a time when they had problems ganging up on them, stupefying arrays of hard decisions to make and businesses that were in danger of disintegrating—those clients were experiencing the long dark night of the soul and they simply had to trust advisors who were reputed to be winners. There was something convincing about the adrenaline coming out of the pores of Wells Rich Greene and the sureness we had. Because we never had a second's doubt in those days that we were right about what we believed. Roy and Bill McNealy and Bill Pickett were happy to have me push and nudge and force and hound them for a time. They wanted help. They had stomachs filled with fire for winning, for staying in business, and they didn't give a damn where a good idea came from, even if it came from their advertising agency. The automobile business is an extremely complicated one at the best of times and there are periods when awareness and imagery are not top priorities, but at that moment in American Motors' life awareness was all-important and Roy believed in us, primarily on the basis of our other successes.

Fortunately, the new attitude and advertising that we gave American Motors played a major role in the reversal of that company's health in 1968, '69, '70 and '71—survival time. The avalanche of orders for Javelins surprised everybody, even us, and 57 percent of the buyers were under 35, a statistic Roy was proud to tell everyone for months. The dealers reported they had never ever had young people shopping for cars and now they were crowded around their Javelins. Even better, 53 percent of the buyers of Javelins were conquests, brand-new buyers who had been driving Mustangs and Volkswagens. Wherever the old American Motors drivers had disappeared to, they reappeared when it was apparent the company was not only surviving, it was swinging.

Doyle Dane's Volkswagen advertising was not understood in Detroit when it first appeared, but our advertising was understood instantly. It was received with glee by American Motors' dealers and workers, but it shocked and irritated the other automobile companies.

When Henry and Cristina Ford saw the Javelin-Mustang advertising, they stopped talking to Roy and Sis Chapin. Lee Iacocca, who was still at Ford, said testily to the *Life* reporter after he saw our comparison advertising and his Mustang crushed into a Javelin, "She'll lose. Any time people try to play dirty, they will lose, even though they might gain a temporary advantage. The public is too smart for that type of approach." As *Life* magazine reported, "Because of fear of greater antitrust attention, nobody in Detroit wants AMC to collapse. However, as Ford officials pointed out to *Life,* its type of approach was backed by some $100 million in ad money against a mere $12 million for AMC." *Life* magazine also said that I was delighted at Ford's outrage. I experienced it firsthand when Rosemarie Kanzler, who married a relative of Henry Ford's, actually uninvited Harding and me to a dinner party because she was giving it in honor of the Fords and Cristina said they wouldn't come if "that woman" was going to be there.

We spent many days and evenings in Detroit in the early years working closely with managers in all areas of the company. There was something gala about our meetings. We always went there looking our best. And they, too, looked as if they spent a little extra time dressing on the days of our visits; there was a sense of fine cologne about it all, as if the return of the company's confidence deserved to be celebrated. Roy and I had long talks and good lunches, we liked each other, and he teased me mercilessly about Wells Rich Greene's bad ear for technical language. His son, Billy, advised us for a while and was a great favorite at the agency, but he couldn't resist telling Roy about our goofs—we called the AB&C pillars "the things that hold up the roof," the instrument panels were "dashboards," the rear decks were "trunk lids" and the glove box was a "cubbyhole." Wells Rich Greene's Detroit office could speak the language, though, and soon enough we all became conversant.

It was a love affair at American Motors for a long while. We enjoyed each other and learned from each other. I learned, for example, that a business based on engineering can be as romantic in the eyes of its people as the movie business, publishing or advertising. I had never thought of sales directors as romantics until I watched Bill Pickett, AMC's sales director, roam the company with an idea a minute. He thought the new Gremlin subcompact wasn't going to come down the line sexy enough and he wanted to decorate it. He thought the Gremlin should have white sidewalls, state-of-the-art air-conditioning, a neat German radio and an unheard-of paint choice of 18 colors that didn't cost the company anything but sounded terrific. We firmly supported him, the Gremlin got decorated and it did well. One day he took me to AMC's design studio and introduced me to another romantic, Dick Teague, who had designed the Javelin and the AMX. Dick Teague was a sculptor of undulating steel, a Frank Gehry of the auto-design business, the Javelin was his Bilbao, his life was filled with grace, every new project was the best one he ever had. Since then I've had my eye out for the romantics in business, they are full of ideas, and I am crazy about people who are happy in their work.

The man that got away

One grey morning later in the game, in 1972, five years after Roy first appeared at Wells Rich Greene, he called to say that he and Bill Luneberg were going to be in New York the following day and would like to talk to me, could they come in for morning coffee? I said yes, of course, and had an ominous, sinking feeling because his voice was so flat. I called Vic Olesen in our Detroit office to learn what he knew about Roy's visit. He was surprised to hear about it and told me about his latest meeting at the company. I went to Charlie's office, closed the door and told him about Roy's call. Charlie was easily terrorized so I usually protected him from my day-to-day worries. But there was something too odd about the fact that Roy was bringing Bill Luneberg with him to keep to myself. Bill was the one executive at American Motors who had always kept a distance from us, he rarely spoke to me whenever we saw each other, and from the pugnacious expression in his eyes and the way he lowered his bull-shaped head when anyone from Wells Rich Greene appeared I used to joke that we shouldn't wear red around him. Bill was cautious when he was with Roy and always let Roy do the talking. But we were told that without Roy he was aggressive. People at the company said he was a bully who made pets of the weaker executives, but the Bill Luneberg I'd known so far was the one who followed Roy about respectfully, and Roy made it obvious to everyone that he thought highly of him.

I think the only time Bill Luneberg ever spoke to me directly was after he saw the *Life* magazine article. To be sensational, *Life* headlined the article "Can Mary Wells Rescue American Motors?" Roy had accepted the sensationalism for what it was—good publicity for the company, great publicity for the Javelin, it came off so well in the story. But Bill stopped me in a hall shortly after the article appeared and said, "Don't believe your press, Mary, I call the shots here." After that I can't remember him saying anything to me. So if Roy was bringing him for a special meeting it could only mean there was trouble and it was serious.

I told Charlie I thought he should be at the meeting and to say a prayer that night. I felt better knowing there were two of us worrying and not able to sleep. By 1972 Wells Rich Greene was living handsomely in the General Motors Building on Fifth Avenue. Roy and Bill arrived a little early, Roy looked tired and Bill looked exultant. I would have dropped a tarantula down his shirt if I'd had one, there was something cheeky about him that morning that told me he felt victorious even before the meeting had begun.

"This is unpleasant for me, Mary," Roy began, and I knew he was going to fire Wells Rich Greene. I barely heard him for the first few minutes. It was a total surprise, a big blow, and I was feeling a wash of fury. Whatever his reasoning, we had risked everything to take on American Motors at its worst hour and we had contributed substantially to their turnaround. We deserved the same largesse we had given them.

Roy was talking to me, turned in my direction, but he was looking thoughtfully at the wall somewhere behind my left ear. He was telling me that the management of American Motors believed that their company had grown to a point where they needed a traditional, multifaceted, country-wide agency. They needed to fix the complicated and tricky dealer-field operations where there were problems. They needed branch-office service throughout the states that could respond quickly to their nationwide challenges. They wanted more in-depth marketing analysis, and—he said hesitantly with a quick glance at Bill—some of the management wanted a relationship with an agency that was more inclined to take direction than give it.

He began to study the back of one of his hands then as he went on to say that they were profoundly aware of the contribution Wells Rich Greene had made at a crucial moment in their history and of the leadership I personally had provided. They all thanked me profusely but they thought they had been as good for us as we had been for them. They didn't need that sort of help now, they were in excellent health, such good health that, unfortunately, they required a different kind of advertising service. He knew how hard and unfeeling this must sound to me but, then, he felt he should remind me that I had not been that close to the account for a while—Wells Rich Greene, too, was doing so well and I was so much in demand. They understood, they had no quarrel with our success and our great growth. They were happy for us, but they didn't want to be in the position where they had to beg for attention. After all, he said proudly, they were a *big automobile company.* They shouldn't have to ask me to make the agency pay attention.

I told them I thought their decision was too abrupt, that we should take time and work closely together to solve their problems now just as we had in the past, there was no need for such a terrible break. Charlie and I were all theirs, today as we had been, but we appreciated it was time for a more traditional agency-client relationship and would give them one. After an hour or so, I knew there was absolutely nothing I could say or do that would keep American Motors from leaving Wells Rich Greene.

As they left, as Roy went out the door, he stopped and looked me in the eye for the first time and said, in a low voice, "Don't you realize how far apart we've gotten? Don't you know how removed you've been?"— leaving me, in the end, with the full weight of the guilt on my head as he walked out of Wells Rich Greene.

Charlie and I floated back into my office like ghosts without any feeling in our bodies and we sat there not saying anything to each other for a long time. Kathie buzzed me on the intercom and brought us to life or we might be sitting there yet. We didn't know where to start and we felt heavy and vulnerable and not up to the long list of melancholy chores ahead, the people who would have to be let go, the end of the Detroit office, telling the staff and the endless media questions. It had been such a splendid season with American Motors; when and why did it go wrong? How in all hell was it possible that we didn't know we had a problem with them as big as this? Where were all our executives, for God's sake, and where was my trusty intuition, where had Charlie and I been?

Charlie and I have always had mental and emotional telepathy, so we didn't have to ask each other these questions out loud, we just sat there scanning the years passing before our eyes. In 1968, when our first campaign for American Motors appeared, our billings were $53 million and growing fast. The new account that was big enough to take my eyes off American Motors was probably the airline, TWA, but I had also spent a lot of time in California persuading Hunt-Wesson to give us Wesson Oil and then Bristol-Myers gave us Score hair cream and Utica Club gave us their beer.

General Mills left Tinker and followed us because we'd given them such a success with their extruded snacks; we'd named them Bugles,

Whistles and Daisies and they were extruded into Bugle, Whistle and Daisy shapes. The test markets had been so rhapsodically successful General Mills had built massive plants filled with expensive extrusion equipment. It was so strange—I left Tinker just about the day the new plants started producing Bugles, Whistles and Daisies and for some inexplicable reason at that moment people stopped buying them. So General Mills had brought them to me to get them going again, to make those new plants pay off. Dick said he thought it was an act of revenge when they gave me the account. ("Let's see what you can do with these little suckers now, Miss Smarty Pants!") But you would never find more sincere, more ambitious executives than Don Swanson and Bruce Atwater. They were clients any agency would covet and I was proud to have their faith.

"P&G," Charlie sighed. Procter & Gamble, as impressive a client as an agency can have, read all about our success with number-two brands and, as they had some of those that they wanted to keep alive, they came in to look around. They not only gave us a toothpaste, Gleem, and Safeguard soap, they became a force within the agency, as they do in all their agencies. Unlike the management of American Motors, everybody at every level at Procter & Gamble demanded attention from everybody at every level at Wells Rich Greene. They keep you on a leash. Then came Samsonite. And Ralston Purina gave us Chex cereals and Tender Vittles cat food. Gordon Sherman and his cousin Howard came to see us and ended up giving us the Midas muffler account before it was an account. Royal Crown Cola had come to us. Bic had called us about their fiber-tip pens and their butane lighters. And Philip Morris never stopped growing.

So there we sat, Charlie and me, in 1972, with Wells Rich Greene billing $115 million going on $150 million, breaking records right and left. Something was buzzing in my head that I couldn't scratch. I knew I had to stand up and walk through the agency soon because the word would be out, the press would be calling and I needed to look like a happy confident chairman to keep everybody's minds on what they were doing. But I couldn't. I looked at Charlie and thought, "What in the world would I do if you were not here?" We never had enough talent, we were hiring the best talent we could find all of the time but our resources were always way behind our growth streak.

Dick Rich had gone, he was interested in creating spectacular television advertising for a few accounts and when he wasn't appreciated he lost interest. The first work he did for Procter & Gamble had not gone well so he didn't want to bother with them. He wouldn't raise a finger for Braniff, the account that put us in business. It always ended up that Charlie was my partner, he was the one I learned I should turn to, so finally Dick left, without tears, to start his own place and Charlie became, first, creative director and, then, president and I became chairman.

Getting new business at a runaway pace is like trying to bite into a double-decker deli sandwich, you can't get a bite of the whole sandwich all at once, you get it into your mouth to chew little by little. Charlie and I had managed to lead every account in the agency so far but sometimes we were like monkeys swinging through trees chattering to one another between the branches. Wells Rich Greene was filled to the brim with new employees, many of them highly gifted and highly paid, but it wasn't a carefully structured army, we barely knew a lot of the people. There was an awful lot of improvisation and masses of egoplasm—my own word for the tiresome hijinks that super talents in creative businesses are capable of. The only truly proven talents, the only ones he and I knew well enough to feel secure about when it mattered, were us, him and me. We had known we could not continue at this obsessive pace much longer without an accident, and we had just had one. Roy had been right, we had turned away from American Motors— not completely but more than we should have—we had turned the authority of the account over to others too soon.

Bill Bernbach had once taken great pains to teach me something relevant. He told me that there was danger in clients who came to an agency desperately in need of direction and guidance because, he said, "the same brilliance, the same guts you use to grab the brass ring and lead that client to a success will be perceived as arrogance and an irritation as soon as the client is successful." I remember him wagging his finger at me, "You have to stay close and take your agency through a transition from leading the client to taking more and more direction from him." He looked at me, an owl: "Mary," he said, "don't imagine that anyone else at the agency will know when to switch from the left foot to the right." Then, ruefully, "I know these things. What I just told you is worth a lot of money."

Agencies are fragile in their early years—the structures are not set, people can still surprise you, the most respected rainmakers let you down. We had hired men who were good account men, smart business-men with excellent marketing and media backgrounds, but they had not yet demonstrated that you could count on them to come up with strategic breakthroughs when they were called for or that they could pull an agency full of raconteurs into a stable, problem-solving adver-tising business. On the other hand, the writers and art directors we were collecting, gifted as they unquestionably were, had not had time to demonstrate that they could lead, not just one or two accounts, but a big chunk of an agency. Few people can, and Charlie and I had no idea yet who we could count on for the long run and also for the real wins. In such a hurtling time, with so many new clients giving us new and large challenges, 40 percent of the people were still doing 90 percent of the work, Charlie and I were doing too much of it ourselves, we needed to discover whom we could safely delegate to.

Suddenly the buzzing in my head became one of my visions. My visions are not as clear as the pictures on my Sony television screen, they are usually more like a pointillist painting, dotted and soft and slightly transparent. They do not come at my calling. I could wear a yellow robe and chant to the moon the rest of my life and get nothing for it. My visions come when I least expect them, when I am feeling turned off because I am out of my depth. After Roy Chapin fired us and Charlie and I went into my office and just sat down, my brain went into some kind of brownout and my intuition produced a picture of the future of Wells Rich Greene in front of my eyes—and it was *no better.* For years to come it was going to be very much as it seemed to be that day, vulnerable and heaped with talent of all kinds, but there would be no real rainmakers I could be sure of other than Charlie Moss and Mary Wells. I have often thought that my psychic intuitions come to provoke me into a positive action. That one made me angry, got me to my feet, got me striding throughout the agency. Control is probably a self-delusion in the advertising business, but I had a new determination to find more strong pillars to hold up Wells Rich Greene.

Up, up and away

Harding and I were in Acapulco when I got the call about the TWA account. Acapulco was our weekend escape when we were feeling stretched. I would take my usual Friday-afternoon flight to Dallas and make the connection there to Braniff's nonstop to Acapulco and get to our house in time to sleep in that light, sensuous Mexican air. Acapulco was growing but it was still a happy-go-lucky place to unwind. It was no Garden of Eden, though. Men in trucks drove through the streets of the new part of Acapulco, where we lived, spraying serious chemicals all around, to push back an army of bugs that George Lucas would appreciate, steely-eyed spiders and tarantulas and scorpions and giant, hairy macropeds. I never put on a pair of shoes without shaking them and knocking them against a chair leg and I never ever walked barefoot in the dark.

The houses were little more than white concrete shelving on the hills to the bay. They were cheap affairs made luscious by the magnificence of the tropical flowers that hung all over them. The only wonderful house was Loel and Gloria Guinness's grass-roofed pavilion. Gloria had been married to a Mexican once, and she knew what life in Acapulco should look like. She knew what life *anyplace* should look like, but she really set the standard in Acapulco. We would have dinner at Gloria's and lunch at Merle's. Merle Oberon had married a Mexican tycoon, Bruno Pagliai, and built a house with cool gardens and palm trees and dolphin-shaped rocks on the sea. She made you take your shoes off if you went inside her house because it was completely carpeted, wall to wall, in snow-white Hollywood plush. We didn't mind, you could see anything crawling on that rug! Harding and I leased a pretty house from Guy Rothschild. It was so easy to live in Acapulco then. Most of the houses were managed by an utterly charming woman from Texas, Marianne Rivas, who had a wide range of resources. She saw to it that the houses had the best Mexican cooks (all of them named Pepe or Maria) and everything else you needed to live like an irresponsible, slightly naughty native.

That's what I was doing the day Herb Fisher called me about TWA. We had been invited to Harold Robbins's house in downtown Acapulco for one of his long and late buffet lunches. I was nervous about going because I'd heard that he had photographers and a PR man at his lunches and I didn't want pictures of me and Harold Robbins, who might be wearing one of his European mini bathing suits, showing up in *Advertising Age*. I went out of my way to dress like a girl scout for that lunch, startling all the other women there, who were wearing the local uniform, a teeny bikini and a handkerchief. I was startled myself, though, when Mrs. Robbins appeared. Harold, who was covered with gold jewelry and not much else, was showing Harding and me photographs taken at past lunches when Mrs. Robbins joined us and said, cheerfully, "Welcome!" She was wearing a thong bathing suit that made a point of revealing her masses of black curls— not the ones on her head. Nobody blinked, nobody cared, Harding and I were the only nervous Nellies at that lunch—and that was when the butler came to tell me I was wanted on the telephone. "New York," he said.

Herb Fisher sounded very, very far away—Mexico was still on the other side of the earth in 1968. "Hello, hello, Mary, is that you?" he shouted as though the telephone had just been invented. "I've got an idea for you. What do you think about handling the TWA account?" I knew I had misunderstood him. It sounded as if he'd asked me what I thought about handling the TWA account. "I can't hear you clearly," I enunciated carefully. Herb shouted again. "I'm serious. They're serious. TWA. They asked us if we were interested in their account. Are you flying back tonight? Tomorrow?" I turned to Harding. "It's Herb

Fisher. He says TWA wants to know if we are interested in handling their advertising business." Nothing has ever surprised Harding. "Tell Herb we'll go back to the house and call him in an hour." We slipped away, carefully avoiding the photographers, and headed back to our house, then to Dallas, and I kept going on to New York to meet with TWA.

Jack Fry, who was the head of TWA in Harry Truman's day, was a buddy of Harry's in Missouri. After one of their Kansas City poker games that was fortunate for Jack, Harry asked him, "Well, Jack, what do you want?" "I want new routes for the airline," Jack said. "OK," said Harry. "What routes do you want?" "All of them," Jack said. "I want to fly all over the world." He got his routes, and for a long time TWA enjoyed the best routes of all the airlines.

TWA had a lot of lives. When Herb Fisher called me about its advertising account, Foote, Cone & Belding was its agency and had just won back the account in one of the first big, expensive shootouts on Madison Avenue, a scandal on the Avenue because so many agencies had spent so much money on presentations only to have Foote, Cone keep the business. Charlie Tillinghast was the chairman and shortly after awarding the account to Foote, Cone for the second time he hired a new marketing vice-president from United Airlines, Blaine Cooke. Blaine didn't like Foote, Cone's campaign, although it featured a popular song of the day that will be forever associated with the airline, "Up, Up and Away." Blaine liked what Wells Rich Greene had done for Braniff and he liked Herb Fisher, whom he had known in an earlier life at Lincoln Mercury. He also thought highly of our research director, Marty Stern, another guru with an accent like Freud's. Blaine didn't think my marriage to Harding or Braniff had anything to do with TWA, the routes were so different, and he invited me to meet with him when I returned from Mexico.

In Acapulco, Harding and I had zipped up our luggage and dashed for the afternoon flight to Dallas, laughing at first, but flying over San Antonio we began to discuss the advantages and disadvantages of separating our marriage from our work. There was no doubt that it would be more relaxing to separate them, although I did feel that Braniff was our love child and we did talk Braniff-talk morning, noon and night on our weekends, just like parents do about their children.

Somewhere between Acapulco and Dallas, Harding and I decided that it might be better all around if I handled TWA. Of course, I didn't know if TWA would give Wells Rich Greene its account. But when I met Blaine Cooke, we just clicked. We could talk, we were sympathetic and easy with one another and we liked each other's ideas. We knew we would work well together.

Wells Rich Greene's meeting with TWA's management went well, too. We were candid about what we thought of their advertising and what we thought it should be, and they were open and interested. We knew from our experience with Braniff that the business traveler had become the most important customer for all the major airlines. Business travelers bought the most profitable tickets, they flew first class then because in those years the difference between fares for first class and coach was not great. (Business class, as a section of the plane, developed later, in the seventies, when fare differences became more extreme in the larger planes and the business traveler could no longer afford first class.) Fliers believed that business travelers were the ones who were *smart* about airlines, they were the authorities, they traveled more than other people, knew who had the best service, and they were the canny ones who cared about getting their money's worth from an airline. The business travel market was the market for an airline to own.

TWA's problem was that, having been owned by Howard Hughes for a while, it was thought of as a Hollywood, international-set airline, an image that was not only passé, it was negative. That dilettantish persona wasn't helped by Foote, Cone's new campaign which, I pointed out at the meeting, was a little too *feminine* in style, too *effete,* to appeal to business travelers, who were mostly serious, hardworking and long-suffering men.

By the end of the meeting we knew that Wells Rich Greene would be invited to be TWA's new advertising agency. Charlie Tillinghast then made a sweet gesture that was typical of him—"Gentleman Charlie," I used to call him—he telephoned Harding at Braniff and asked him for my hand. He asked if it was agreeable with Harding if Wells Rich Greene handled TWA's advertising and he told Harding that as far as he and Blaine were concerned, as the two airlines' route structures were so different, they saw no problem at all if Wells Rich Greene handled the advertising for both airlines.

Harding and I saw problems with that idea, though. We knew Harding's plans for Braniff and in time there could well be conflicts of interest. We decided it was best if Wells Rich Greene simply accepted the TWA account and Braniff found a new agency. So on August 15, 1968, I held a secret meeting in the sanctuary of my office and told most of Wells Rich Greene that the agency would be going to work for TWA and Braniff would be getting another agency.

August 16, the news appeared in the press and it was just as shocking as if aliens had landed on Madison Avenue. After all the money that had been spent by so many agencies in the big shootout, after all the bruises Foote, Cone had suffered, TWA was going to give its account to Wells Rich Greene, a new agency that already had an airline account. That was the day some of Madison Avenue's old guard decided women were dangerous to the advertising community and that I was not only an arriviste but the queen of black widow spiders. I don't think I am overstating it. I was about to drive to Utica that morning to try to persuade Walter Matt, who owned Utica Club beer, to build a Utica Club disco in New York City with all the inherent possibilities such a club would have in a disco era for promoting his beer, when I got a call from *Fortune* magazine that resulted in a nine-page story with an amusing headline: "As the World Turns—on Madison Avenue: Or, What Happened in the Ad Biz When Mary Wells Got Married."

What happened in the ad biz was that Braniff hired the George Lois Agency, I had known George at Doyle Dane and he was a major talent, and then Mary Wells, Charlie Moss, Stan Dragoti, Herb Fisher and Marty Stern went to work with Blaine Cooke and his group to replace TWA's campaign with maniacal fervor, as if there would be no tomorrow if the old advertising ran one more day. I suppose that is when I began to slip out of the intense relationship I had with American Motors. But Gordon Sherman had something to do with it.

Nobody does it better

Wells Rich Greene's clients came in all shapes and sizes, with endless flavors of personalities, like Häagen-Dazs ice cream. Just about the time Blaine, "The Professor," gave us the TWA account, Gordon and Howard Sherman came to see us about turning Midas into a powerful brand name for automobile mufflers. They were cousins with the same last name and a familial dark attractiveness, but it was immediately apparent when we met them that although Howard was bright and engaging, Gordon was a prince. Princes rarely visit advertising agencies, but there is no doubting one. Gordon and Howard were leaning against the backs of the chairs, their hands deep into their suit pockets when I walked into the room. Gordon was smiling at Howard in a lazy, nonchalant way, an amiable comrade, radiating an air of absolute authority in all directions, ready to hold court.

He was born a prince. It wasn't that he was the spoiled son of a successful Chicago family. It wasn't that. Gordon's father, Nate Sherman, had founded a company that turned out mufflers and tailpipes professionally in the thirties when auto-parts makers were a sooty, careless, even negligent group of small-timers. His little company thrived in the automobile boom after the war, but the Shermans weren't super-rich or Chicago social leaders. It was simply that from his first breath Gordon wanted to do everything, try everything, he seemed to think the world had been created a gymnasium for him to work out in. When he was still a kid, with the help of a library book, he taught himself the art of taxidermy on the animals his father brought back from hunting. He built his own bagpipes and mastered them, then moved on to the oboe, then to the English horn. He might have been a concert pianist or a Talmudic professor, he was so intent on those interests. But after his stint at the University of Chicago business school, a prestigious grad school that was on the leading edge of humanized economic thinking, he chose to join the family business, he said he had "such moving ideas about what could be done with it every waking morning." When Gordon's eyes opened mornings, he saw a picture of an idea that would rush him out of bed, and one morning he imagined the Midas franchising system for that sooty, rugged muffler industry. He got up and built it, starting with 22 or 23 dealers. He hit the ball out of the park with what became an international network of Midas shops, where customers could lounge in comfort watching their cars receive new, golden mufflers in a few minutes.

By 1961 Midas was successful enough to take public. The Sherman family kept the majority of the stock and Gordon continued waking up with ideas of offering brakes and tires in shops and then of creating a higher-level, more idealistic and communicative kind of management for Midas than he had seen in the auto-parts world. He wrote poetic want ads and placed them in unlikely magazines like *Saturday Review* and *Psychology Today,* snaring people for his management like Hugh MacLean, a psychotherapist who had studied with Carl Jung. Gordon's father viewed him with a cool, maybe competitive, eye, but Gordon's success as an explorer of modern franchising made him the star of all the early books written to teach young people how to succeed in that business, not his father.

Gordon's cousin Howard was his vice-president of marketing. Howard was up to the minute on who was doing what in creative businesses and he was looking for an express route to making Midas the powerful brand name that Gordon had in mind. "If anyone can help us pull off the miracle we envision, it's Wells Rich Greene," he said melodically, conning me into attention at a time when he had no real account, no real budget for one.

But very soon Howard started to bring Midas dealers in to teach us the muffler business: Harold Forkas from Long Island, Howie Lichterman from New Jersey, Jerry Orns from Tampa and Charles Margolin from Chicago—we called them the Four Musketeers. They may have been Midas muffler dealers but they were about to be chieftains, czars, they would build muffler universes and fortunes. The four of them walked into Wells Rich Greene the first time rippling their muscles and looked around as if they were appraising the agency as a possible acquisition. We knew right away we better show respect.

What other business teaches you how much aspirin it takes to reach the threshold of pain one day and the art of replacing a muffler in a car the next?

The Midas dealers adopted us and we found ourselves touring Midas shops and the competition, as they saw it, the muffler shops on the back streets, gritty little places with no inventory, run by amateurs. We saw their mistake immediately, that Midas had no competition at all in the muffler business. So who *was* the competition? It was the thousands and thousands of service stations on almost every corner of every main road in America—and powerful competition that was. People drove in and out of those service stations to buy gasoline and other services regularly and would automatically head there when their mufflers acted up.

But when we tried to discuss the idea of the service station as the real competition that Midas had to address in its advertising, the Musketeers told us bluntly to forget it! move off! They told us that most of their business came from those friendly nearby service stations who were too busy to do a muffler job or didn't have the right muffler on hand. They were not about to cut off the hands that fed them.

We didn't think we could build a big brand image for Midas without recognizing its true competition, the service stations. It was our experience that taking on the establishment was not only the fastest way to get attention for a new business but also a first step towards creating trust for it—and trust is what branding is all about, trust is the payoff for the investment it takes to build a big-name brand. You would trust a McDonald's hamburger in Calcutta, wouldn't you? You would trust that it would taste pretty much the same and be as safe to eat as the Big Mac you ate in Chicago. It cost McDonald's a lot of advertising money to persuade you to trust them wherever you found them. We thought we could create the same trust for Midas muffler shops by taking on those powerful service stations, by believing enough in ourselves to have the nerve to do it. After all, service stations were busy places that pumped gas, installed batteries, changed oil, changed tires, washed cars and did 40 or 50 other jobs as well as replace mufflers. Midas installed mufflers for a living, that's all they did in most Midas shops; they simply had to do a better job than the busy service stations.

And that became our theme: "At Midas we install mufflers for a living—we have to do a better job." It was an audacious position that was sure to be appreciated by television viewers. In the sixties America still loved the little guy who was fighting the giant. Wells Rich Greene's conservatives weren't happy about taking on big boys like the service stations. Dammit, they reminded us, the Midas dealers had forbidden us to attack them. Well, none of us relished the idea of defying the dealers. I started to think fondly of rottweilers. But we were sure we were right, that taking on the service stations would clearly position Midas as the muffler specialist, El Supremo, the best, and would build a great brand name in short order.

Wells Rich Greene commercials were always created by teams, a writer and an art director. The first Midas campaign was created by Charlie Ashby, a soft-spoken writer from North Carolina who had a gift for making the characters in his commercials sympathetic and believable, and Bob Reitzfeld, an art director who was a closet intellectual, the agency's lightning rod for what was happening in all the arts at any given second. They dreamed up a campaign that was fun, which would come as a surprise in the world of mufflers, but that demonstrated to you without a doubt how superior Midas was to a service station when you needed a muffler.

In the first commercial the owner of an Edsel drives noisily from one service station to another, desperately trying to find a muffler for his Edsel. One service station attendant says, "The last time I saw a muffler for an Edsel was ten years ago." At another station all the attendants leap to attention, salute, spray his windshield, lift up the front to inspect the engine and ready the gas pump until they hear that what the driver wants is a muffler for his Edsel—at which point they stop short, back away and ask, "Have you ever considered trading cars?" Another station attendant says, "I might have something I could put in sideways." At another, when the attendant sees the Edsel, he slyly removes the sign that says "mufflers" from his list of services and hides it behind his back, shaking his head no. The last attendant does a take-off on Jack Benny's Rochester:

EDSEL DRIVER: I need a—
GAS STATION ATTENDANT: I know you do. Do you think—
EDSEL DRIVER: They used to.
GAS STATION ATTENDANT: Why don't you—
EDSEL DRIVER: I tried them.
GAS STATION ATTENDANT: Oh yeah?

The announcer says: "Gas stations install mufflers as a sideline. At Midas we do it for a living. We have to do a better job. So when you come to us for a muffler we'll have the kind you need for almost any kind of car." Super (title on screen): "Midas. We install mufflers for a living. We have to do a better job."

We told Gordon and Howard that the dealers had forbidden us to take on the service stations. "Oh, don't worry," they laughed—and suggested we were imagining things. Ha. The following day we presented the same strategy and campaign to the dealers and all hell broke loose. One of the Italian dealers attacked us with an "Achugh!"—a guttural shout so loud General Motors executives heard him on the floor above. "Absolutely not!" those dealers raged. What did we want to do, put them out of business? Gordon Sherman and his imperialist ideas! What did he know! He wasn't there on the sites under those cars that had been sent to Midas by the friendly corner-gas-station guys. He was up there in his utopian ivory tower smoking Bach! And who did I think I was, a woman telling successful, experienced Midas muffler dealers who had been through the hard knocks what to do! I didn't know what a muffler was or where to find it until they taught me! Did I? Did I? I was just a woman, for God's sake! What kind of an agency were we anyway?! And four or five dealers walked out of the meeting, redfaced, veins popping, arms flying.

Howard Sherman, the scout at the meeting, the emissary from the culturati at Midas headquarters in Chicago, was shaken. He was surprised at the depth of feeling and the dealers' fear of service stations.

Always quick-witted, he decided then and there that the dealers' reactions were proof of the power in our combative position. He herded the Musketeers and the other dealers still in the room out the door of the agency, talking animatedly, with growing conviction. In that entire meeting I never got a word in. I figured we'd lost the account before we ever really had it, and although Midas hadn't been around long enough to reach my heart, I was disappointed. I was looking forward to a high-profile campaign war with America's gas stations and saw a juicy, profitable future in selling a lot of Midas mufflers.

I was scheduled to be interviewed on *The Mike Douglas Show* later that day and a makeup man was waiting in my office to give me false eyelashes. On occasion there is something of the circus in the advertising business. The agency's Midas group followed me to the little powder room outside my office as Damon Michaels began gluing one eyelash at a time onto my lids for the TV cameras. "What do you think?" we asked each other. We didn't know anyone at Midas well enough yet to sense how far Gordon was willing to go against an army of furious dealers. We didn't hear a peep out of any of them for a week, and then dealers came straggling back to see the presentation again and one by one they decided they loved it. Nobody ever told us what changed the tides, but we heard rumors that there had been fights serious enough to make Jerry Orns, the Godfather of the dealers, decide that pulling the dealers together into a positive force was more important than any advertising position could ever be and he used his considerable gifts to persuade the dealers to back the advertising.

We hunkered down to turn out all the materials required to launch Midas as a big brand—and then I got a call from Stew. "Have you heard? Gordon's talking about resigning. He and his father are fighting. Everybody's taking sides in Chicago and they say the whole Sherman family is siding with Gordon against Nate. Even Mrs. Sherman."

Gordon had developed passionate concerns about social reform and pollution over the years and had been contributing serious money to controversial leaders like Saul Alinsky, who was battling the big industrial polluters, all of them powerful businesses. Now Alinsky was opening a school for organizers and dissidents, and rumor had it he'd gotten the money for the school from Gordon. Gordon was also supporting Ralph Nader, who was happily telling the press that his goal was to eliminate the internal-combustion engine—which would eliminate the need for mufflers, too. The Chicago media was critical of the way Gordon was stirring up trouble in "his cheeky, royalist way" with his donations. Midas dealers began to grumble that Gordon was getting a little odd and too intellectual and elegant for a nuts-and-bolts business like mufflers. They said Gordon gave short shrift to technical expertise, to the day-to-day muffler business, that he looked down at the dealers as his subjects who needed him to light their way. "He's dangerous," some of them said. The fact that Gordon was the one who had the original vision, the one who had built the system that was more than 700 dealers strong by then and growing fast, was forgotten all too easily, it seemed to me.

Three bottles of red wine arrived without warning. They had working labels on them that read something like "St-Emilion 1945 classification number 6667328." A small note from Gordon: "Mary, save this wine for our meeting next week, it is a surprise." The wine was from Pomerol, the best in all the world, probably; it was produced in a small batch from a small vineyard by a family who have been in Bordeaux for what they believe is eternity. Today, the French call wines like that *vins de garage,* although none of them are made in garages and they cost a fortune per bottle if you can find one to buy. I don't know what they called them when Gordon sent them; I looked at them and thought, "Ah, nectar for the gods."

Gordon arrived with a good friend, Abbie Hoffman, at his side. In the early days of the Yippie movement, Abbie was no fugitive, he was a sure and secure producer of what only appeared to be an impromptu tour de force but was really manipulation of the media. The press made a lot of his outfits but today we pay a high price for the same jeans and jackets made by Helmut Lang. Gordon had come up with the surprise wine for Abbie, he was excited by Abbie and anyone else who did not accept the status quo. For some reason I locked the door and the three of us huddled, slowly drinking Gordon's precious wine, while Abbie gave us his thoughts about Midas advertising. After a while he apologized and said he couldn't get his mind around selling mufflers or soap or beer, he was overwhelmed with the challenge of selling people on living, on waking up and seeing clearly what was going on in their governments and courts and in the big businesses that controlled them. Whenever he referred to the courts he held his nose, his only freakish act the whole afternoon. I liked him. He was interesting and he was fun. He looked at me and grinned slyly and said he thought New York was for children who ran away from home, his impression of me, I guess. When the wine was finished he and Gordon left and as I closed the door, for absolutely no reason, I had a hint of coming catastrophe.

A few weeks later Gordon cheerfully took Abbie and Jerry Rubin and Tom Hayden, the entire Chicago Seven, all friends of Gordon's, to lunch at his father's ultra-conservative downtown-Chicago business club, giving the club members a roaring fit and the press a field day. This time Nate blew up. Father and son got into a primal fight that after a while turned into an all-out proxy war. Every day we received bulletins—who was in, who was out. After a prolonged painful time for the Sherman family, Nate finally won the proxy fight, if not anyone's devotion. Gordon resigned, moved to California and we never saw him again. We searched for him, we didn't want to lose him, but he just disappeared completely from our view, and it was years before we heard anything more about him. His entire management team resigned and followed him, leaving the company in a big mess and the marketing department headless.

"We're working for the dealers now," I said to Charlie the day that our advertising declared war on service stations all over America. Luckily, the strategy and the advertising made Midas the big name in mufflers so quickly the dealers embraced it and us. That was the beginning of a beautiful friendship between the dealers and us, and it saved our bacon, because after Gordon left we were given a new Midas president every three years. First up to bat was Milt Shamitz, a glinty man who demanded a Chicago branch office and got one, as well as Larry Singer, a young man we hired who had automotive experience and was eager and willing to live with Milt and the dealers to keep the day-to-day relationship relatively calm. Milt finally revealed to me that he was only in the job to help Midas be acquired, as it was, by IC Industries. Then we received Ralph Wiger, a dramatic, six-foot-four giant who played Lawrence of Arabia with us in his long cashmere greatcoats. Charlie gave Ralph a campaign based on a word he created, "Midasize," that promoted Midas's new lifetime guarantee, and Ralph became a friend and a fan. He was full of promotion ideas; once he went around the world in chartered planes promoting the idea of dressing for down-hill skiing wrapped in big yellow wool mufflers with Midas logos on them. He gave out enough of those mufflers to tent Aspen and I still have glowing pictures of him posing with gorgeous skiers in yellow Midas mufflers.

Charlie and I enjoyed Ralph. But his relationship with the dealers was rocky, even brutal, so he was president only three years when he was replaced by Dick de Camara, who, when he came in to inspect us, startled me by crushing me in a big bear hug and patting Charlie on the head. "I think you've done a crackerjack job for Midas and I guarantee we are going to have a great and productive relationship," he said with a big smile and dancing eyes. Dick was cheerful, tough and shrewd and he had the good sense to form the first real working partnership between the Midas executives and the Midas dealers.

But three years later Dick turned 65, Midas's retirement age, and once again we were hoping to survive a new president. Our love affair with the original dealers, who were now the power brokers, helped us with each rebirth, and I became friends with the head of IC, Bill Johnson, who was a gentleman, intelligent and graceful. He was helpful, but we were always nervous when a president we had learned to love left us exposed to a new man who could be a wolf. Happily, Ron Moore replaced Dick as president and broke the three-year spell; he lasted a long time. He was the best of the presidents and smart enough to survive the most terrifying threat of all, the dealers' sons. "You can bet they're going to want control and you can bet they're going to get it," he told us.

After a long, successful run of the "Midasize" campaign we had a bleak period of mediocre advertising at the worst possible time—when Midas growth had cooled during a bad recession. The dealers' kids were critical and suggested that Midas had an obligation to examine everything that could help increase sales and, in particular, to consider a new advertising agency.

In such a testy atmosphere we did everything but light candles around the agency to inspire a breakthrough campaign for the new Midas year. Weeks passed, ideas came and went but nothing moved us. In the face of possible disaster Charlie and I would always grope our way to each other's offices to sit and stare at each other. That seemed to help. We were sitting there one afternoon clicking our Bic pens—Bic was a big client by that time—and Charlie said, "I don't know why they are so worried about Meineke these days. The fact is, nobody beats Midas." We looked at each other for a long time, tasting that line. For one thing, the Wiz electronics department store was saying that "Nobody Beats the Wiz." But something rang true about "Nobody beats Midas," maybe because in the case of Midas, it was a cold fact at a serious time. Or maybe because it forced us to think about doing a tough-talk campaign, which would be a profound change from the humorous advertising we had been doing with such success since the beginning. Or maybe we were just desperate. Charlie talked to Bill Mullin and Bill Lower, the art director and writer, who after frustrating months of trying to solve the problem were suffering a flameout and were testy with us. I remember one of them looking at Charlie accusingly and saying, "Chee-rist! That's the Wiz line." They morosely toyed with the line for a couple of days and then said, "How about, 'Nobody beats Midas. Nobody.' " Adding that extra "Nobody" made them feel less like thieves, but it also gave the line a vehement, narrow-eyed aggression and would certainly militarize the tone of Midas advertising. I thought the dealers' kids would love the way it felt.

The campaign became what I call eyeball-to-eyeball advertising, with Midas dealers committing themselves to you, close up, on your television screen, something they did convincingly when they greeted you in their shops. The commercials were undeniable. They communicated, with cold certainty, that nobody in the world beat Midas and that it mattered, it was worth caring about. Sometimes the simplest bare-bones advertising can make a fact become a bigger, more important fact. But that technique is tricky; it requires just the right timing, the right editing and the right mood effects, whatever they may be—music, sirens, bells, grunts, shrieks or loud silence—to produce the right emotion.

The morning I presented that new campaign at the convention there were a lot of sullen Midas dealers suffering from what had become a painful recession. I looked down from the stage and I saw 1,000 restless gorillas. I knew a lot of them personally and I could tell they weren't as welcoming as in the past, they weren't as certain that Wells Rich Greene still had the magic to make things right. I started out using my cool, secure voice. I reminded them, "We're in a recession. Money is tight. People aren't fooling around, they want their money's worth. And now, after all those years asleep, the competition is awake and getting mean." I wasn't telling the dealers anything they didn't know, I was just reassuring them that Wells Rich Greene knew what they knew and that we were on their wavelength, we were not dancing on the moon. I told them that Midas needed a conspicuous change in its advertising, it needed advertising so dominating it would wipe Meineke off the map. I was just about to switch on the advertising when my intuition kicked in. "Go over the top," it told me. So I leaned down and whispered into the microphone, "This is Mary talking, fellows. This is not hype. This is Mary. Mary is telling you that this advertising is going to work, this is the magic you are looking for. Mary guarantees that you are going to have a big year with this advertising. I know that you know Mary would never lie to you." The 1,000 gorillas were shocked by this Mary business coming out of me. They became quiet and stared at me with their 2,000 eyes. Then you could *feel* their expectations growing. The advertising began on all the giant screens around the room—thank God, because I suddenly felt like a nut saying that Mary stuff. At the end, the applause was more than appreciative. It was love. I was so relieved tears streamed down my face. And, oh Lord, thank you, that eyeball-to-eyeball advertising worked so well nobody would allow us to change it for years.

Weekend nights in Dallas, long after Harding had curled into sleep and the girls had cuddled up with their poodles, with all the soft sounds of a Texas night lapping at the windows, I would lie three feet off the bed doing reruns of the past week's happenings, mulling over special moments when one client or another sparked a meeting, led us with his insight and, for one moment or two, enlarged us with his conviction—and his intensity. I was searching for the Business Grail, the reason that some businessmen were more successful than others, as a clue to what I needed to become to continue Wells Rich Greene's howling success. Intelligence wasn't enough. Talent wasn't enough. I would lie there doing flashbacks of the leaders I had known—Dr. Land and Bill Bernbach, for example, Harding and the Philip Morris crowd. I was getting a priceless, close-up view of many of America's top businessmen at work (and they *were* men, it was a man's world) and I wondered why so few of them were able to suffuse a business with light, to do something people would talk about for years. You could tell when a company had a great leader and guide; you could sense his presence in the halls, and the heart of him was evident in every development at the place.

Everything old is new again

At Procter & Gamble it wasn't a man who was the leader, it was a philosophy, and that was so powerful it transformed the people who worked there, turning a lot of individuals into one mind and one voice.

In 1968, when we went to work for P&G, it set the standard in the package-goods world for controlled, scientific marketing—religious consumer research, self-discipline, relentless will and staying power. The mystique of Procter & Gamble was so dynamic that each executive was viewed as an atomic part of a huge omniscient power by the outside world. Procter's executives, once they had trained there, were in such demand they could move to almost any other company and increase their fortunes.

Advertising agencies who worked for Procter were viewed as sophisticates who could be counted on to work scientifically and maturely.

However, like the Catholic Church, the company kept a pragmatic eye out for small miracles beyond their control and invested, warmly but warily, in one or two of the more intuitive, spontaneous agencies.

It was the press touting our success with troubled brands that caught their eye. One of Procter's laws was that a product had too much invested in it to be allowed to die and if it was given the right branding idea and the right advertising it never would. So an exorbitant amount of time and expense was invested to bring back the dead and to give rebirth to brands that began to droop. Procter's Crest toothpaste with fluoride to fight cavities had received the ADA claim and was winning the sweepstakes. Procter's other toothpaste, Gleem, had once enjoyed a 45 percent share of the toothpaste market. After Crest appeared with fluoride, Gleem steadily lost share of market and was becoming an emergency. Ed Harness, who was soon to become chairman, liked the idea of trying a hot creative agency for Gleem. Ed Lotspeich, the corporate advertising manager, was sent to take a look at Wells Rich Greene to see how far-out we might be. He looked us over with a dry eye, but we passed his test and were duly invited to Cincinnati to meet the toothpaste executives at the Queens City Club, where for years agencies were hired and fired, encouraged or warned, while breakfast or lunch was served by sweet little ladies in crisp green uniforms with lace caps. I had no idea of what we were taking on when we went to work for Procter & Gamble—it was so different from any account I had ever wrapped myself around, it was so structured and so sure of its infallibility. It would take me and most of Wells Rich Greene years to enjoy their ways, and Procter would worry and shake its head about us until we did.

We hired Al Wolfe to manage the account because he had strong package-goods experience and when I met him I thought he was smart and sensitive enough to loosen up and swing with us. He had a hard time. He did learn to appreciate the flamboyant creativity but I think he despaired of us ever getting into Procter's formulaic groove.

"The Blonde," he called me: "The Blonde" thinks this, "The Blonde" said that. I imagine this cheeky expression gave him some distance from the emotions he felt working for a woman—in person, he was unfailingly polite to me. I couldn't have cared less what monikers Al or anyone else at the agency found therapeutic, I was aware of the difficulties some of the men had working for me. There were no other women creating agencies as I was with large, big-time, big-budget accounts. Women-in-business was just becoming a big issue. A few talented men resigned from the agency because they found the idea of working for a woman intolerable. Herb Fisher, whom I admired and had big plans for, confronted me in the middle of a busy hallway on a difficult day when I was wishing I had been born with ten heads. "Mary, I've made up my mind about something and the sooner I tell you the better. I can't do this. I can't work for a woman. I don't think you can handle all this. I have to run this agency—or I have to leave." And so, of course, he left.

Marty Stern, our marketing director, was ecstatic when we got the Gleem account. Dick Rich was not. He liked to feel like a star with clients and Procter's controlling science made him crazy. When his first campaign for Gleem was not received well at P&G, he reacted with a New York shrug and disinterest and I found myself in Charlie Moss's office with yet another opportunity for him and Stan.

Charlie was working 25-hour days at the time but he and Stan began staying even later, had burgers and fries sent up every midnight, and finally came up with a taste strategy for Gleem that I liked a lot. Crest, the competition, had fluoride, a real ingredient in an era when toothpastes contained ghost ingredients that worked more on your mind than on your teeth. Fortunately, from Wells Rich Greene's point of view, fluoride toothpaste did not taste good at first and a lot of kids didn't want to brush their teeth with it. Charlie and Stan's idea was to exaggerate the delicious taste of Gleem, a toothpaste without fluoride, in television commercials where mothers chased their sons and daughters up and down and around the house, caught them, made them brush their teeth with Gleem, whereupon the kids discovered they loved the taste of Gleem and brushed their teeth happily ever after. The point was that it is better to have your kids brushing their teeth with a toothpaste they like than to have them refuse to brush their teeth at all with a fluoride toothpaste. Charlie's "Best Tasting Toothpaste in the World" campaign was a hit at Procter and it was a hit with television viewers, too—even by Procter's standards the commercials got extremely high recall scores—and it was a hit with mothers and kids. We firmly held our own against Crest.

A few years later, however, Procter decided that they should put fluoride into Gleem. There went the good-taste strategy that was saving Gleem's business! Gleem began to taste like any other fluoride toothpaste, and we were back to square one. By that time Procter had assigned us Safeguard soap, Prell shampoo, Sure deodorant and a long line of other products and we found ourselves having a love affair with a client who cherished us for challenging them with big ideas and arresting advertising but who constantly reproached us, in an ideological struggle filled with long sermons, for not really getting their act.

We agreed with the basic underpinnings of Procter's creed but they had created a painfully slow, Byzantine organization with layers of management that had to be convinced not only that advertising was on-strategy but that each word, each nuance was Proctercorrect. Procter believed that these different levels of control kept intuition and creativity on the right track. Unfortunately, the executives at different levels had different levels of experience and ability. The agency was expected to escort its creativity through the ascending levels of Procter up to the authorities at the top, using all the persuasion it could muster. It was also expected to help train Procter's young executives along the way, those who, in their early years, were inexperienced so, naturally, were opinionated.

When the agency finally reached the powerful guys on the top floors—the Bob Whelings, Bob Goldsteins, Steve Donovans, Sandy Weiners, Bill Connells, John Smales, John Peppers, Tom Lacos and Bob Blanchards—Procter & Gamble marketing became individual and courageous and tried to resurrect any magic lost along the way. These names may not mean as much to you as Sting, Mick, Bono or Bowie, but that only means you don't know the package-goods business. They

OPPOSITE: One of our first commercials for P&G dramatized the success a determined mother could have with a toothpaste as good-tasting as Gleem.

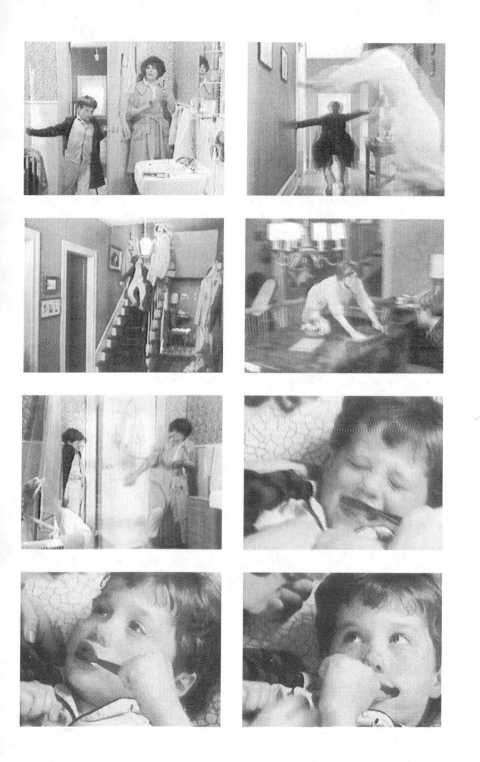

are package-goods stars. And good guys, the kind you want for blood buddies or husbands and fathers of your children.

I spent a lot of time with those good guys and I wondered why I never met a wife. So I organized a lunch for wives only and I invited Mrs. Ed Harness, who was then the wife of the chairman. It seemed a perfectly natural thing to do as a female head of one of their agencies, although no one had done such a thing before, so my lunch was viewed nervously in Cincinnati. We were a little itchy together at first but we all quickly dropped our hair, the way women do, and had a great time. I made friends I cherish, like Nancy Donovan, a bright light of a businesswoman. But best of all was what I learned in the long discussions the group of us had, taking us late into the dinner hour—candid information I would never have learned any other way—women are so communicative. I have never revealed one precious word from that charming lunch and I certainly won't now.

The most tedious P&G meetings were inside Wells Rich Greene—boring struggles when our Procter & Gamble account representatives tried to control our feisty creatives. Al Wolfe felt trapped between P&G's system and what he saw as Charlie Moss's arrogant dismissal of it. One of his biggest gripes was what I called Charlie's "comfort boys," an expression Charlie loathes. They were the less talented people who bought the agency time for the superachievers to get around to producing the right stuff. They were enablers, and everyone who has ever run an agency has enablers to fill up time until a superior talent is free. No matter how hard we searched, no matter how much money we paid—and we paid extraordinary salaries—we were never uniformly talented. No agency is. There isn't enough talent in the business. The knowing use of enablers, who are not talented enough but are sweetly willing, is one of the darker sides of creative businesses.

Looking back, as though from the window of a rocket, I see Procter & Gamble as a space station in its own galaxy, a world all its own, filled with converts who had been screened for uninhibited, exhibitionist, mercurial traits or anything that might pollute the environment. Life in the space station was civilized—sensible, rational, smart enough to be interesting and full of good guys who generally agreed with one another. Life was in control. If you had a problem, you could take it to the high priests of research—their reports were viewed as safe and sure guides to success.

What I did for love

The way I'm telling it you'd think each account was a distinct experience and that we focused on each of them one at a time. But that's not how it was. They all happened at the same time in an explosion. Jack Landry and Roy Chapin rode up to our offices in the same elevator on the same day and when they got out on our floor, Charlie Tillinghast, Gordon Sherman and Peter Godfrey got in and went down.

Here is the rhythm of the gentle chaos in a typical 48-hour period of my advertising days, which could be technically demanding, terribly dull and inconsequential; the world didn't always tilt. Still—48 advertising hours could be amazing, with arialike moments and not without farce.

I got off the plane from Detroit after that first press conference we had at American Motors and dashed to Grand Central Station, where we were hanging a spectacular, three-dimensional ad for Boodles gin over the main waiting room. A gin martini was the only drink I ever learned to like other than wine and I felt strongly about what gin should be, so when we got the Boodles business I did a test run comparing it to the gins I knew and loved and discovered that Boodles was better. Drier. Harding put it on all Braniff flights and I talked it up all over town. I explained to Charlie, who didn't know gin, that Boodles was great because it made a martini without flowers—you know, that slightly floral aftertaste you can get with gin. Charlie blew that visual picture up into a vast red mouth with flowers coming out of it and gave it the words "Martinis Without Flowers" and hung it high at Grand Central Station. I wanted to see it before heading back to the office, where I was due to see ideas for new snacks I was going to present the next morning to General Mills in Minneapolis. When I walked into Grand Central I was pleased to see there were crowds standing under the big red mouth with flowers, everybody seemed to be nodding their heads in understanding. So I rushed on to the agency.

The snack people were getting impatient and rambunctious outside my office and Kathie was giving me her infuriated look, but Jack Landry had come up from Philip Morris and was waiting to see me. "Come on, Little Tiger, come have a drink with me. We have to talk." Jack and I liked each other, trusted each other, we had become each other's security blankets in the political wear and tear at Philip Morris. I thought his marketing abilities at Philip Morris were extraordinary. He never got enough credit for that company's success. He was a late-day drinker, though, and I always tried to meet with him in the morning. The Leo Burnett Marlboro men handled their late-day bar meetings with Jack with gusto and style, but I couldn't do that (a distinct advantage in being a woman).

I followed him out of the office that evening because I knew what he wanted to talk about. Benson & Hedges sales had soared to record heights on the strength of our television commercials. But the TV ban on cigarette advertising had forced us to take our campaign off television and into print, and Dick didn't have the same gift for print he had for television. Herb Green and George D'Amato, who had come with us when we left Jack Tinker, had tried to adapt the campaign into print but a lot was lost in the translation. At the bar, downstairs, Jack said he had to level with me, he didn't believe the Benson & Hedges television campaign was ever going to make it in print. "It's a television idea, Mary," he said, "you can't make a silk purse out of it." What to do? We talked for an hour or so, I tried to change his mind and he was sympathetic, but I left with palpitations, promising to get back to him within the week. It was getting dark, I had a few thousand other things to do besides save the Benson & Hedges account, I had to sample and select snacks to take to Minneapolis, name them (Monkeys, Rabbits and Squirrels, maybe?) and write the speech I was due to give shortly. (I was forever giving speeches. When clients asked me to give them I couldn't say no and as I was the advertising flavor of the day, I was invited to speak to advertising and sales executive clubs all over America. We were trying to build awareness of the agency in all areas of the country so it also seemed smart to accept invitations to speak to Rotary groups and newspaper associations and bank conferences, even a meatpackers' convention—I spent one entire flight home to Dallas studying America's meatpackers' problems, but I came down on the side of the cows and that just added to my worries. The problem was that I couldn't give speeches that were written for me by someone else with any va-voom, I had to write them myself to bring out Mary Wells the Actress, so I was always writing them in snatches on napkins, notepads, Kleenex, anything available anywhere.)

When I got to the agency I saw Stan Dragoti about to leave for the night and I was struck by a monumental hunch. I grabbed him and told him about Jack's fears about Benson & Hedges and said I thought that he, Stan, was the one who could reassure Jack that we could keep the brand growing in print. "I don't even know Jack. Why am I the magic messenger? How could I know what to say to convince him?" Stan protested. I insisted that Jack would appreciate his great, prizewinning reputation in print, and anyway, I just knew he was Jack's kind of guy, he could give Jack a little more faith and buy us the time we needed. Shaking his head, Stan hurried over to the bar, introduced himself to Jack, and found a way to reassure him that if he gave us time we would find the answer to the Benson & Hedges print campaign. I don't know where that hunch came from, the agency business is so fast-moving and so full of emergencies, you learn when to jump without looking and when to fly without wings.

The next morning, while I was in Minneapolis presenting snack ideas to General Mills, Bob Adler, who ran the Bic business, called the agency and gave us their felt-tip pen to advertise. We named it the Bic Banana and Mel Brooks became the voice-over for the commercials. "Some tree!" Mel said, walking by our grand spiraling wood stairway in the entrance hall on his way to meet Bob Adler.

Bob Adler was a master at promoting disposable, impulse pens and lighters and razors. His idea was to put all his money behind one Bic product, sensationalize it, and it would then sell all the other Bic products. He chose the right agency. "Flick your Bic" was Charlie's line. He had to force it down the throats of his creative team, Adam Hanft and Maurice Mahler, but once they gave in and accepted it, they were otherworldly wonderful. Their commercials put Gillette's Cricket lighter, the established one, out of business for a time. Lew Wechsler, our head of TV programming, flooded Hollywood with the lighters and we got about 100 prime-time jokes from stars like Bob Hope using the line "Flick your Bic." We thought of it as free advertising.

It gets a lot worse than cold in Minneapolis. When I got up the morning of my snack meetings it was so far below zero the radio reported people were freezing to death on their way from their homes to their cars. My motel room was not connected under cover to the lobby and I faced a life-threatening walk to the taxi that would take me to General Mills. I called the agency to see if anyone had found a way to solve Jack's Benson & Hedges print problem, but no one had. No one had by the time I reached Wells Rich Greene, either, that afternoon. Charlie and Stan were meeting with a group from American Motors, so I looked around the buzzing agency and I couldn't find anybody who was rethinking the Benson & Hedges print. I would have had a tantrum, but I knew Charlie. So instead, at about seven p.m. I went out and sat very quietly in the chair outside my office and stopped breathing. In a few minutes Charlie and Stan came shuffling down the hall on their way home. They had to pass me and by that time I was grey from not breathing. They stopped to say goodnight, looked at me, took a few more steps. Then Charlie said, "We can't go." Stan: "Why? What's wrong?" Charlie: "She'll get sick. She's so depressed about Benson & Hedges. She's all alone, she won't go home, she'll stay all night like that. We can't go. We've gotta find an answer." They returned to their offices. I went into mine, ordered up pizzas and wrote my speech. About midnight they were back and they had a line, "America's favorite cigarette break," and ideas for breaking cigarettes that finally made the television work in print and we all went home.

Waiting for Charlie and Stan, I had telephoned Dorothy Carter, the smart doctor who was a consultant at Miles Laboratories. I'd thought of her on the plane from Minneapolis because I'd seen an Alka-Seltzer commercial the night before at the motel. It was a very funny commercial about spicy meatballs that was getting raves in the agency world and would win many awards. But I knew that Walter Compton would be unhappy with it. He didn't want humor to be so extreme it was all you remembered about an Alka-Seltzer commercial. Then Dorothy Carter jumped into my mind. She was happy to hear from me. She said that Alka-Seltzer sales had been off, Walter Compton had left Tinker and gone to Doyle Dane Bernbach looking for another sales turnaround, but he wasn't happy, he was always telling her that I was the only one who understood Alka-Seltzer the way he did. "Perhaps," she said, "you and I should meet and have a talk about Alka-Seltzer's future?" I made a date. I was pleased with myself; I went to bed and dreamt of hurdles.

Life has its hallucinatory moments, or certainly mine has, but in the sixties and early seventies you had to work a little harder to stay focused, so many large questions had been let loose—protest, authority, war, death, civil rights, women's rights, freedom, individuality. They weren't new questions but they were being presented so regularly on television you couldn't look away as you might have before. Awareness is at the very core of the advertising business, you have to be aware of what is happening today, now, this minute, to be connected, to be effective, not only about the issues but also about style, trends, art. So in my head Alka-Seltzer, long cigarettes and making Midas a household word were bumping up against Vietnam, the Kennedy assassinations, Martin Luther King and Neil Armstrong padding around in moon dust—not to mention Andy Warhol, Alice Cooper and what had become of Abbie Hoffman. And I had added the quagmire of taking Wells Rich Greene public.

We took the stock over the counter on Halloween, 1968, not long after we'd gotten the TWA account and in the glow of the publicity we'd received for the American Motors campaign and the success of Benson & Hedges. We believed that stock options would give us a gold stick to throw out in front of talents we would want to hire as well as help us hang on to the valuable talent we already had. We innocently thought that the leverage in options would make Wells Rich Greene tighten up expenses and exercise restraints. We thought our people would mature. Well, that never happened. Paul Hallingby of White Weld & Co. had been suggested to me as an investment banker by Harding's banker, Gus Levy, at Goldman Sachs and he led us through the offering. Our IPO had a business plan behind it but no real track record, just like the IPOs of the nineties. The stock opened at $17 a share. Dick and Stew and I each sold shares worth a little more than $1,200,000. Then we sailed into stockholders' meetings, board of directors' meetings and meetings with investment bankers in all the big cities.

I invited Harding's lawyer, Arnold Grant, to be a member of Wells Rich Greene's board. He said, "You know, Leland Hayward is a client of mine and I bet he'd get a kick out of being on an advertising agency board. He'd certainly get the gist of it. Why don't you take him to lunch and talk to him about it?" So I took Leland to the Colony Club and proposed to him and he was tickled pink to become a board member. Troy Post, still the head of GreatAmerica, and Emilio Pucci were also happy to join the board. It was a merry group; the outside directors were fond of us and very helpful. The disciplines and long-term planning and financial reporting that accompanied public ownership and the time that took out of my overpromised life might have sunk me but for their help and, more important, Harding's. Harding was always a beam of clear vision to help me machete my way through the jungles in each year's financial plans and results.

To make the stock easier to buy, we planned to move it from over the counter to the American Stock Exchange; Paul Hallingby had completed the plans and wanted to meet the next morning. We met so early that the cleaning lady hadn't reached my office yet and that pizza Charlie and Stan and I'd had the night before was still hanging around. Paul wrinkled his nose and left as soon as he could. I was speaking at the New York Sales Executive lunch that day and needed to shine my speech. Bill Claggett, a major executive at Ralston Purina, would be sitting next to me and I wanted to impress him and persuade him to give us some of his dog-food business. Also on my Do It Immediately list was my speech for the coming TWA road show, the presentation I had to make in Detroit to sell American Motors on a nervy idea we had for the next campaign, the speech I would need in a couple of weeks when I would be inducted into the Copywriters Hall of Fame, a speech to the American Marketing Association in Atlanta—part of the deal I'd made with Bill Durkee when he gave us the RC Cola and Diet Rite business—and an emergency trip to California I had to make, preferably yesterday, to untangle a knot in our new relationship with Al Crossin, a smart, highly expectant executive at Hunt-Wesson.

Add to that the waves of advertising the agency produced every day that had to be seen by me or Dick or Charlie. That work had to be considered, approved, improved or tossed out or replaced by work we did ourselves. Add to that the waves of information we had to digest in stolen moments so that we knew what to illuminate about the products or services we were selling—or what to hide about them—and exactly what miracles were called for.

Add the potential disasters that hovered like spooks in our dark corners, for example: the fact that I did not like, in fact I did not even understand, the work we had done so far on RC Cola and I had promised Bill Durkee that our campaign would put RC Cola right up there with Coke and Pepsi. Add my belief that the group handling Love Cosmetics was falling apart. Love had grown into an extended line of products that required us to advertise more heavily in print ads. They were being written by a choir of ladies, an odd group, some of them older, Revlon Fire & Ice types and some of them kohl-eyed, go-go Mary Quant types, one of whom put a hex on Charlie and his children when we fired her, making Charlie unbearable for a couple of weeks. It was not easy to find great fashion advertising writers. But Peter Godfrey was becoming as uneasy about the ladies as I was, so somewhere in the world we had to find replacements soon or that account would fall into the arms of another agency that was wooing Peter Godfrey, just waiting for us to fail.

Add to that the surprises—like the call I got from Don Swanson and Bruce Atwater saying they had decided to hurry up the launch of the new snacks I'd presented to them in Minneapolis so we needed advertising for them immediately, how soon could I return to Minneapolis? And, finally, add the unexpected blows like Charlie and Stan's announcement, mid-pizza, that they had to have a vacation or die. They'd rented a house in St. Tropez for three weeks, where they were going to go come hell or high water to write a movie. In the late sixties and the seventies everybody on Madison Avenue wanted to make movies and a few were actually making them.

These days there are smart ways to deal with stress. In those days and for many years I dealt with it by dancing. When I got to my apartment nights I turned on Sly Stone and "I Want to Take You Higher" and I hoofed, I strutted and pranced and boogied and stomped and shimmied and sometimes I slipped in a hula or a tango. Later I shook my booty with the Sunshine Band. I shook until I could get out of my head and into the tub. Then I would sit in the water, a zombie. People in the building averted their eyes when we shared an elevator. God knows what they thought. The best song I ever found for shaking my psyche into shape was "I Will Survive." It's still better than any pill.

Harding and I had a pact we would talk to each other every night no matter how late before we went to sleep. I called the kids earlier, when they got home from school, but Harding and I talked late into every night, wherever he was in the world, calming each other, loving each other, promising each other anything.

By 1971 I knew these things: that there were few people who could build a hot advertising agency, and I would not be able to hire one of them to help me build mine because he would be building one of his own—and that in the real world there was no one who would be a better creative director for Wells Rich Greene than Charlie Moss—and that if I lost Charlie Moss to the movie business I was stupid.

My buddy

L ike me, Charlie had elocution lessons when he was four. When he was 11 he saw a play given by the school drama club and thought to himself, "I want to do that." So his father drove him to New York every Tuesday evening, where he studied acting, tap dancing, singing and ventriloquism at the Marie Moser Theatre Television Institute. He was good with the dummy and they toured Elks clubs, Mason lodges, hospitals and mental institutions. Presenting to mental patients may have been the best training he could have had for the advertising business, where so often you make presentations to groups that just sit there and look at you with no expression. The dummy's name was Algy and he was fast and flip and hilariously funny, unlike Charlie, who was very shy. When Charlie realized that all the cute teenagers he had eyes for preferred Algy to him he packed Algy away in a box and got serious as an ensemble actor. "It's lonely up there with a dummy," he says. "It looks like there are two of you but there's only you with yourself." He auditioned and got a part in a movie, *The Little Fugitive,* and it was a surprise hit. Then there were a few television shows and college productions and he was sure he was a younger, thinner Montgomery Clift. But when he graduated there were no real acting prospects, no money, his dad had big problems and couldn't help him and his girlfriend expected marriage. That's when he walked into my office with the orange floor at Doyle Dane Bernbach, a skinny kid looking for a job as a copy trainee. I remember that when I first saw him I thought to myself, "Buy that boy a steak dinner, Mary, before he starves to death."

Charlie listened with his entire mind, his entire being, so he heard clearly. I loved that. So did clients. He was more intelligent than most trainees, silly on the surface but absolutely serious underneath, funny the way great clowns are funny and earnest the way great clowns are earnest. Those characteristics appear in all of his work as they do in his life. He is still brilliantly funny on television and in person but he is still not a funny man. As a copy trainee at Doyle Dane, his opportunities were meager, but even the trade ads he wrote stopped you. It was Dick who thought to hire him at Jack Tinker & Partners. And it was while he was working on the Braniff business that he began to emerge, an impresario of ideas and a television natural.

I was too focused on Wells Rich Greene's survival to witness all the larking and sometimes outrageous behavior in our early creative department, which was as hedonistic as any other creative business in the sixties and early seventies. My loss, probably. So there may have been sides to young Charlie that I missed. What I saw was that I could trust him. I could trust him to do wonderful work most of the time. I could trust his ability to digest information correctly—even demanding stuff, highly technical information—and to develop advertising that solved problems for our clients, not just for the fun of it. I could trust him to invent new types of television advertising, to keep stretching. I could trust him to help others understand their clients and to do better work than they could do without him. I could trust his serious heart, his responsible intention and his elasticity. He could change direction, if necessary, without giving me too much guff. I could always be honest with him. And I knew without a doubt that he would be there, like Butch Cassidy, to jump off the cliff with me.

Stan Dragoti added a touch of elegance. As a team, they fill each other out. Stan was a cartoonist in grade school, tramping around with his portfolio of cartoons until he became a mascot for the big talents at Marvel Comics and King Features. He was a kid movie buff and he remembers seeing Charlie in *The Little Fugitive,* although, he says, bells didn't ring. He went into television advertising before anyone thought it would amount to much and became the youngest vice-president at Young & Rubicam after lifting everybody's idea of advertising grace with his glamorous Eastern Airlines ads and commercials. He was always a relentless force, a tidal wave, so determined he could produce a six-week campaign in a weekend if he really had to. And as he never gave up, he could make me sigh and alter my plans, and that wasn't easy to do. He was street-wise, steady, and blessed with a chuckle about everything in life. He was also a swell dresser and you could take him anywhere.

They went to St. Tropez—Charlie, Stan, and Stan's wife, Cheryl Tiegs, who was temporarily retired as a model and was for a short time plump. Cheryl is beautiful thin but she was world-class gorgeous when she was plump. They had been working on the movie about five days when I called. I never let Charlie go anywhere for very long—first of all, I needed him at the agency—but, also, I didn't think it was a good idea for him to get used to anything else. He says he always felt like a runaway slave. So when the advertising for RC Cola went from bad to worse I called them in St. Tropez. I said, "Listen, guys, we have catastrophic trouble. They are expecting a Wells Rich Greene miracle and the work is not just bad, it is insane. It is grotesque. It is trash. It could destabilize everything we have worked for here. You have got to come back this minute. Now. Right now. Don't talk. Don't even pack. Take the next plane. I promise you, I swear, you can go back to St. Tropez in a couple of days and you can take an extra week. I'll pay. But you have to be in that studio by tomorrow afternoon. We are out of time." They would have called the Mafia and taken out a contract on me if they had known how to do that, but instead they returned in a rage and went to the studio to see the footage for the campaign that I was so upset about.

The idea of the campaign was "RC Cola Cools Off the Hot Cities." Translated, that means that RC was creating the smart scene, it was the catalyst that turned a city into the hip place to be. This theme allowed us to limit our spending to the cities that offered RC Cola the most potential and to compliment those cities, to make the people there feel hip and to make them think about RC Cola, probably for the first time. The promotion potential was phenomenal. The local RC Cola bottlers were thrilled with the idea and the presentation of the new advertising was scheduled for Las Vegas as if it were *Gone With the Wind*. But campaigns like that need a virtuosic Cecil B. DeMille creating them. What had been produced while Charlie and Stan were in St. Tropez was madness. When they reached the studio they found Bert Stern, normally a truly great photographer, viewing miles and miles of footage of nothing but the yellow line that runs up the middle of Sunset Boulevard. Do not ask why. I asked why for years and I still do not have an answer that makes any sense at all. The original scripts had been Cecil B. DeMille material. But somewhere along Sunset Boulevard Phil Parker, who was the art director, had simply walked off and never returned. That was when I called St. Tropez and ordered my movie moguls back to the agency. I didn't know what to do with all that footage of Sunset Boulevard's yellow lines. Stan and Charlie took the film available, added what they could, and reinvented the campaign. Cecil B. DeMille it wasn't, but at least they didn't lynch us after the presentation in Las Vegas.

Watching all those miles of Sunset Boulevard kept my mind on incentives I might offer Charlie and Stan to make them forget the movie business. I had one horrifying idea but I knew it would work: Wells Rich Greene could produce the movie Charlie and Stan wanted to make. I discussed the idea with Harding. He said, "You know, it would take a doozy of an incentive to keep those boys down on the farm now that they have Hollywooditis. They're movie-struck, and even a million-dollar bonus, enormous as that is, might not settle them down. And it would certainly spoil them forever." He agreed that the money would be better spent producing a movie if I could find a partner to produce one with. If the movie failed, the boys would return to Wells Rich Greene, cured. If it did well, Wells Rich Greene would make a profit on its investment and, as he said, "After all, the movie business isn't that far afield. Maybe you'd like the movie business, Mary." I could always count on the gambler in Harding's psyche to keep the future alluring. We agreed that there should be no movie deal unless Charlie and Stan agreed to devote an equal amount of time to Wells Rich Greene advertising.

Movie partner? I was in luck. Arnie Grant, Harding's lawyer and my board of directors member, was a brilliant tax lawyer and financial manager for Hollywood stars and studio heads, Jack Warner, for example. Arnie had a reputation for using Stalin's techniques to achieve what he desired for his clients. But the Arnie Grant I knew was charming and easy and fun to know. He had a low, murmuring voice and a little dry chuckle so you had to lean close to hear his stories, but they were worth the trouble. He wasn't handsome, he had pink Pinocchio ears, but he was nice looking, tall and slim and immaculate. All the years that I knew him he was madly in love with Bess Myerson, he married her twice and the second time he divorced her he went into such a state of shock I thought he might not live. He spent a couple of terrible days at the agency telling me about a diary he'd found, tears streaming down his face. He never really recovered from that.

But earlier, the day we talked about Jack Warner, he was his happy self, brokering a deal between two people he adored. He told me that nobody was going to the movies anymore and a revolution was tearing up Hollywood. "All the studio bosses are scared. Jack's scared," he said. "He's afraid he's lost it, he's afraid he's old and doesn't know anymore. He made *Bonnie and Clyde* because Warren got down on his knees, but he hated it. He doesn't understand why anybody would want to see these crazy movies they're making—you know the ones I mean. *Love Story*—she's got leukemia, for God's sake. *The Graduate*—he does it with a friend of his mother's!" Then, whispering, as though he were telling me something really off-color, "Jack says there's a bunch of drug-crazed loonies out there making pictures now. He can't talk to them. They don't have respect. They don't love the business." "Well," I said, "Jack should come in and talk to *us*, Arnie. Wells Rich Greene could make a better movie than *Bonnie and Clyde*." I really thought so. Arnie said he would bring Jack to the agency. Jack wasn't running the studio anymore but he was still producing and, after all, Wells Rich Greene was the coolest new-wave agency around. Arnie lit up. We would be the new wave for Jack.

You ought to be in pictures

He brought Jack to our offices one hot day in August 1969. The elevators in the General Motors Building were tall and Jack was a little fellow but when the doors opened there stood a real mogul, the last of the moguls, 77 years old, smiling with the world's whitest teeth and flashing his eyes at us as if they were cameras. Here was Hollywood in person. He hummed through the hall to the reception room where he patted our best chair. "You can't beat good French!" he said. He told Arnie later that he was enormously reassured by the quality and style of our interior decoration, something he knew about. He could tell that we were not drug crazies by looking at our furniture. He seemed to be thrilled to be meeting such famous advertising kids. When he learned that he and I were both from Youngstown, Ohio, he closed his eyes and said, "I feel it—I tell you I feel it—from the top of my head to the bottom of my feet, this meeting was meant to be, heaven itself is pulling us together!" I thought he was going to jump up and down. We roughed out a theoretical three-picture deal: Jack would put up half the money and Wells Rich Greene would put up half. Then we celebrated the idea with champagne.

He was dying to read the script. Only there wasn't any script, because I nixed the first one Charlie wrote. The basic idea for the script came from an article about the Old West that Stan read that burst all the balloons. That outlaw period in history lasted only about 15 years, although it stimulated hundreds of movies. It wasn't what it was cracked up to be. It wasn't easy to kill anybody with the ubiquitous six-gun that any outlaw worth his salt was supposed to have had on his hip. Six-guns could only shoot straight for short distances and they were usually dirty and grimy with sand, highly unreliable. To kill anybody with one you had to belly up close. According to the article Stan read, one of the reasons for Billy the Kid's success was that he was so little and looked like such a baby the big guys didn't worry about him and let him get close enough to kill them. Charlie and Stan saw hilarious potential in all that and wrote about 180 pages cartooning the Old West and Billy's close-up shooting career. I nixed their first script because they had just tossed it off, it was too thin, too silly. I thought the movie should be more than a cute cartoon, it should be a serious comedy. It should seat the comedy on the reality of that ridiculous, inefficient outlaw world and the humor should be the kind of sweet funniness Charlie and Stan could create with such success for television.

As I was the one coming up with the money, I was taking a hard line, and they were just beginning a new approach. But they did have a title to give Jack: *Dirty Little Billy.* "I like that title! It's got blood and guts! That could be very good, very commercial! I'm in!" Jack always talked with exclamation marks. "OK!" he said. "So what's the story?" Charlie looked at me for help. "Tell him the story, Charlie," I said, giving him a bright smile. So Charlie did about a half-hour synopsis of a story he created on the spot, an act he was used to performing at clients' in emergencies. "I like that! Then the kid does this and the kid does that! It's a deal! Come out to California, to my office, right away and we'll get it rolling!" Jack left Wells Rich Greene feeling young, waving at everybody and throwing kisses all the way to the elevator. Arnie followed him, grinning from ear to ear. As soon as the elevator door closed Charlie and Stan and I collapsed in nervous hysteria. Could it really be true? Just like that we're in the movie business with Jack Warner? We must be dreaming. The only thing real about that half hour with Jack Warner was that it happened. I supposed it could happen because Jack believed in Arnie, Arnie believed in us, and we believed in ourselves.

We created a subsidiary, WRG/Dragoti, Ltd., and announced the formation of a joint venture with Jack Warner, founder and former president of Warner Brothers, Inc., for the purpose of producing, from time to time, creative, low-budget motion pictures. *Dirty Little Billy* was budgeted at less than $1 million—the bonus money I didn't give Charlie and Stan.

The telepathic rapport between Charlie Moss and me crashed only a few times over the years. It crashed then, big-time. Charlie thought I believed *Dirty Little Billy* should be a serious film, whereas I thought he and Stan were creating a new script based on their sweet way of making a serious idea funny. Stan just wanted a good script, serious or funny was OK with him. By that time he was obsessed with the idea of directing a film. I was only obsessed with Wells Rich Greene and disappeared back into the agency business, leaving *Dirty Little Billy* to evolve into an intensely serious, unbelievably muddy film about the West not too different from *Unforgiven,* another muddy movie made not so long ago that at least had Clint Eastwood.

Dorothy Carter had gone to Walter Compton and told him that I was important to Alka-Seltzer and that Walter owed it to himself to see me and talk to me about it, which was exactly what he wanted to hear, she told me afterwards. Walter called and we had a date. So I didn't go with Charlie and Stan when they went to Los Angeles to Jack's private offices. They really weren't offices. He had taken his whole studio world with him as easily as somebody who retires takes family pictures from his desk. There were rooms full of photographs of his stars, Cagney,

Bogart, Gary Cooper. One of the rooms was the barbershop he'd had at the studio. It had been precisely rebuilt for him and his barber was right there by his chair. All his assistants had gone with him, too, and had retired into the complex with him like the wives of the pharaohs.

"Come in, kids!" Jack was lathered up in the barber's chair watching the astronauts on television. "So who's the star? Wattayagot?" Charlie and Stan had been studying Michael J. Pollard movies and they thought he was such an unlikely Billy the Kid that he'd be a good, shocking choice. "Don't know him! Who's Michael J. Pollard?" Jack asked the assistants who hovered with notepads. In fact Michael Pollard had been in *Bonnie and Clyde,* but Jack hated that movie so much he had it withdrawn from distribution almost immediately after its initial release because he felt that it had no commercial potential whatsoever. A bright marketing man at Warners pestered Jack until Jack finally agreed to a limited re-release. The rest, as they say, is history. Jack never noticed Michael Pollard in the film, he was too busy hating Warren Beatty. "Michael Pollard would be a perfect Billy," Jack's assistants agreed, winking at Stan and Charlie. "Cheap, too," they added. "Great!" shouted Jack, bounding out of the chair. "Perfect choice! And cheap, too! Come on, I'll take you to lunch!"

Michael J. Pollard didn't turn out to be perfect, he had energy problems and he was in the hands of a Dr. Feelgood who flew in regularly to give him vitamin-cocktail shots that seemed to keep him fit and appearing on the set. If Robert Taylor was Hollywood's archetypal Billy, Michael Pollard looked like a sweet little kid clown playing with his guns, too small for his boots.

The new script moved forward, but Charlie was having serious problems with his marriage, he had a painful broken wrist that wouldn't heal and he was being pulled one direction as the creative director at Wells Rich Greene in New York while Stan pulled him to Los Angeles to get more pages of script. Tensions between them escalated and Charlie went into a creative coma, he had little enthusiasm for anything. I watched him trying to sort out who he was and what he was going to do with his marriage and his life but around me he wore a No Trespassing sign. He appeared on the movie set less and less. Jack would always yell

"Norman Maine, you're back!" when he saw him, referring to the husband in *A Star Is Born,* who walks into the sea and never returns. One evening Harding, Charlie and Stan and I went to the extravagant screening room in Jack's home to see the first scenes Stan had shot. Bugsy Siegel was found and arrested in that room while he was watching a movie. Jack enjoyed living dangerously from a distance, he would grow a foot taller right in front of your eyes when he was telling stories about his Mafia friends. We all settled into his luxurious chairs and I remember how glamorous I felt sitting in that room screening a movie I was producing with Jack Warner. I wished my mother could see me. Jack was happy with the first scenes. Harding liked them. Stan had discovered heaven. I didn't know what to make of those muddy scenes, beautifully shot, but so downbeat, and Michael Pollard, not untalented but so ugly in all that sepia dirt. What had happened to sweet humor? That was not *my* movie, I thought. As for Charlie, he was at his all-time emotional low point and really didn't care. For a while he removed himself from the movie completely and Stan moved on without him. They got their act together to complete the film, the fraternity between them reignited itself, but by that time the issue was settled: Charlie's future was in the advertising business and Stan had become a Hollywood director.

The only difficult time we ever had with Jack was over the advertising theme. We wanted the advertising to say, "John Wayne would hate this movie." But Jack had never liked John Wayne and wasn't about to give him any free publicity. Eventually we agreed on "Billy the Kid was a punk." Stan previewed it at the Sorbonne in Paris. The students loved it, they gave it a thunderous ovation and carried Stan around on their shoulders, calling him a true genius in film. The reviews were enthralling. "I think we may be in big trouble," Stan said to me, agitated, when he called from Paris that night. "You know how a French film can be like watching paint dry? I mean, their idea of a sexy film is of three people sitting around a table debating adultery for an hour. Mary, trust me, it is not good that they like this film so much! It means it's slow."

In October of 1972 we all went to San Francisco for the first Ameri-

This picture of Jack Warner and me dressed up for the premiere of our movie, *Dirty Little Billy,* was taken before the hissing began.

can preview of *Dirty Little Billy* at the San Francisco Film Festival. Traditionally, hundreds of students attended the festival screenings. They were hotbeds of gleefully radical, anti-authoritarian youth, and I was warned there would be no holds barred, no prisoners taken. Somebody very wise suggested that we should sit near an exit door. Jack wasn't worried, though, he thought *Dirty Little Billy* was so much better than *Bonnie and Clyde* that we were going to make motion-picture history. The publicity folks had invited prestigious film press to a black-tie-and-caviar supper party after the screening, so we were all made gorgeous and we arrived at the theatre looking as if we were part of Queen Elizabeth's coronation and had gotten lost in Haight-Ashbury. Seats had been reserved for us in the center, in the eye of what turned into a hurricane. Twenty minutes into the film the first rows of blue jeans began to gently hiss, and like a bolt of lightning everybody in the theatre was hissing. The sound grew until there were waves of hissing at force 8—9—10 and growing. The publicity executives panicked. One of them grabbed me and dragged me out of our row of seats. Jack was seated beside me, stunned. He bent his knees so that he would be shorter than the seats and invisible and he crawled out behind me, hanging on to my skirt and yelling something like "Kids! Kids! Kids!" When we reached the exit he was green. I turned back for a last look at the crowd. All those happy hissers had reached force 12. They could have knocked down trees with that sound. Jack was whisked away in a limousine by his assistants, the rest of us returned to what was to have been a celebratory late supper but was now a funeral. We were deaf. And beyond conversation.

I love New York

But I wasn't so far gone that night that I didn't see a familiar gleam in Stan's eye. Mr. Never-Give-Up was a Hollywood director now. He would go on and escort the film through all its openings, learn all about local movie reviewers and how to get a good review in a town like St. Louis, and, more important, he learned about the profits that get hijacked in the motion-picture business and how to protect yourself. He would direct a string of megahits like *Love at First Bite* and *Mr. Mom,* but he would never really leave Wells Rich Greene. In fact, just a few years after The Big Hiss, as we called it, he and Charlie were given special Tony Awards and thunderous applause for creating and directing the "I Love New York" campaign.

That was one of the agency's finest hours, but I wasn't tickled pink when we first got the account. New York was a mess and in a lot more financial trouble than American Motors had been. I was never comfortable when clients were poor and New York was broke. The troubles started earlier, in John Lindsay's time, but it was hard to look at those posters of handsome John Lindsay with his coat slung over his shoulders, the sun giving him a halo, strolling down Manhattan's most dangerous streets, and not have hope. By the time Hugh Carey became governor, the city faced a billion-dollar operating deficit and bankruptcy and you had to scratch hard to find anybody with hope. Three hundred thousand workers were let go. Schools closed down and teachers became ugly. Every day headlines counted the New York businesses that were leaving the town and the state. The ultimate rejection came when President Ford turned his back on the state's plea for financial aid. The *Daily News*'s front page said it: "Ford to City: Drop Dead!"—although the president came through with the loan when Carey personally guaranteed it. New Yorkers walked around disgusted, depressed.

The height of horrors was reached during the long weeks of a garbage strike that covered New York City in piles of unmentionables. The city smelled so bad some people took to wearing surgeon's masks in the streets. That's when Marty Stern, the most hopeful man I knew and by then our marketing director, came to me with New York's senior deputy commissioner, Bill Doyle, and what I saw as a hopeless proposition. Bill Doyle was a temporary helping hand in the governor's offices, on loan from Chase Manhattan Bank, trying to bolster his Vietnam buddy John Dyson. John was the commissioner of commerce, a great choice of Carey's—the governor was clever about people. John, like everybody else around the governor in those days, was looking for a fast buck—anything that would help get the economy going and wouldn't require serious investment by the state. He saw that tourism had everything in place to be exploited—roads, bridges, upstate beauty, museums, hotels and, above all, Broadway. "New York spends less per person on tourism than any state in the country. We need a plan," he told Bill Doyle. "We have to squeeze money for tourism out of this penniless legislature with a good, foolproof plan." Bill had gone to see Marty Stern and they had come up with the idea of spending the few thousand dollars left in the state's tourism budget for research geared to benchmarks that would measure, reliably, what an investment in tourism advertising would produce for the state's coffers in tax income. Out of respect for Marty I approved the idea and agreed to contribute the agency's work on the project as charity.

The research results were surprising. People never even thought of vacationing in New York, yet when you brought it to their attention, they were crazy to see a Broadway show. As for the outdoor wonders of New York State, they were a big secret. When they were revealed to people they instantly wanted to visit them. The research study was given to Stanley Steingut, the speaker of the legislature, with the promise that four million in advertising would yield eight million in revenue (it produced much much more). While Stanley Steingut was thinking about those $4 million profits, I was invited to have lunch with the governor at his mansion in Albany. His invitation finally got me to focus on New York, the numbers, the names, the potential and what seemed to me to be the hot button, the emotions that New York brought out in people everywhere. Marry and I chartered a slow helicopter to Albany because I knew nothing about the state outside the city and the Hamptons and I wanted to sound smarter than that when I talked to the governor.

What is it about smiling Irishmen? They smile with such enthusiasm. They may be plotting your ruin but when they look at you, their blue eyes gleam with affection and joy. Hugh Carey was at his very best about the time I met him. He and a group of the city's warriors—bankers, politicians and businessmen—were masterminding the deals that finally kept New York afloat, and he and Bob Wagner were getting the unions together into a supportive position that made a rescue possible. I was seated next to Bob, surely one of New York's sagest politicians, at dinner one night and he told our table, "Hugh Carey was brilliant, he rose to it, he's the one who should get credit for saving New York." The governor came down the stairs of the mansion to greet me, full of welcome, and took me on a tour of the place rattling off funny, intimate stories about every picture and every rocking chair. We were admiring what he called the "Rockefeller begonias" when he said, "You know, Virginia claims it is the state for lovers, but when you drive through Virginia all they give you is a ticket for speeding. New

York is the state for lovers, I love it and I want everybody to love it. If I get you the money, will you give me advertising that makes everybody love New York?" We had a deal. We shook hands on it in the begonia garden.

They still hadn't picked up the garbage on 58th Street when I got back from Albany but I had new eyes for New York. I told Charlie, "Governor Carey loves New York and he wants everybody else to love it. I know everybody hates New York right now, people get more emotional about New York than any city I can think of. We've got to use that emotion and turn it around, from strong hate to strong love." "What about the garbage?" Charlie asked. He was getting ready to love New York, since I obviously did. "There is no garbage," I said. "Remember your very first time in New York City? The thrill it was? That's New York. Forget the garbage. Everybody loves New York, deep down inside." Charlie was sold. He once spent days looking for a beach outside Lima, Peru, that I told him was pink to photograph for a Braniff campaign touting South America as "the Next Place." When he returned he told me he couldn't find a pink beach. I sent him back to Peru. "The pink beach is there, Charlie, go at sunset!" At sunset every beach in Peru is pink. After making a second trip to Peru Charlie understood my visions and how to turn them into advertising. White-lie advertising, we called it. He assigned the advertising for New York's beautiful outdoors to an art director who had been smartening up our TWA advertising, Jerry Ranson, and a stylish writer, Peter Ognibene. After their first couple of ideas didn't fly with Bill Doyle, Charlie said, "Why don't you do a testimonial, have different people from different states doing different outdoor activities in New York and have them say things like, 'I live in New Hampshire, but I love New York'?"

I adored the campaign, and Steve Karmen got the music for it just right—an emotional anthem, the kind of music that is spiritual, lifts your heart, lifts your soul and changes your attitude. I think the "I Love New York" music is what changed people's attitudes towards New York so quickly. There was a distinct shift as soon as that music took over, and it did take over. It was played everywhere for a while. In the movie *Wag the Dog,* a fake war is created for political reasons and an anthem is created to move people and make them believe there really is a war. For me, watching that movie is like reliving the "I Love New York" days at Wells Rich Greene. Charlie was Dustin Hoffman and I was Robert De Niro and we had New Yorkers marching right past all the garbage singing "I Love New York."

That is how the words "I Love New York" became the campaign for New York. I lost count of the people who claimed to have created the line "I love New York." We even heard from the son of an aide to Harry Truman who claimed that Harry was the first person to say "I love New York," on a campaign visit to the state. Nobody *created* the expression; it is what people have been saying since I can remember, because that's the way people feel about New York. Charlie simply took the words out of their mouths and put them into context.

Creative businesses are full of marvelous accidents. Milton Glaser, who is a very elegant, modern designer, was asked to create posters for New York because the state had nothing to help its tourist program, no posters, no maps for gas stations, no bumper stickers for taxis and no money to make such things. It was love for New York that brought Milton to our offices with a batch of posters, and while we were oohing and aahing over them he pulled a piece of paper out of his pocket and said, "I like this, what do you think?" It was the "I Love New York" logo with a heart in place of the word "Love." The state paid him a pittance for it, and shabam!—"I ♥ New York" was so contagious that people all over the world adopted it and half the world copied it, substituting the name of their country or city or hamburger stand for "New York." The state did not license the logo. The Department of Commerce preferred to encourage its use. The more often it appeared, the better, they said, and at no cost to the state. That logo shows up in the most unexpected places. I have seen I Love Everything, including "I ♥ Zimbabwe" on T-shirts.

Charlie and Stan created an "I Love New York" campaign starring Broadway. Traditionally, Broadway shows were advertised in a representational style as you would see them in a performance from somewhere in the audience. Stan wanted to do something really new, and he thought of directing the stars of the shows in a *presentational* style, they would present themselves *to you* while singing the "I Love New York" anthem. The presentational style would create an exultant connection between the Broadway stars and you, the television viewer, that would not only make you feel you absolutely had to see those shows but also remind you that you loved New York.

Jerry Schoenfeld, the head of the Shubert Theatre Organization, and Jimmy Nederlander, the two czars of Broadway, understood instantly what those commercials would do for ticket sales, but when we held a meeting with the producers of the shows themselves, there was only silence and suspicion in the room. "Um . . . what order do you plan to present the shows in—who comes first in the commercial?" asked the man from *Annie*. "Well," Stan said, "that depends on the footage, we want the commercial to ebb and flow, you know, maybe it starts with *A Chorus Line* and then—" "Wait a minute!" said the man from *Annie*. "You mean *Chorus Line* would come before *Annie*? Why would *Chorus Line* come before *Annie*?" He was outraged. If you looked around that table you didn't see one expression of joy or gratitude for what the commercials would do to sell tickets to all those shows. There was only sour suspicion about which show would appear first in each commercial. Finally Jerry Schoenfeld said, "Look, guys, this is going to be fantastic. We've never had anything this big to sell tickets for us!" and slowly, cooperation spread through the room. There was only one holdout, *The King and I.* Yul Brynner didn't want to bother with the commercials, he didn't want to take the time. Harvey Sabinson, the executive director of the League of New York Theatres and Producers, called him and said, "Listen, Yul, every other show is going to be in the campaign. You are the only one who is not going to be in a spot. Think about how that is going to look to the public. You better change your mind." And he did.

The first commercial we made ended with Frank Langella as Dracula. Swirling in his Dracula cape he looks into your eyes and says thrillingly, "I love New York—especially in the evening." Frank wanted to say the word "night" instead of "evening," he wanted to say "especially at night." But Charlie and Stan thought the word "night" in that commercial would be ghoulish, whereas the word "evening" was a glamorous word and less scary for Dracula to say on television. "We don't want to scare little kids," Charlie said. Finally Frank agreed. But he was uneasy. The day of the Dracula shoot New York had one of its big blizzards, all the limousines for the performers broke down and Volkswagen buses were sent out to pick them up. Stan set up a fog machine to make the snow appear moodier, "like Venice in winter when the vampires are out," he said. When Frank Langella appeared in his Dracula makeup and his cape he was a very imposing figure and people backed away from him nervously. Just before they shot the scene he grabbed Stan's arm and whispered to him, "Don't hurt me." Stan realized that Frank was a serious actor, an artist who did not appear in commercials, and suddenly there he was in a Dracula cape with a fog machine in the middle of a blizzard terrified that he was going to look ridiculous in a television commercial. Later, we staged a screening for all the actors so they could see the commercials ahead of everyone else. They came up to the agency in droves to see themselves. When Frank appeared, he rolled his eyes at Stan, but he was delighted with his bit in the commercial and sent a charming note.

When we were certain the commercials would be a success we suggested that the state get Bobby Zarem, an expert public-relations man, for the campaign. Bobby arranged to launch the commercials at the Tavern on the Green and followed that with a midnight launch at Studio 54. For reasons none of us can fathom he is another one who claims to have created the line "I Love New York." I don't know what to say to such poor souls except "Get a life." The governor, Mayor Ed Koch and all the other political, financial and social stars of New York were at one launch or the other. The din at the first launch was deafening until the first commercial appeared, then the crowd became mesmerized and silent. Almost everyone in New York, let alone at the Tavern on the Green, had a vested interest in the advertising by that time. Fortunately, it was a wild and wonderful hit. Wells Rich Greene had experienced its share of heartfelt applause for campaigns but nothing like the reaction to those first "I Love New York" commercials, because they mattered so much to so many people. At that time in New York, it was impossible not to love commercials that made you love New York again.

Frank Langella worried about playing Dracula in this "I Love New York" commercial.

The campaign continued for years. Almost every major Broadway production appeared in it. Do you remember the commercial that had Sandy Duncan flying over the Brooklyn Bridge? Steve Horne directed that one and Tom Heck and Marcia Grace produced it for Wells Rich Greene. All of the productions were headaches, scheduling nightmares, backbreaking in detail. The account was blessed with a wiz of an account supervisor, Jane Maas, who wrote a book about those magic days. By the time we reached the second stage of the campaign, with commercials that featured stars of not only the stage but also Hollywood, the Metropolitan Opera and even politics—stars like Beverly Sills, Frank Sinatra, Gregory Peck, Pearl Bailey, Carol Channing and Henry Kissinger—we had the big-time help of Phyllis Wagner, Bob Wagner's wife, who was a PR expert. I hired Phyllis in one of those moments of pure prescience. I hired her because she is smart and I had a vague notion that she could introduce us to people we might otherwise never know or even think to know. I thought she would stir something up. She did all those things, but she also talked Frank Sinatra into doing a New York State commercial and kept him drinking and eating and happy at "21" until almost midnight one night so that Stan could set up a late shot.

Frank, who would be surrounded by beautiful girls in his commercial, was to say, "I love New York because it's open all night." Setting up took longer than expected, because word got out about the shooting, thousands of fans appeared and had to be controlled. Finally, Frank drove up in a sheriff's car with armed guards. He was a little bit huffy by then and not exactly sober. The fans went crazy at the sight of him. Stan said, "Mr. Sinatra, the girls are going to dance around you. Be careful that you don't bang into them when you say your line." "Fine," said Frank. "One take, that's all you'll need, one take!" He'd been waiting for hours to say one line and he was getting impatient. So they started filming, he said the line and banged right into the girls. "OK," he said, "that's it. Goodbye." Stan stopped him. "Mr. Sinatra, we have to shoot it again. You banged into the girls." "No. No more." He was getting testy. Stan gave a secret sign to the prettiest of the girls, who went up to Frank and said, "Oh, please, Frank, my mother will be watching. I told her I was making this shot with you and she is so thrilled." "OK," said Frank. "I'll do it for you. For you and your mother!" (Frank loved mothers, he adored mine—he was always trying to fix her up with George Burns. "How's your cooking? George wants a good cook," he would say to my mother.) He then said the line perfectly: "I love New York because it's open all night. *All night!*" He added a second "all night" and he came off as a pussycat in the commercial. The instant he finished, the heavens roared, thunder and lightning appeared out of nowhere and rain flooded the set. Frank called Stan into his car and told him that throughout his entire career he had had near-misses with thunderous downpours happening the minute after he finished his performances. "I take it personally," he said, looking up into the heavens.

The stars were as cooperative as one expects great stars to be. Gregory Peck, Stan's particular favorite, was filmed on the roof of the Rainbow Room. He told Stan not to worry that the shoot was going late into a bitter-cold night. "I've got my long johns on, partner," he said in a western-movie drawl. "You keep shootin' and I'll keep actin'."

Henry Kissinger, when asked by the press why he made a commercial for New York State, said, "Because Phyllis Wagner told me to."

The "I Love New York" campaign moved people to believe in New York again. Optimism grew and businesses thought twice about leaving New York, very few ever did, and the state's economic health began to improve.

When the day arrived for me to have lunch with Walter Compton, he was so excited to see me that he dropped his briefcase and all the notes that he'd made for me. Five waiters at La Côte Basque scrambled to pick up the papers flying through the air. The maître d'hôtel, whom I was tipping generously by those days, forced himself to be charming about the Charlie Chaplinesque goings-on at prime time in his restaurant and all the advertising executives who ate at Côte Basque regularly took note that Mary Wells was about to get the Alka-Seltzer account again. The following morning there were headlines about us in the advertising press because in our world we were making significant

Stars from stage and screen like Frank Sinatra were happy to be in the "I Love New York" campaign.

news. Doyle Dane Bernbach, where Alka-Seltzer had moved when it left Jack Tinker & Partners, had become more and more beloved as it aged. The advertising community revered the commercials Doyle Dane had created for Alka-Seltzer, the "Spicy Meatballs" commercial and another one called "The Newlyweds," in which Alice Playten, as a bride, enjoys the seeming success of her melon-size dumplings and makes plans for marshmallowed meatballs and poached oysters to the dismay of the groom. Walter Compton thought the commercials were so extreme you wouldn't take them or Alka-Seltzer seriously. He didn't want to talk about them. He poured out his problems and he had major problems. The Food and Drug Administration was about to investigate all over-the-counter medicines and was particularly interested in aspirin's effect on the stomach. Walter, who was a doctor and a scientist, said that in the relatively near future aspirin would be found to be nature's great gift to mankind, if for nothing else, for the good of the heart. In his opinion, the Food and Drug administrators at that moment in time were a political group. Few were knowledgeable enough to handle the weighty responsibilities they had been given and many products would have to hide their strengths under a bushel for a time. "There are going to be witch trials," he said. "There'll be malcontent informers coming out of every lab in every drug company making up all sorts of nonsense that we'll have to prove false. It could become a dangerous business."

His passion, Alka-Seltzer, was so effective because it worked on combinations of upsets, which is the way you usually get upsets. Upsets are rarely discrete. Aspirin was an important ingredient in the relief Alka-Seltzer provided. He predicted that if Alka-Seltzer advertising was perceived as encouraging the use of aspirin the FDA might remove it from the market altogether. "It is not only what you say that will be questioned, it is what they think you *mean*. They will be subjective, facts will have nothing to do with anything." "Walter," I said, "it's a kind of game. And it will pass. But right now we have to outwit them. We have to sell Alka-Seltzer however we can but we also have to protect it."

"How should I handle this?" he asked me. Seamlessly, we were partners again. I knew he needed a reason for moving the account to Wells

Rich Greene that would sound good to his executives. I was wired for that one. "You are running a campaign of, mostly, 60-second commercials. That is a very expensive media plan. Bring your marketing group to see us. We will present a 30-second media plan that will save you millions. Your fellows have been trying to get a 30-second media plan out of every agency they've had for years. They'll jump to Wells Rich Greene to get one." We smiled at each other. We clinked our glasses. And that is how Wells Rich Greene got the Alka-Seltzer account, not because we were the people who had created a miracle turnaround for them once before, back when we were at Jack Tinker & Partners in 1965, but because we offered them a 30-second commercial media plan.

We hired a package-goods pro from Lever Brothers who had a warm, appealing manner to supervise the business, Bill Luceno. He played many important roles for us over time, but the memory of him that makes me smile is that he brought a secret weapon—he won every golf game he played. He won at basketball, too, but you don't get many clients that play basketball. Every agency likes to have at least one great golfer on staff for special occasions.

Our first two commercials for Alka-Seltzer were created by two of the most talented people we ever had, Howie Cohen and Bob Pasqualina. One featured a man in a restaurant who tells you how he was saved by Alka-Seltzer. "Try it. You'll like it," he says. The other featured a husband sitting on the side of his bed moaning, "I can't believe I ate the whole thing." "You ate it, Ralph," says his wife, who is trying to sleep. "Take two Alka-Seltzer." He takes the Alka-Seltzer and his wife says, "Did you take the Alka-Seltzer?" He beams happily at you, the viewer. "The whole thing," he says.

These first two commercials stopped the sales slide for Alka-Seltzer and sales started up again. I've been asked many times why those commercials, which were funny, sold more Alka-Seltzer than the hilarious spicy-meatball and dumpling commercials. My guess is that the spicy-meatball and dumpling commercials were funny in a manic, deranged way, and although they were fabulous attention grabbers and delightfully entertaining, they were not as believable, as earnestly

Wells, Rich, Greene, Inc./767 Fifth Avenue/New York, N.Y. 10022/Plaza 8-4300

CLIENT: MILES LABORATORIES	TITLE: "WHOLE THING" (REV.)
PRODUCT: ALKA-SELTZER	CODE NO: MIAS2403
	DATE: 11/8/77 LENGTH: 30 SECONDS

1. HUSBAND: I can't believe I ate that whole thing.

2. WIFE: You ate it Ralph.

3. HUSBAND: I can't believe I ate that whole thing.

4. WIFE: No Ralph, I ate it!

5. HUSBAND: I can't believe

6. I ate that whole thing.

7. WIFE: Take two Alka-Seltzer.

8. (SFX: PLOP, PLOP... FIZZ.)

9. ANNCR: (VO) Alka-Seltzer neutralizes all the acid your stomach has churned out.

10. For your upset stomach and headache, take Alka-Seltzer, and feel better fast.

11. WIFE: Did you drink your Alka-Seltzer?

12. HUSBAND: The whole thing.

One of the most loved commercials of all time, Alka-Seltzer's "I Can't Believe I Ate the Whole Thing."

sincere and therefore not as persuasive as Howie and Bob's sweet-funny commercials—especially "I ate the whole thing." Humor attracts a crowd, and that's good, but I think that most of the time funny advertising needs to have a serious heart to move you to buy, not just to laugh.

Just as we were celebrating new sales figures for Alka-Seltzer, Ralph Nader and the FDA rode over the hill and with all the press they encouraged and the monograph regulations that were issued, aspirin was viewed as snake poison for a while. We feared a meteoric sales decline and we got busy trying to find ways to simply keep Alka-Seltzer on television. Walter wanted to go onto television himself and talk to people honestly about Alka-Seltzer, from his view as a scientist. We thought that was an idea worth exploring if we could find something interesting for people to watch as Walter talked to them. One suggestion was to have Salvador Dalí create surreal paintings of the stomach as Walter described what Alka-Seltzer was doing in there that worked so well.

Dalí and his wife, Gala, flew in from Port-Lligat, where they lived, on the coast of Spain. He arrived looking like Salvador Dalí, I didn't think anyone could and assumed there was something fake going on, but he really looked like Salvador Dalí. He was wearing a loose white cotton jacket with a red scarf tied around his shoulders and he was carrying an empty, diamond-studded leash that had once belonged to an ocelot he traveled with. Gala was the one I worried about. I was warned by friends who knew her that she was apt to bare one of her breasts at the meeting and I didn't know what Walter Compton would think about that, although he was highly intrigued with the idea of meeting the Dalís.

Salvador Dalí's first words to us were worrying. "Dalí go pee-pee." Noel Duffy had dropped by our offices, curious to see the great painter, and she nervously directed him to the nearest men's room. Whatever he did in there, the men already in the room left like a shot and said they wouldn't forget Salvador Dalí soon. Just as the Dalís arrived I was struck by a violent virus that put me flat for a short time so Charlie led the group into my office. Gala didn't like Charlie on sight and insisted on sitting next to him so that she could kick his leg with her dagger-sharp shoes. Whenever he moved to avoid her, trying to pretend nothing unusual was happening, she followed him and continued to kick until his leg bled so badly he had to excuse himself to find a bandage. According to Walter, Gala began screeching when Charlie left the room, whereupon, as if on cue, Salvador fell over his own lap, dead asleep. I managed to get back onto my feet in time to see Charlie rushing by with blood flowing down his leg, followed by Walter and his associates making a fast and furious exit muttering "mad birds" and "mad as hatters" to me as they rushed out to the elevators. It took Kathie the rest of the morning to remove the Dalís. As they left, Gala carefully picked up every pencil and pen on my desk and put them in the bag she was carrying. I bet that bag was full of goodies by the end of the day. One of the pens she took from my desk had been a serious gift but, as Kathie shrugged, what do you say?

Charlie discovered the pylorus as a replacement for the Dalís. The pylorus is the opening from the stomach into the intestine. Walter fell in love with it. Charlie's office walls became wallpapered with grotesque drawings of stomachs in different states of disrepair and he was forever listening to the sounds that stomachs might make when the pylorus is not happy as well as the crooning of a happy pylorus soaking in Alka-Seltzer bubbles. He thought he had found gold in the pylorus but after a few weeks of development Miles's Washington lawyers called and told us that sensitivities had escalated at the FDA and any quasi-medical claim Alka-Seltzer could make then, even one as mild and factual as the pylorus claim, could quickly lead to a ruling to take Alka-Seltzer off the air, perhaps even off the market. "We better do something to just keep Alka-Seltzer's name alive until this blows over," I said. "Have you seen anything anyone is doing that is worth developing?" "Yes, maybe." Charlie began packing away his pylorus sketches. "Paul and Bob may have something."

It is a big treat when creative people surprise you with work that isn't anything like work they have done before or that you ever expected them to do. In a flash you realize they are even more talented than you had thought and they realize they are even more talented than they had thought. A kind of euphoria sets in. Paul Margulies and Bob Wilvers were two high-intensity super-talents who won all the contests at the agency when it came to Wagnerian passion and religiosity in advertising. They, of all people, had created a frothy, gossamer, luminous commercial of nothing but two Alka-Seltzers dropping into a crystal glass, creating sparkling bubbles, with an amusing ditty playing behind them: "Plop Plop Fizz Fizz—oh, what a relief it is." On the surface it appeared to be a glamorous shrug of self-confidence, a reminder of what commercials used to tell you about Alka-Seltzer. But in fact bubbles had always said great things, subliminally, about the effectiveness of Alka-Seltzer to people who got stomach upsets. When the commercials appeared, the bubbles went to work on people's imaginations and "Plop Plop Fizz Fizz" became as effective and famous as any advertising we ever created for a client in trouble. Everybody on television was Plop Plop Fizz Fizzing.

B ill Claggett had liked the speech I gave at the New York Sales Executive lunch and had seen to it that Wells Rich Greene was given a pet-food account, Ralston's Tender Vittles. It was a great new piece of business because the product was state of the art, a moist cat food in a foil pouch, a breakthough at the time. They'd given us more pet-food business soon after and I had become friendly with Ken Griggy, who was the head of marketing, and Hal Dean, the chairman, who enjoyed talking to women and to me. After a while Hal asked me what I thought about joining Ralston's board of directors, an unusual suggestion, agency executives are rarely asked onto client boards, there is usually a conflict-of-interest issue.

I was trying to stay off boards of directors. In the seventies, with the women's movement in high gear, a lot of boards were looking for women members and I received many invitations. But I was colossally laden with guilt as I divided myself into thinner and thinner pieces at home. I was not interested in increasing my celebrity or my business credentials. I didn't want to add anything to my life that was not valuable to either my family or Wells Rich Greene. Besides, I hated all the second-rate hotels that had crept into my lifestyle. Many of our clients' office buildings were not in the garden spots of America, they were in the cheaper sections of towns. The walls of the hotels in those areas were so thin I could never really sleep, waiting for some group of late-night drunks to gurgle and pound their way down the hall, lost, looking for their rooms, any rooms, sometimes banging on my door. The carpets were cleaned every decade, maybe, and had to be covered with towels, and more than once I had to deal with a large crawling thing by covering it with an ashtray. I always called Harding to report those terrors. He could never understand why I was paralyzed by roaches but fearless with clients. Wherever he was, though, he would stop what he was doing or saying or reading and calm me down about the roaches.

Harding: "OK. How big is it? How fast is it moving?"

Me: "What do you mean, how fast is it moving? It's a roach—it's fast."

Harding, patient now: "Where is the nearest ashtray? Or a bowl? A bowl will do. Drop it over the roach. Let the maid deal with it tomorrow."

I got so that I was good at it.

But a steady diet of grim living had dampened my enthusiasm for travel. Sometimes Kathie went with me, we got a lot of the agency's tedious backstage work done on planes and in those hotels, and our occasional giggles kept me seeing the funny sides of life. Still, from time to time we stumbled into creepy situations. We seemed to have bad luck in St. Louis. We were often given keys to rooms that were already occupied and would find ourselves witnessing everything from a saleman's efforts to service one of his buyers in a king-size bed to a room full of guns, hundreds of them, but only one furious occupant. More than once I thought of my father's life as a salesman on the road and felt a wash of pity and connection.

One morning I heard from Ken Griggy asking me to fly to St. Louis to see him about what he called an acute, highly charged matter. He had been talking to our Ralston account group about the possibility of Wells Rich Greene acquiring the Gardner agency in St. Louis. Gardner had been handling a lot of Ralston's advertising for many years—originally there had been a family connection between the companies.

Ralston felt responsible for Gardner and loyal to the point of caring about its health. Now Ken was worried about the quality of the work Gardner was doing and its serious dependency on Ralston. He wanted to move the responsibility for the agency's survival someplace else. As we were the eager new agency from New York, we looked like a good candidate to him. I had not had time to study Gardner thoroughly so I didn't know enough about it yet to have a smart position in my pocket, but Ken Griggy was a particularly civil, polite man who rarely made command calls, so I hurried to his office. His first words were "I am in favor of Wells Rich Greene acquiring Gardner, Mary—I think it would be a good move for Gardner, for you and for us. I'm willing to guarantee you that all of Ralston's accounts now at both agencies will stay at them for a full year while you absorb the Gardner agency and I'll put heavy pressure on Warren Kratky and Kelly O'Neill to be realistic about purchase terms. I just don't think Ralston can cradle Gardner to the grave."

Gardner was a full-service agency with an array of modular agency services it sold either as a package or individually. The core agency appeared to offer us some good growth prospects. But the modular services had surreal techno names like "Advanswers." At first glance I was suspicious of how useful they would turn out to be and I knew only a smattering about the two leaders, Kratky and O'Neill. I was about to negotiate when Ken said ominously, "I better warn you, three of our marketing men are about to join us. I invited them because they are dead set against this plan and they are very angry that I am determined to go ahead with it. I thought you should hear their concerns straight from them." "Whoops," I thought. I had just been about to say firmly that a one-year guaranty was not enough time, but my negotiating power suddenly felt threatened. "What am I doing here?" was my next thought. "Do I really want to buy the Gardner agency?"

Before I could answer myself the marketing executives were walking through the door. If they were not gnashing their teeth—and I seem to recall they were—they were making silent vows that they would get me, get Wells Rich Greene, just give them time! It was written all over them. They wanted the control they believed they should have to hire and fire agencies they chose, including Gardner and Wells Rich Greene. If Wells Rich Greene purchased Gardner, their hands would be tied for at least a year and they saw themselves ethically saddled with both agencies for longer than that, putting them in a captive position that dampened their illusions of having any power.

Ken turned to the one who looked angriest, Bill Stiritz. "Why don't you give Mary chapter and verse on your misgivings?" Bill Stiritz and I would have a long and interesting relationship in the years ahead. At that moment he looked at me with open distaste. His good manners finally came to our rescue and he began a dry explanation of everything he did not like about Wells Rich Greene's operation. When he was finished with that list he began an equally dry explanation of everything he did not like about Gardner's operation. There is nothing one can do in those situations but take notes like a court reporter. I remember looking around the room, thinking, "My God, these offices are dreadful, dark, dispiriting." I wished I had been better prepared for such a meeting, I would have liked to sling a few fish back in his face—sweetly, of course, he was a client. I took careful note of his complaints, though. No one had ever been clearer about an agency's weaknesses, so I was able to return to Wells Rich Greene armed for bear with Wells Rich Greene's Ralston group. And I got an education about Gardner that I couldn't have paid for and that turned out to be valuable, because we made a much better deal when we acquired them.

We all shook hands on our good intentions at the end of that meeting, but the air hadn't really been cleared as Ken had planned it to be. I thought we would run into those bitter feelings in Ralston's marketing group for a long time to come. I was sure of that after the meeting we had a little later to present advertising for a new kind of cat food. I'd told Bert Neufeld, one of our bright lights, that I'd read an article in a psychology journal that dogs are members of the family but cats are like guests you're never sure of and are always trying to please. He created insightful commercials showing the lengths people will go to in order to get their cats to eat. In test screenings cat owners were excited about the commercials and said things like, "Yep, that's me, that's the nut I am with that cat of mine, she is impossible but she is the boss in our home. I will definitely try that cat food. Might work. She might eat that." After showing the commercials to Ken Griggy and Bill Stiritz, Bert, who never quite got over his hippie period and always presented advertising straight from his heart, told them that if they would just do what Wells Rich Greene told them to do, his cat-food commercials would "put Ralston on the map." Ken Griggy was amused but Bill Stiritz looked pained.

"OK," I said. "We have to come to grips with it. Let's look at every facet of the Gardner agency and all those modules of theirs with those disembodied names."

I had just begun a meeting with the Gardner acquisition group I had assembled when Ned Doyle called. I hadn't talked to Ned Doyle in years. He sounded a little forced, maybe he was calling on the sly from an outdoor pay phone. "It's been a long time, kid. Are you still beautiful or have you got a big head now?" It was Ned Doyle all right. "Well, Ned, love of my life, you left me, you disappeared and you promised to take me to lunch every month, do you remember that?" We picked up easily, we had parted good friends. "Listen, I have an idea, kid, I don't know if it's any good or not but it's worth your time. Bernbach is having problems. He wants an easier, lighter role at the agency but there is nobody he trusts to run it. Time hasn't made anybody shine any brighter, he's fed up with the whole bunch there. Now he wants to get his money out of the place and he's worried that he won't. He doesn't say so but I think he's mad that I did so well selling early and now, with the stock price down and those damn boats, there's a good chance he won't make what I made. He can't stand that." Long pause. I knew what he was going to say and my heart skipped a beat.

He went on. "You're not as smart as you think you are but you're not bad for a dame. Do you think you can come up with a good idea for Bill? He knows I'm calling. He says you're the only one he thinks can handle the place now—you're just willful enough, he says, to deal with all the people who've stuck with him so long. Every one of them expects to be his successor. We talked about you for a long time the other day and you will be surprised to learn that you were always one of his favorites. Don't laugh," he laughed. I could just see him on the other end of the phone. "The point is that he's ready. Do you think you can manage something? Do you want to? Here's how it could go. We think Wells Rich Greene should buy Doyle Dane Bernbach, Bill will be chairman and chief creative officer and he will do only what he wants to do, he can oversee creative work but he doesn't have to unless he wants to. He and Evelyn want to travel. There are a lot of places they want to see. You can be CEO and pull it all together. The trick is that Bill has to come out as good as I did. You've got to use that devious mind of yours to come up with a plan that makes it possible. He has to come out a lot better than he could with just a stock sale."

I don't recall what I said, there weren't any words for that moment. "Well," he said after a while, "are you still there? Are you going to call him? Ask him to lunch. He's expecting you to call him to ask him to lunch." "Yes, I'll call him in the morning, Ned." Another long pause. I said, for no reason, "I've missed you, Ned." I wanted to cry. "I'll see you, kid," he said. And then, very kindly, "You can do this, Mary." He hung up. He really did talk like Humphrey Bogart most of the time. I pulled myself together and returned to the meeting room, where the Gardner acquisition group was laboriously estimating Gardner's sources of income.

Only a few months before my trip to Ralston and Ned Doyle's call I had spent an afternoon with Frank Lowe of Collett Dickenson Pearce exploring the possibility of Wells Rich Greene acquiring that agency, a particularly fine creative agency in England. They were going through a troubled patch and thought merging with us would be a good idea. It was an expensive proposition but I had not put it down yet. I was taken with Frank Lowe, I thought we'd do well together, and Wells Rich Greene needed to be in England and Europe in a more important way. Most of our clients were international, although nobody was using the word "global" yet. The devil started dancing a sexy little rumba in my head. Acquiring Doyle Dane Bernbach and Collett Dickenson Pearce were possibilities that promised us months of thrills and chills. Merging Gardner into Wells Rich Greene was a smart move to make, but that day the idea just made me sleepy.

I'm a fool to want you

Charlie could not imagine Wells Rich Greene acquiring Doyle Dane Bernbach and Bill Bernbach arriving in our offices at the General Motors Building as the chief creative officer or how in the world we would relate to Bob Gage, let alone Joe Daly. It sounded like complete chaos or Transylvania to him, or World War III. But the idea was blooming in me. Bill was so charming when we met, almost like equals, at La Côte Basque. He looked barbered and massaged, well tailored and cologned, and his eyes were amused, not wary as I remembered them, signaling that he was in a good mood. He was optimistic, he knew about the success at Wells Rich Greene, our profits, our growth, the high quality of our clients, he even admired some of our work. "I never doubted your good mind and your relentless determination, Mary," he said, "or your marvelous ability to talk anyone into anything. I admired that more than you knew." I was just giddy enough at that lunch to be flattered. Little by little, we began dreaming of a new agency composed of our two agencies and as we inched along we had so many laughs, so much fun imagining what a surprise we would give the advertising world and the fabulous possibilities, that we sat there, blissfully intimate, two minds utterly absorbed with one idea, until the restaurant began setting up for dinner.

I invited a small trusted group of consultants to help me strategize a way to acquire control of Doyle Dane Bernbach and pay Bill what he wanted. To meet his requirements at a time when Doyle Dane's stock was at a low we needed a formula, some combination of very high salary, multi-bonuses, profit sharing, options, insurance, deferred income, retirement income. The cost of paying Bill what he wanted over and above the sale of his stock had to be added to Doyle Dane's cost of operation at a time when their profits were nil for a variety of reasons, one being some bad investments that would probably have to be written off. Whether or not Wells Rich Greene could afford the total final cost was the issue. Ned slipped secret information to me, regularly, in hand-delivered envelopes. Once, devilishly, he sent a handsome folio of color photographs of sailing boats from a company Doyle Dane had bought that would be one of the necessary write-offs. "I want you to know the whole truth," he said. "I don't want you and Bill going belly up."

Harding thought I would be certifiably crazy to jeopardize Wells Rich Greene, when we were in such strong financial shape and growing by leaps and bounds, to take on an agency that was in a difficult financial condition, particularly as the merger would have conflicts to deal with. He kept reminding me that the actual melding of the two groups of executives could only be a pain in the neck—mine. "What is this, some leftover parental complex?" he asked me. "Why do you have to be the one to make Bill Bernbach's dreams come true?" A good question, but I was in a state of thrall and, anyway, Harding was too busy taking Braniff to cities throughout the world, negotiating with presidents, senators, governors and city council members, to think much about it. I knew that in the end, if I believed in the idea, he would be supportive.

Once a week, for a little while, Bill and I had a picnic lunch in a limousine and drove around and around and around Central Park discussing the status of the formula, drawing organization charts on yellow pads, conceiving ways to hold accounts that were conflicts as well as ways to hold executives we thought essential who might feel betrayed by the idea of a new company. We talked about accounts at other agencies we were certain we could shake loose. We would be powerful, together. He was like a man falling in love, he had persuaded himself that I could and would find a way to put the right financial offer together giving him all that he deserved, and he was certain I would be able to manage any hysterics during the first year of the merger itself. But what moved me, killed me, was that little by little he became so enamored of the new merged agency we were creating in our minds that he felt a renewed vigor for the entire advertising business and for himself as the dominant creative force in it. He smiled all the time.

It was February 1975, and in those limousines, as the bare trees and the cold lakes of Central Park passed by, he told me his thoughts about the people at his agency. So many years with the same executives around him—so many feuds and political games and bad decisions—he said he was tired of carrying Doyle Dane Bernbach and everyone around him, except for Mac Dane and Bob Gage, who were perfect. He was infuriated that everybody else was so expectant. When Bill was feeling easy and confident his eyes turned silky. "We'll take care of each other," he said, looking at me with those silky eyes, "we'll fly to some higher ground with this agency." During those weeks I would have followed him if he jumped off a bridge.

As both of our agencies were publicly owned, any serious negotiation would have to be reported. We had to be very careful because we had conflicting accounts—most of our package-goods accounts were conflicts. If the press discovered our talks we would have to reveal them to the public and then our conflicting accounts would see themselves as pawns, they could rebel and fire us. No account wants to be put in that position.

At first Bill was cautious, he told only a handful of people, including Josh Levine, perhaps the best agency lawyer in the business. But as our plans developed and his enthusiasm grew, he thought I should talk to his most important executives, he wanted me to understand their individual positions so that I would be informed enough to put together the best possible organization. He shouldn't have, but before we were ready, he told all those executives about our talks, asked them to call me and make a date to visit me at Wells Rich Greene. He told me that Bob Gage would do whatever was good for him, Bill, so he didn't need to call, I could count on Bob. He was certain Mac felt the same way. And Phyllis was gone, she was with her husband someplace in Italy. But I would hear from the others. God. If he had dropped a bomb on them it would have had less impact. Some of them, like Ted Factor and Ed Russell, had been pals of mine, and although they were shocked, to put it gently, they came right up to see me and talk. Joe Daly was outraged and made it clear he thought the idea was a terrible one and wanted no part of it—no way! When I told Ned about Joe he said he knew Joe would be troublesome. "But the bets will be on you and Bernbach," he said, "not Joe."

In 1971 I had become the first woman chief executive officer to have a company listed on the New York Stock Exchange. The day Wells Rich Greene was listed, Robert Haack, the president of the Exchange, gave a jaunty toast and there were pleasant little jokes about the ERA and *The Feminine Mystique* and NOW, but by 1975, when Bill and I were talking, the women's movement was becoming powerful and I was no longer an oddity to the financial community. I had met and talked with almost every financial power broker who ate lunch or dinner, so Wells Rich Greene's performance was well known. Paul Hallingby's view was that although the combined agency numbers we were seeing weren't pretty, we stood an excellent chance of raising the necessary funds for the deal on the basis of Wells Rich Greene's strong performance and Bill's great stature. We had talked to our own banks, without revealing everything, and we came away confident. We had a lot of work to do, not only to complete the deal but also to be absolutely certain we would be comfortable living with it and that we would all be safe. I believed the two agencies would do well together, even with the obvious problems. But it was a complicated and expensive deal, I intended to dot every *i* and cross every *t,* to take the time we needed before making a final, irrevocable decision.

So it shook me up when I got a tense call from Bill and Josh Levine asking me to set up a telephone meeting with all who were working, in confidence, on the concept. They told us, then, that the *New York Times* had called and said that the *Times* had reliable information about our talks. They planned to release the story the following morning and wanted to know—well, what about it? Bill needed to know, before he returned that call, if we were in a position to rush things and say, yes, we were negotiating? Did we have the necessary funds behind us and were they firm enough to allow both agencies to make such an announcement? They supposed that we were still a distance from a firm, final commitment but they were trying to determine, from a legal point of view, what position they should take. I had to say, "Bill, it is too soon. We do not have solid commitments yet. We are close and we are working very quickly but we need more time." Josh Levine said, in his kind voice, "Mary, I'm sorry, but in that case we are going to have to deny that you and Bill are talking seriously and that means the two of you will, in fact, have to stop talking altogether for a while." "Mary—" Bill did not want to lose our momentum—"Mary, somebody must have talked, why don't we go ahead and merge on an ordinary basis and you and I can work everything out afterwards?" But I had come too far, worked too hard, and too many others at Wells Rich Greene had come too far, worked too hard, to gamble on a merger without having control of the final agency. I kept seeing Joe Daly's face. "We can't do that, Bill." I felt ice stream down my spine. It would all fall apart now. I knew it. Both agencies would have to get busy denying the story as "stupid, are you kidding? That's insane!" to reassure our big clients who were conflicts. Our dream would go poof! And I was sure that all the king's horses and all the king's men couldn't put it back together again. In a fast-moving business like advertising, things change in a couple of months whether you want them to or not. That night Bill called me at home: "I am counting on you to put it together, Mary. I will wait for you." Then Ned called: "Too bad. Maybe it can still happen. Take it easy for a couple of months. I'll call you, kid." Then Harding called from Mexico: "Congratulations, darling. You were saved."

I am woman

The day the Sun Oil Company gave us their account I had a frightening rock-and-roll flight from Philadelphia to Newark and on to Dallas. Leaving the restroom, I was forced to sit on the floor of the plane and hang on to the side of a seat, the surprise turbulence was wild and terrifying. Everyone on board expected to die. We survived and I even arrived in time to drive to the Hockaday School and park in the driveway with the other mothers to be there when Katy and Pam would fly out the door. Fridays were treat times, I was full of bribes for all the other times that mattered to them that I'd missed during the week.

After buying treasures at Toy World we would have ice cream and french fries while they gave me minute-by-minute accounts of each day I'd been away.

Fridays were also dinner-on-trays-in-bed nights with television, the greatest luxury for Harding and me, and somewhere I found the energy to be the woman he married. That night, late, we were watching a rerun of the day's Dallas news. Gloria Steinem was in town and she was being interviewed. She was asked if, as a feminist, she was proud of me, a local resident. She replied, "Oh, well, Mary Wells Uncle Tommed it to the top." Harding was incredulous. I thought, "What a silly woman—is that really Gloria Steinem???" Feminism, like any movement, has its politicians and its actors and its soldiers. I was one of the few women I knew in those days who had bit off what businessmen were chewing, who was performing a man's job in a man's world, in a business I had created from scratch the way men did. I didn't think I had to change my clothing or my personality or have a sex change to be successful. I was willing to do what it took—to work hard, make decisions, accept the ultimate responsibility, provide the leadership and the goals, whatever that cost in hours or comfort or personal pleasure. I was also willing to accept the guilt of not giving enough of myself to almost anybody, just as businessmen were used to doing. I wanted a big life. I worked as a man worked. I didn't preach it, I did it. I simply acted as I saw others in business act—at the time, they happened to be, primarily, men. In my corner of the universe, America, I found them welcoming and helpful, I liked them and I just accepted their culture. Gloria Steinem was right that I didn't declare war on men. But I didn't witness offensive male bonding against women. From what I could see, men in business were competitive with anything that walked or talked. They had learned, as boys do, to play games all-out with the idea of winning, so in business they would stretch their psyches to the breaking point to be successful. But there were no mean-spirited bigots getting in my way or holding me down.

I didn't think that businessmen's lives were rosier than women's lives, either, as many women supposed. If anything, what I saw made me sympathize with the chief executive officers of large corporations.

They are often lonely fellows. The high offices they work so hard to obtain are full of decision making—that power is the real prize of the game. Respect for their opinions fills the air of those offices and makes them heady. But there is that infernal loneliness. Because behind every CEO's office, in the offices to the left and right of him, are executives who are working night and day to replace him as the next chief executive officer. It is only natural that CEOs become slightly defensive with their successors, to keep some important thoughts to themselves, to be careful. Ahead is retirement. Retirement is death to many CEOs. One executive described it as falling into the Grand Canyon. The instant he was no longer the chief executive officer, nobody called him for a decision or an approval, nobody even wanted his opinion. The telephone never rang. The President of the United States knows what it is like. When it is over, it is over. So no CEO wants to be pushed, the goal is to stay in power as long as possible. Few CEOs have developed alternative lives that excite them, so they aren't eager to jump into their futures. Instinctively, they play their cards close to their vests and hang on, lonely. That's why so many infuse their boards of directors with friends they trust. It is all part of the game of business that women were clamoring to join in the sixties and seventies.

Gloria Steinem made me consider the issue of women who Uncle Tommed it. I knew a few women executives who inherited their businesses from their fathers or husbands but over time became effective leaders. On occasion I would hear that old song that women could only be successful in a man's world by having the right love affairs. Well, advertising was and still is a man's world if there ever was one, and a sexy female chief executive officer of an advertising agency would be viewed as a horror show—a nuisance, an embarrassment and even a danger to men interested in powerful business careers. My highly publicized marriage and my low gender awareness were two of the reasons I was trusted by the CEOs who controlled America's most important advertising accounts and was able to build a large, international agency. They saw me as one of their own.

You don't hear anyone talk about female Uncle Toms anymore. Many more women are running businesses, although there are still only a few female CEOs among the Fortune 500 companies (like Carly Fiorina, who runs Hewlett-Packard), and there are still too few female heads of advertising agencies, the communicative type of business women do so well in because they are often less inhibited and bring their life experiences to their campaigns. From the start Wells Rich Greene hired feisty, audacious women who wanted it all and more: Jayne Eastman, an inventive and theatrical research executive; Paula Forman, one of the best managers of P&G business in any agency anywhere; Marcia Grace, who levitated clients with her strategic coherence; Jackie End, with her sweetness shot with energy and shtick; and Nancy Vaughan, who scorched and sizzled her great advertising campaigns onto nervous clients who ended up on their knees thanking her. All natural-born winners. It's just a matter of time, women are starting new companies at twice the rate of men today, according to a 1997 NASDAQ survey, the Internet economy by itself is changing the rules of the game.

When I thought about it at all, I thought that much of my success had to do with timing. I came along just as the world became willing to accept a woman as the chairman of an advertising agency and when advertising was moving to television, a theatrical medium I understood. But success can be born of necessity, too. I had to invent my life, an American tradition. No one invented a life and handed it to me. My parents had an unusually silent marriage, they didn't say much to each other or to me and they didn't say anything about what my life could be or should be. They never talked to me about me, philosophically, or indicated they had any specific dreams for me. My identity, my universe was mine to create. They didn't give me road maps or goals and they certainly didn't suggest there would be trouble ahead or I would run into a ceiling, that I could never be a priest or a rabbi or President of the United States because I was born a female. They simply didn't talk.

My father, Wally Berg, a Norwegian from Minnesota, had done well in good schools, Exeter and the University of Pennsylvania. His family expected him to be a business success. But he had the terrible luck to spend the First World War in the ambulance corps tramping through hundreds of miles of trenches picking up shredded, mutilated, screaming bodies at the front line. By the time he returned from France he had lost his gut strength and accepted an undemanding job as a salesman traveling in a car around Pennsylvania and Ohio selling furniture. He was no Willy Loman, he didn't have grand dreams of being wonderful. At first he just thought he was recuperating, but when he met my mother at her grandfather's hotel in Youngstown, he fell in love and decided to marry and settle into the little life he was making.

My mother had her gut strength when she married him, though. He was ten years older but she married him thinking he was an exotic stranger who was sweeping her off her feet into a new world. She had grown up German during the war when it was hard to be German in the United States. Her family withdrew into a corner ghetto of Ohio and clung to old-world ideas, they didn't believe in educating daughters, even though my mother begged them to let her go to school to become a teacher. She developed a complex about education and she felt helpless, hopeless, until she met my father. Out of the blue came this educated, well-read foreigner, a Norwegian from Minnesota, who had been to France and seen Paris, who she thought would kiss her and not only wake her up but catapult her into a new dimension. My father thought he was marrying a pretty, undemanding young woman who would soothe his tremors, maybe even erase his memories. But what he got was a smart, ambitious young woman who became extremely unhappy as soon as she understood him and the small life that he wanted.

My father's way of dealing with the fears he couldn't conquer was to become a recluse. I don't think he ever had a pal, a companion. He wanted to be alone. I went up to him once when he was sitting on the back step of our house, I thought he was ill, when I touched him he murmured, "There was nothing left, broken glass, just broken glass." I had no idea what he was talking about, years later I understood he was talking about what he'd seen in France. He rigged up a hideaway in the cellar of our home where he carved and painted beautiful decoys for duck hunting back in Minnesota. This became his private chapel for worshipping Roosevelt and his New Deal and his reluctance to take the country into a second world war. He also created a paradisiacal garden of wildflowers he found in the forest nearby. Weekends he would go off in his car and return covered with mud, laden with masses of sparkling lavender lace, tiny twinkling lilies, froths of the palest yellow diamonds and the most amazing sensual ivy. He became the conductor of an orchestra of flowers without names, all of them demonstrably happy to have been transplanted to our home. That was enough Eden for him.

They had me but no other children and my mother adored me and for a while she was satisfied. She didn't give up on herself, though; she went to the library and educated herself. Then she learned to play bridge and became a semiprofessional player and she joined women's organizations, where, over time, she found her voice and learned how to manage groups of people. After I went away to college she got a job in a department store and built a successful career for herself as a buyer, finally as a highly respected buyer in New York. But when I was small, she was quiet and he hid.

I never doubted for a moment that they loved me or that I was important to them. Until my mother's last breath I had that girlish thought tucked away somewhere in the back of my mind: "I can always go home." In the end, that may be everything, to know you are loved. Still, they were not interested in what I thought, what I read or who I was becoming. They weren't interested in my school and neither of them ever asked me about my work there or about homework. My mother felt too uneducated to trust herself about my schooling and my father was out of sight, carving decoys. Our house sounded empty. There was music, no conversation, no noise except for rare and terrible fights—my father returned from the war with a sudden, shocking temper that made me think of lightning. Our dinners could have been in the middle of the Sahara desert, they were so remote, any family talk was about what chores needed doing, how money was to be made and saved. I don't remember ever being asked what I thought about anything until I returned from college.

So I didn't start life playing in a field of intellectual ideas from my mother or father. But neither did anyone else I knew. Somewhere children were brought up with Shakespeare and opera and Matisse drawings, reading good books and taking part in stimulating dinner conversations—but no one that I knew when I was a child in Youngstown, Ohio. My world began when people didn't have much, children didn't have music players and television and computers, there were no *Lion Kings*. Our imaginations were our Sony PlayStations. Lack of stuff didn't stunt our imaginations. On the other hand, my grandchildren, whom I overstimulate every way that I can, with every new excitement that appears and every idea that comes into my head, do not appear to be stunted by overstimulation, either. Still, I see that silent start in my life as at least the second greatest gift from my parents: freedom from their ideas about who I should be and what I should become, an independence of mind.

My mother surprised us all with two prods that she must have understood would do something to light my way, though she never said. She found an elocution teacher for me when I was five. Then, when I was ten, she approached the director of the Youngstown Playhouse and introduced us. The Youngstown Playhouse was a well-funded, highly respected local theatre group that attracted audiences from all over Ohio and Pennsylvania. The directors it lured there were always professionals from much larger towns. It was brilliant of my mother to think of the Playhouse. I don't know where she learned of it. No one else in our world even knew it existed and she knew nothing about the theatre. It was supported by a wealthier, more cultured society in Ohio. The director allowed me to play occasional roles of young children. As I grew older I played young women of whatever age he thought I could get away with. My mother spent hours in the dark theatre waiting out the tedious rehearsals and performances. She spent hours driving to and from the Playhouse. I didn't like spending all those nights there and my mother never told me what she had in mind, why she was putting us through that ordeal, although, of course, she hoped it would stimulate me to want a more exciting life than she had. We spent years together saying almost nothing, but we were comfortable together, I trusted her and I would never have rebelled. Only once, when I was home on vacation from college and we were taking a late-evening walk together, she startled me by saying she was considering a divorce. We talked about her feelings for perhaps five minutes. She still had hopes for a better education, a more exciting life, more fun. It was a little dip in the finger bowl, not a plunge into intimacy. She did not divorce my father. She never talked about it again. Shortly before she died I found letters my father had written to her when they were just married from all over his sales territory in Pennsylvania, love letters—stacks of them—that made me realize I didn't have the complete picture of that marriage. Even when we were older and she was with me a lot and was a second mother to my children, my mother and I rarely talked personally. I tried but she just couldn't. It was OK. She loved me, I loved her and we managed without words.

Light my fire

The first intellectual stimulation I was conscious of was at the Neighborhood Playhouse School of Theatre in New York. The director of the Youngstown Playhouse persuaded my parents that I was talented and should attend the drama school he admired. My father took me to New York for an interview with the guru there, Sanford Meisner. Sanford—Sandy—had been a member of the Group Theatre along with Elia Kazan, Lee Strasberg, Harold Clurman and Stella Adler. The Group Theatre was an American descendant of Stanislavsky's revered Moscow Art Theatre, where a group of talented mavericks gathered to try to lift the art of theatre up a peg or two—and where the "System" was born. Konstantin Stanislavsky, the giant of the group, thought that an actor must truly believe in everything that takes place on stage. Most of all, he must believe in what he himself is doing there; his emotion must be real, not pretended, in order to give you, the audience, a genuine experience. What happens on stage then happens to you—in you.

He developed a system for actors so that they could always find that imagined truth in the roles they were to play. This was a revolutionary approach to acting. Using psychological and even spiritual ideas and exercises, he produced a different kind of actor than had ever been seen and more believable, more emotional performances. His system was huge, complicated, visionary. The actors and directors of the Group Theatre in America translated it into what they called the Method. When the Group Theatre broke up in 1940, some of its members became teachers of acting. Each personalized the Method, although they all espoused the power of an experience genuinely felt by an actor, a power that doesn't happen in the usual simulated, stylized performance. In one way or another, all taught actors to launch their performances by remembering and refeeling the emotional experiences in their lives that corresponded to the emotions of the scene they were about to play.

A typical Method exercise would help you to remember those experiences and to store the memories in a way so that you could pull them up again when you needed them. Other exercises taught you to feel emotions that were completely new to you so that you could store them, too, to use when needed. I remember one exercise at the Neighborhood Playhouse that incited a group of us to crawl up a fire-escape ladder to the top of a four-story building in the West 40s, enter a window and force open a door in order to steal a note from the pocket of a sleeping man who had been instructed to wake up at the slightest sound. We felt silly climbing the fire escape. But there was no doubting the fear we felt trying to steal that note without waking the sleeper. If I want to feel fear today I can still pull up the exact way I felt entering that room where that man slept and approaching him—which was the point of the exercise, and the idea behind the Method.

The day I read for Sandy Meisner at my interview I knew little about anything, let alone about Stanislavsky, the Group Theatre or Method acting. In Youngstown I had merely played a role as directed. Turn right. Turn left. That sort of thing. What possessed Sandy Meisner, who ran an extremely sophisticated, razor-edge operation at the Neighborhood Playhouse, to accept me as a student is a question. Of course, Sandy was famous for running the place like a brilliant sadistic cat playing with marvelous mice—and a few masochists. Maybe he decided to include a little girl from Ohio in his highly motivated group of terrific talents for his own amusement.

It was a knockout place at the time. Almost everyone I saw there had already been important in the theatre or would be: Marian Seldes, Richard Boone, Darren McGavin, Nancy Marchand. There were classes in clarity of speech, developing style, movement and agility as well as emotional and psychological techniques for acting. Martha Graham taught our dance classes and those classes were a hoot as well as agonizing. Few of us could achieve anything like the positions she pushed us into. We moaned most of the time. Martha had long, sharpened nails and was pleased to scratch us into better shape. She had a furious temper and seemed like a witch to me. I had never seen anyone remotely like her in Youngstown, Ohio. But she was an inspiration. None of us would ever forget her total focus and her religious belief in herself.

I met her again later, in the seventies, at Halston's home in New York. He introduced us and she said she had heard about me, giving me the courage to remind her of my classes with her at the Playhouse. She laughed a witchy laugh and said that at the time she was scratching us into position she was miserable in her relationship with her partner, Erick Hawkins. Erick taught our classes, too, and Martha married him for a while. She told me that it hadn't been peaches and cream between them, and in her enthusiasm for the story she grabbed my wrist. I barely heard what she said because I was looking at her fingers digging into me. She still had panther nails—and a panther attitude. I knew she could still scratch anybody into position. "One mustn't grow old sweetly," Karl Lagerfeld told Mia de Riencourt, a friend of mine, and I understood what he meant: I remembered the vibrancy, the hunger for everything that pervaded Martha Graham in her older years and pray that I will have it.

She sailed off to Studio 54 with Halston, leaving me with an appreciation for the vivid impression that the Neighborhood Playhouse had made on me. I may not have heard of the luminous creatures I met there but I knew I was in a rarefied atmosphere and I knew I was having a major experience. So although I went through my Neighborhood Playhouse year moon-eyed and unready, all the teaching, all the ideas, the exercises, the attitude and the thrill of working with world-class talent sunk in. I internalized all of it. And at the right time, when I was running an advertising agency—which is like producing, directing and acting in a different Broadway show every day of the year—I reached into where it was all stored, the emotional resources in me that I could awaken by using memories of feelings in order to be convincing and persuasive with my audiences, my clients and my agency—the way I could manipulate my voice—the instinct I'd developed that made me walk or turn or gesture to suit the role I was playing from moment to moment—the inner control board that Sandy had taken great pains to make me understand, that I had finally understood as the monumental focus it takes to stay in control as the director. It was all there waiting.

After a year Sandy told me I needed more work before I could profit further from the Neighborhood Playhouse. There was no doubt about that. By that time the director of the Youngstown Playhouse had left to become the head of the theatre school at Carnegie Institute of Technology in Pittsburgh. Carnegie Tech was willing to accredit my year in New York so I enrolled there a sophomore. It was a pleasant place with a green campus and big Pennsylvania shade trees. Most of the students were men, engineering and design students, and there was a small fine-arts school for women. The theatre school was self-absorbed, indifferent to the fraternity and sorority life, even to the smart, arty life of the design students. At first I thought I would suffocate in that drama school filled with amateurs infatuated with elementary ideas of the theatre. I was insufferably proud of having spent one year in New York at a meteoric school filled with genius and it took me a while to see just how talented my classmates were at Carnegie Tech. They were younger than the students that Sandy normally accepted at the Neighborhood Playhouse, they had no professional experience, but the best of the lot had the same samurai-like will that I had seen at the Neighborhood Playhouse, and most were gifted. I realized that when I also realized that the problem was not the school, it was me. I not only didn't care about becoming an actress—a realization that left me feeling direction-less, vacant, with absolutely nothing to hang on to—I didn't know what I wanted to study or be or who I was.

Today it is not unusual to find college students who have not found paths for themselves. But these are rich days. Those were poor days, and it took everything I had earned and a lot that my parents had saved to enroll me in Carnegie Tech. If I was not an actress, I had to find out what I was right away—before the money ran out. So although I made dutiful efforts to become part of the theatre school, I started to look around like a homeless person for a place to hide from the storm I was feeling, my first awareness of my self. I didn't know how to think, reflect, analyze. Introspection terrified me. I filled up my hours with people, joining a sorority, dating fraternity boys, going to parties. Noise, I wanted a lot of noise.

In Carnegie Tech's theatre school almost no one dated. Groups gathered to eat and drink and talk animatedly with one another, but the theatre students were single-minded and intense about their futures and they thought they were above parties. The engineers and fine-arts students snickered at them, at their bohemian clothes, at their eccentric individualism. The sea between them and me got bigger and it is only now, as I write about them, that I have a bittersweet longing to go back and be one of those ferocious, determined individuals who knew just exactly what he or she was doing in Carnegie Tech's theatre school.

But I slid into the role of a college girl looking for someone to marry on graduation day. I wasn't exactly like Blanche looking for the kindness of strangers, I wasn't crazy, I was just buying time to find a direction, leaning on the strongest support I could find. The most interesting possibility of an immediate life that I could see was with a good-looking industrial design student, Bert Wells, head of his fraternity, an active doer. He was intense and focused, he finished what he started in a grown-up way and he made me feel secure when I was with him. He hadn't planned to have a serious relationship so soon, he was ambitious and he wanted a career, success, money, he was a little behind schedule because of the time he had spent in the army. He didn't want to fall in love with me, he wouldn't call for a week or two and would have fights with himself about me, I should have left him alone. But when I learned that he planned to have a career in New York, I threw myself in front of his train, he gave up and we became engaged. Then, having committed himself, he became as intense about me as he was about everything else. He would run his hands through his hair and say things like, "You're different from anyone I've met, I won't meet any-one like you again, I'm seriously in love, this is not just a sexy romance anymore, you are becoming my life. Do you understand me?" No, I didn't understand him. I didn't love him as I should have, but I was enthusiastic, exuberant about the idea I had of our future as a married couple in New York. How many young women have married thought-lessly, simply because they want to marry? A zillion? I was an ordinary young woman.

Nice work if you can get it

But I was lucky. I left Carnegie Tech in order to work, to make money Bert and I would need for a new life in New York, while he finished school and graduated. I moved back into my parents' Cape Cod cottage in Poland, Ohio, and began looking for a job. In my teens I had worked summers selling hats at McKelvey's department store in Youngstown, so I went there first. Vera Friedman was running Mc-Kelvey's advertising department and needed a writer. She said she hired me because I had theatre training and could type—the perfect combi-nation of resources, she thought, for a trainee copywriter. In all the years that young people have asked me how to become a copywriter in an advertising agency I have always told them to get a job writing for a department store or another retail business. I still think that is the best place to learn about advertising, because it puts the problem so clearly before you. How do you persuade people to buy a store's pants and shirts, pots and pans, with only a few words in a newspaper? How can you find, how can there be, a few words so powerful they will make somebody get up out of their chair, pull out their Amex card and buy the pants or shirt that you want them to buy? There is something mys-tical in the process. There are so many pants, so many shirts, so many things being sold out there—how you can put 10 or 20 words together that will lead buyers to your pants or your shirt in your store? In a department store you learn how to persuade in a few words. You learn from the buyers themselves, their necks are on the line. They must sell pants and shirts day after day after day or it is over for them. They are heatedly dependent on those words you write for the newspapers. The buyers don't have the words. *You* must have the words, *you* must produce the magic. You get so you can feel a buyer's pulse—it becomes your pulse. Any languid ideas you may have had are quickly dumped.

Picture it. All over America copywriters are writing words so powerful they make people stand up and go to a store and buy pants and shirts. From the first minute I loved the challenge of motivating 500 people I couldn't see, and who couldn't see me, to buy 500 pairs of $8.95 wash slacks within 24 hours of when the newspapers hit the streets. There is a dynamic in this challenge that is essential to absorb if you want to succeed in advertising; it is an intuitive line between you and the store buyers and the shoppers. You've got to have it—even later when you are a big star, computing frogs to sell beer on television, you've got to have it. The best place to develop it is in the retail business, a relentless wheel of buying and selling. Day after day after day after day you have to have the words. A success every week or every month is not enough. You have to come through with the words every day for every buyer who is counting on you.

Vera hired me to write advertising copy for the bargain basement floor of McKelvey's. The merchandise manager, who was a dictator there, was a short, muscled fellow with eyes that snapped at me like little whips. He wanted results and he didn't mean maybe. "Sale!" he would yell at me. "Say it louder." *"SALE!"* "No, say it bigger, louder." "SALE!" He thrilled me. It is impossible not to become intoxicated in a department store advertising department with so much riding on you.

Vera was educated, well traveled, articulate. She was married to Fred Friedman, the editor of the leading newspaper, who was involved in local politics, and their dinner table conversations were bristling with opinions and debates. They had no children, I would do just fine, she spent hours after McKelvey's closed evenings teaching me the fine art of advertising the store's tonier, upstairs fashions: how to create a climate on a newspaper page that attracts an experienced customer; how to be interesting, irresistible, haunting so that customers cannot forget an idea you have given them; how to create a recognizable style for a store, how to build a strong and lasting image. She was appalled at all the books I hadn't read, and to give me a taste of what I was missing, she persuaded me to tackle the *Odyssey,* analyzing Telemachus over tuna salad sandwiches at lunch.

Years later, after I started Wells Rich Greene, I was adopted by another goddess, Mary Lasker, and I was finally introduced to Matisse paintings. Mary, one of the world's most creative givers, who planted trees and flowers up and down Park Avenue and groves of cherry trees in Washington, who did more than anyone else to force Congress to fund cancer research (her prestigious Lasker Awards still set the standard in the medical world)—Mary decided one day over tea that it was her mission to correct my dreary ignorance of art. She had been an art dealer in Paris when she met and married Albert Lasker, head of the Lord & Thomas advertising agency. She corrected his ignorance of art, too, and they assembled a collection that was not only immensely valuable but lyrical, luscious, lovely to live with. The most beautiful experience you could have had in the sixties was to be invited to Mary Lasker's townhouse to revel in the Matisses that leaped and lounged and sang boisterously, tenderly, seductively, passionately all over her white walls from floor to floor. If I could give one art lesson to an innocent, it would be to take her to Mary Lasker's house of Matisses. You would not be the same afterwards, your heart would go bang-bang-bang at the very prospect of seeing a Matisse.

Mary could be a general, imperious if need be, to achieve her goals. She was a warrior in Washington, wielding her money like a holy sword to do the impossible, to eliminate cancer. She knew just how strong-willed she was and mostly didn't mind if she came off as intimidating, but she was careful not to squoosh people she adored. She was proud that she was not a patient woman, I think, because after her husband died of cancer she developed what she told me was an agonizing sense of how little time there was to save people's lives from that evil disease. She felt responsible for each and every person who had it and she believed that if she put enough money into the right places she could turn the tide—if only other people would get off their duff and do what she told them to do.

Her husband's great success in the advertising business interested her in it and in me, another woman general to her eyes. She would drop in when I was free at the agency, we would have our tea and she would surprise me with confidential girl talk—sometimes about men she had fancied, like Adlai Stevenson—but she would never leave without giving me a lecture about the modern art she thought I should buy as investments for the agency. Sooner or later, with her opening my wallet, I bought Gottliebs, Klines, Motherwells, de Koonings, Pollocks, Averys, Okados and a vibrant blue Mark Rothko at their early prices. They hung in our halls, giving the agency a gorgeous illusion of security and wealth. Once she called me from California, interrupting a new business presentation. "I don't care who you are presenting to," she said firmly from Los Angeles, "get on a plane this afternoon, I have found a Sam Francis here and a man named Feeley, you must buy him before everyone else does. You will make more when you sell your paintings than you will make from those clients." Not quite true, but close. When we sold Wells Rich Greene's impressive collection we made a couple of million in profits. I was out of touch with the art world at the time, and Mary had died. If I had waited as long as she had instructed me to we would have made the huge fortune she promised. She had practical views about art. Years after she had introduced me to contemporary art and had pushed it, I said to her, casually, frivolously, "I would really prefer to have Cézanne trees in my living room, Boldinis in my bedroom and Vermeer or Manet in my entrance hall." She said, "Paintings that expensive belong in museums, not in your entrance hall." She was selling her great Matisses at the time to fund more cancer research and was investing in the same contemporary artists she was introducing to me. She had no interest in anonymous art and dismissed photographs or sketches I found in flea markets as entertainments, although when, purely by accident, I discovered that a drawing I had found in an obscure place was a Picasso, she wanted to throw a big dinner party to celebrate.

I fully appreciated and was devoted to my goddesses. With Vera, at

McKelvey's, I was a puppy, ardent with ideas, and I gave her headaches. I heard about the Dallas newspapers with their Neiman Marcus ads. Neiman Marcus advertising in the fifties was the crème de la crème of department-store advertising. It was world-class retail advertising, smart and amusing and an eye opener for me. It made me try to get that same sophistication into my ads for the bargain basement floor of McKelvey's. The merchandise manager would always hit the ceiling and go howling to Vera. "Where does she get these ideas?" he asked her morosely. "Where does she think she is, on the Champs-Elysées?" Vera carefully reminded me that Neiman Marcus style was an inappropriate way to sell pants from a place people counted on to charge the best price. She pointed out that their particular dream was to find a great bargain. She taught me to imagine and sympathize with the people who were the customers for McKelvey's bargain pants and shirts, to put myself in their place, to imagine their lives, to talk to them and not to myself; she made me understand that they were as exciting and mean-ingful a target for McKelvey's as the women who bought expensive fashions in the upstairs store and that the customers who had precious little money were an even greater challenge than the rich ones. They had more suitors. They had learned to be discriminating. So if I won their trust I had achieved something to be proud of. Vera taught me to be a detective and a psychiatrist before allowing myself to be an artist with the few words I had to persuade people to buy from me.

Alone together

Bert and I were married over the Christmas holidays in the pretty white Presbyterian church in Poland, Ohio. I was not a peaceful bride. Working at McKelvey's had taught me something about myself as well as about advertising and I wasn't ready to marry. I felt like a flower that was just beginning to bloom and I wanted to stay on course and develop whatever talent I had for the advertising business under Vera Friedman. I hadn't seen much of Bert that year. He had been working hard at school and at part-time jobs. His imagination had been working overtime too, his intensity about our relationship had grown into full-blown fanaticism with baseless suspicions that frightened me. I was having a romance with advertising, not the young men in Youngstown, there was no reason for jealousy, and I started to see his intensity as a kind of craziness. As Christmas loomed I knew I should think twice about the wedding. But I was still too silly, too thoughtless, ready to do the wrong thing in order to do the apparently right thing. Our friends from Carnegie Tech Don and Wilma Ervin were going to be the best man and maid of honor, they were going to New York with us as part of a grand plan. There was too much for me to dismantle and I was frozen.

Just before I was to walk down the aisle at the church I had serious trouble breathing. My father and I were alone in a small room the church set aside for brides. We had become closer since I returned from school and had gone to work. Time, distance from the war and from the Depression had faded his memories, and my weekly paycheck and prospective marriage lessened his financial responsibilities; he was developing the beginning of a what-the-hell attitude that allowed him to express himself with warmth, even some humor, even affection. I could feel that a lot of the pain he'd always had in his mind was gone. My mother was making speeches at the League of Women Voters meetings and was talking about getting a job, she was clearly happier and he seemed relieved, almost peaceful. At the church he studied me and he said, "Mary, we can leave right now if you don't want to get married today. It's fine with me if we go home now. You don't have to worry. We can straighten it all out tomorrow."

But the church was packed with our friends from Pittsburgh as well as Poland. My mother had been seated and she had bought the first really expensive dress of her life for this moment. The music swelled. Wilma, my maid of honor, had started down the aisle. At home, all our wedding gifts had been displayed by my mother as if she and I had conquered Fort Knox. This minute, writing about that minute, I feel the helplessness I felt then. I know that at least a million women have felt as I did, stretched in all directions on the rack, desperate to escape, but going forward down the aisle on my father's arm.

In fact, marriage wasn't so bad for a while. My parents drove me to New York with almost everything I owned piled on top of their car. We drove through the fields of smelly fuel tanks outside the city certain we were entering heaven. Bert had found a shiny new one-bedroom apartment on 14th Street and that first night we all slept in our new apartment on inflated rubber mattresses after unpacking and eating my mother's cold meat loaf. Bert and I didn't have much. He was a design snob out of Carnegie Tech's industrial design school, so we had spent our wedding gift money on a Knoll sofa, a Saarinen chair, four red Eames chairs and a table. It didn't matter that we didn't have curtains or a rug, we were smug that everything we had was good design. We set it up as though the apartment was a stage set and then we became New Yorkers. New Yorkers never stayed home, no one that we knew nested at home. New York was open all night just for us. We became part of a young group that was expert on what was going on. We loved the clubs. Before disco, clubs were small and almost shabby, but Mabel Mercer sang "Just One of Those Things" in them and Mike Nichols and Elaine May performed their high-wire improvisations there. A lot of cabaret thrills happened in those clubs, they were about talent, not décor. The smartest one was the Blue Angel, a narrow shaft of black space with tables too small to get your knees under. We were so proud to be allowed into the Blue Angel by one of the world's first nightclub people choosers. He ended up a millionaire from the entrance tips he received. When we got to know him on a first-name basis and he gave us his telephone number, we felt we had arrived. We danced in some of the clubs, a slow, sexy one-step, to bands that had saxophones playing sad, hopeless love songs. Before the Beatles and the Stones, before the youthquake that was just around the corner, we enjoyed feeling experienced in New York. We tried to look older, not younger. Our gang clubbed the nights away and then split in the mornings, busing to our careers.

The hungry years

Bambergers hired me right away for their advertising department. Bambergers was a big, fashionable store in Newark and I liked working there. But I left to make more money at McCreery's in Manhattan. I always had an eye out for a better salary. A year later, when I was hired by Nan Findlow in the grand advertising department at Macy's for what seemed like a fortune to me, it was as if I had climbed Everest, I was sure I would never, ever leave. Macy's was a profoundly professional place. It was no training school, you were expected to know how to deliver results demanded by some of the world's shrewdest buyers. I was honored when I was promoted to copy chief of the fashion division. Macy's copy chiefs were responsible not only for a buyer's ultimate success, but also for the accuracy of each ad when it appeared. If you made a mistake and advertised a dress for $9 that should have been advertised for $99, the responsibility was all yours. The guillotine sat in an office nearby—the supreme advertising manager, a big executive at Macy's and a man with no jokes.

I don't remember Macy's advertising department ever being cleaned; it had the aura of a busy newspaper office, the clacking of typewriters, the dull shine of cheap olive metal desks, large dusty windows, the left-over smoke of old cigarettes, precarious stacks of papers and myriad forms all over the place, they just collected and grew. You knew that one day the people would move, not the stacks of papers. Every area had a domineering wall clock and none of them told the same time. Still, there was nothing emotionally disorderly about the place, it was self-disciplined and self-important. Thousands of dresses, hundreds of thousands of white shirts, untold numbers of underpants and socks were sold there, millions and millions of dollars were made in that advertising department.

Every day, starting very early, I met with the buyers on the different fashion floors. They would show me what they were planning to advertise and they would give me information about it, they would sell me on it.

It was important to them that I see the appeal of what they had to sell and to understand exactly whom they bought it to sell to. They wanted me to see that what they had to sell was a jewel and I always did, I always saw their dresses or coats or shoes as transcendent offerings. I became such an enthusiastic, understanding partner for them that in time they trusted me, they even trusted my instincts about what they should choose to advertise, they would call me at home nights after Macy's closed to get my opinions.

Fashion was prospering in the fifties. Times were good, people had money to spend and they were enjoying new clothes. It was then that I began to theatricalize what I sold. Life is, after all, the way you see it. I began to see the dresses and coats they brought to me as potential dramas. It wasn't enough to just describe them accurately. I needed to make them important and meaningful. If they brought me a plain grey dress, for example, I would see that the grey dress was a far more exciting basic dress than the basic black dress that every woman already owned. I would write that the "little grey dress" was the rage with smart women who knew about such things and that this little grey dress in particular was the one to wear.

If they brought me a coat with a mousy fur collar, I transformed it into the new way to wear fur—quietly, like young royalty. Flat shoes became "just like Audrey Hepburn's." When we received a carload of jackets that were all the wrong size, extra-large, and the manufacturer went out of business at the same time, I persuaded the buyer to take a full-page ad in the papers and I sold the whole lot by announcing that the hot Parisian jacket for winter had arrived, I named it the Soufflé Jacket, and said it was blown up, divinely out of proportion, as only the French could do, to make you look thinner, fashionably skinny, underneath. The women who bought those coats felt stylish in them, so they looked stylish in them, *were* stylish in them. Fashion is about sacramentalizing the ordinary, it's about wearing your dreams. I grew to see that everything for sale on the fashion floors at Macy's could enlarge a woman's life if I created an idea, a drama for it. That, I realized, is what fashion advertising and marketing are supposed to do—enlarge someone's life through her or his imagination.

The snake in my paradise was television. People were gathering around the first sets that appeared, not because the programs were enthralling, but because the pictures moved. The first time I watched television I felt exactly as if something important had taken an elevator ride up to my head and gotten off and turned on the light in my mind. I knew that I was going to do something in television. It was in my cards. I remember feeling the warm relief of knowing where my future was.

I didn't know anyone who was creating television programs or commercials. Nevertheless, whatever got off in my mind that day was very clear, I knew that one way or another I had to get into television while it was still new. I didn't know how to do that until I got a telephone call from a headhunter who was working for McCann Erickson, an advertising agency with a lot of retail business. "Ever heard of Margo Sherman?" he asked me. "She's a top-drawer agency copy chief, Mary, and McCann's one of the majors. They have a lot of women's products, retail businesses. Mrs. Sherman says she's been reading your ads in the papers and she wants to interview you for an opening she's going to have. It's God-given, that's all I can tell you." Maybe it was. He said, "McCann Erickson is creating television advertising, you should give some thought to that."

I went to see Margo Sherman, a tall, handsome woman, who was gracious, complimented my work, taught me how to put a portfolio together and how to organize a professional résumé and then offered me a job. I struggled for a minute with that offer because I felt so alive at Macy's, I felt smart and energized and there was a clear future for me there, but something in the theatrical possibilities for me in television was irresistible. Finally, in blissful ignorance of what it would be like to work in a big agency that made TV commercials in the early fifties, I left 34th Street and went uptown to Rockefeller Center and McCann Erickson, where I arrived when the big agencies were creating some of the worst advertising the world has ever known.

Advertising agencies are always quick to adapt to the climate of an era and to their clients' psyches. After the war, after V-E Day and V-J

Day and the carnage at Omaha Beach and the atom bomb, there was a sweeping need for sanity and safety and reason and organization in the United States. People craved order and everything that goes with it—politeness, respect for authority, good manners, cooperation. They wanted to feel safe. Committees were in charge of the big decisions, because group thinking was perceived as safer and wiser than any one person's. Conformity was deeply comforting. Bill Levitt cloned $6,900 houses with such success that pseudo Levittowns popped up all over America. Individualism was often seen as dangerous, and in business, hierarchy, loyalty and the Boss were devoutly honored. This postwar caution and conservatism coincided with a great surge in postwar needs and desires. People wanted to live well, they wanted comforts and beauty and ease and they were so eager to buy, so receptive to being sold, that advertising agencies grew like weeds. The big agencies put up their periscopes, looked around, understood what was going on and carefully structured themselves so that they mirrored their clients' conservative ideas and even their organizations, their hierarchies. As a result, for a short time in history, advertising agencies were primarily concerned with taking a scientific and safe approach to selling.

They developed large, powerful marketing-research departments charged with making their work more predictable and on target. All sorts of testing techniques appeared: simple polling, telephone and door-to-door questionnaires, complicated psychological sessions with individuals and groups, instant-recall testing, test markets, even an eye machine that claimed to be able to tell a subject's true reactions. Some research techniques became so important that they developed sinister reputations. Motivational research, for example, became notorious; people thought that agencies were motivating consumers subliminally to buy things they didn't need or want. Television viewers began to believe that commercials were brainwashing them with secret symbols. Stories ran around wildly about the hidden messages that would control your mind. Pure paranoia, it's funny now but it wasn't then. I was always being grilled by people who were certain I was in a business that had an evil eye or considered the consumer a dumbhead.

Like all the big agencies, McCann Erickson was full of intelligent people trying to squeeze their talents into the girdle of science, trying to make the art of persuasion safe—an oxymoron if there ever was one. Marion Harper knew as much or more about advertising research and quantifying a campaign as anyone, and he was looming as the big power at McCann when I arrived there. He had an inventive mind and plenty of ego and he was exploring a wide variety of original ideas he hoped would bring in new accounts. He may have been the first to integrate a range of marketing services to enlarge and enrich the scope of the advertising he could offer prospective clients: public relations, direct response, sales promotion, package design. He was always actively soliciting new business and would cast around for new gimmicks as bait. He had a weakness for people who were good on their feet with fast, engaging talk, smart ones and fools, some of them betrayed him, but without doubt he was visionary. He was the first to seriously consider an agency holding company that would allow different divisions to handle conflicting accounts. Globalization is a requirement for a big agency today, but Marion was already planning to globalize when I went to McCann in the fifties.

I rarely saw him; McCann was a little like the army then, rigidly structured, and Marion was on a higher peg. There wasn't a lot of camaraderie inside the agency. People talked to each other mostly at lunch or at cocktails out of the office. The advertising itself was created in a lonely manner. The copy chief and the creative director were kept informed, but the top account executives, who were the liaisons with the clients, pretty much ran the show. They would tell a copywriter what an ad should be and say. The copywriter would then put the words for the ad on paper and take it to or slip it under the door of the art director who was to make the layout for the ad. The research department would examine and tailor a campaign as it progressed. Eventually important ads and campaigns would reach the agency's Creative Review Board; members of this board were the top executives of the company, and all of them were running for president in their minds, so they were very competitive. They would try to outdo one another by criticizing the advertising that was presented to them and would remake the ads on the spot, squabbling and fussing. Ads and campaigns were massacred in those meetings. You could hear the tomtoms behind the closed doors. Unless the writer and art director who had the campaign being reviewed were top rung, they rarely attended those board meetings. Sometimes they waited, spooked, outside, to be called in for questioning. Campaigns rarely had mothers or fathers, as they would later, in the sixties, people who had created them with a knowing purpose and with passion and would shepherd them, personally, held close to their hearts, all the way through the agency right on to the clients. So when a campaign finally limped out of a Creative Review Board meeting, covered in Band-Aids, it was usually chopped liver— unless, of course, it was exactly like a campaign that the client had liked and approved before. As the account executives were responsible for selling advertising to clients and for bringing in revenues, they urged the agency to clone ads the clients had liked and seemed ready to buy over and over again, one of the reasons advertising in the fifties was so boring.

Mary Reilly, Alice Mosely, Jo Foxworth, Chet Posey, Trav Hand, Nils Berg, Vic Ratner, Wade Hancock, Bill Free, Bob Wall, Tom Heck, Don Calhoun—there was exceptional talent at McCann. Bob Pliskin was one of the best art directors I ever knew, ever worked with. Most of the big talents were at the big agencies. They were all frustrated about the state of advertising in the fifties. But that was the way the industry was, the way the country was, the way people wanted things to be. Tom Johnson, one of the few writers at McCann when I was there who actually made important television commercials, threw in the towel and with his wife, who was in the research department, flew off to Bequia in the West Indies to build cave houses in Moonhole as a personal act of protest. Most of the people who bought his caves and lived in them came out of McCann.

Jack Tinker was the creative director and the first one to shake my hand and wish me well when I arrived. He was adored. He was McCann's symbol that creativity and intuition and art were still alive at the agency. He had the best office in the place. Most big-agency offices were utilitarian, rows of identical offices with pens of secretaries and grey file cabinets outside their doors. Jack had furniture made of real wood and decorator fabrics and he had a handsome and expensive art director's work stand sitting defiantly in the center of his office, a statement that he was, in an agency that worshipped account executives, an art director, a *creative*. He was also a talented salesman and the account executives would stand him up front at presentations to lend an air of genius to the presentation and to sell the work, as he could so effectively, with both flair and cunning. He had charm, he would be greeted with little smiles and soft eyes wherever he walked, but he couldn't revolutionize the agency. Jack understood that the system was destroying the effectiveness of the advertising. I once overheard him shouting and pounding on the table at a Creative Review Board meeting. "All the heart, all the fire in our advertising is stamped out here, in this room, month after month after month!" he yelled. "What have we done here today? We've killed this campaign. It's dead! Can't you see? We've killed it!" When they came out of the boardroom Jack was flushed and his short hair was prickly. The other big honchos came out patting him on the back but they were embarrassed—for him, not themselves. He didn't get anywhere. He swallowed a lot for years. Later, when we worked together at Jack Tinker & Partners, he tried to defend McCann's structure in the fifties. "Look at Picasso," he said. "He subdued art to his will, didn't he? Control takes art to a higher level." We were great friends by then, we took a minute to reconsider advertising in the fifties and then we just laughed and laughed.

I was a novice, gawky in the big-time agency world, I was thrilled to be taken in at McCann. It took me quite a while to care whether or not I would ever be able to do great work there or that the big agencies were making boring advertising. I was proud to have been hired to write expensive, national advertising copy and I was respectful. I figured out who McCann's talents were and made friends with them to learn from them. If they wanted me to finish some of their work so they could leave early, I was delighted. If Mary Reilly, a major writer, wanted me to have cocktails to listen to her tales of woe about a married art director she was having an affair with, I was happy to sympathize. (I didn't like to drink, but agency people used to drink like characters in Irish novels. I knew that a Shirley Temple wouldn't do anything for me. I looked around and decided that martinis looked sophisticated, especially if you were holding a cigarette and maybe even wearing a hat. I concentrated on martinis until, finally, I enjoyed them.) Mary helped me get better copy assignments and to become a copy group head with my own permanent accounts. But I never saw a television studio. Margo had hired me to write copy for her retail accounts, cosmetics, soaps, women's personal products, Holmes & Edwards DeepSilver, Fiberglas curtains and draperies, and they weren't on television. I wrote a lot of radio scripts, but I was too far down the ladder to handle the accounts where the television was, so after a while I became restless.

David Ogilvy appeared on the scene about the same time as Leo Burnett, but Leo was in Chicago and that was on Mars. New York was advertising land the way Hollywood was movie land. David introduced "The Man in the Hathaway Shirt" wearing an eyepatch and it was such an obviously great branding idea it got everybody's attention even though his agency was small. Then he turned his client the mustached, bearded Commander Whitehead into a stylish symbol for Schweppes tonic, a mixer few Americans had heard of. When Schweppes tonic began creating a new market for itself, and when David's Rolls-Royce ad appeared ("At 60 miles an hour the loudest noise in this new Rolls-Royce comes from the electric clock") and won every award for a print ad ever given, the big agencies took him seriously.

Suddenly, like buzz: "Have you heard of that small agency called Ogilvy? I'm not sure where it is but it's doing very good work, excellent writing—he's English, I hear, and charismatic—imagine an Englishman writing American advertising!" The big agencies liked the elegance of David's advertising and, after all, David was a scientist, he had worked for Dr. Gallup at Gallup & Robinson, an important research firm. In fact, he had his own guidelines. No, they were *rules* for making successful advertising. Years later he protested that he'd never had rules, but in the fifties he was busy promoting his rules, a "how to" approach to making ads: how to write a headline, how to write copy, how to make a layout. His way was as methodical as McCann's. So the big agencies saw him as a fellow scientist who happened to have clients who wanted upper-class style. "Lucky David," they said to one another, "to have such clients." And then there was the way David Ogilvy looked: "so English, so well bred, so attractive."

I met him when Bert went to work for him as an art director. David didn't think highly of McCann or any other agency that I can recall, he was more than a little imperious, but he was also curious, so he would offer me tea, puff on his pipe and question me. "Tell me about Marion Harper, what do you think he's up to? Clever fellow, is he?" David was a god to the workers in his agency, he chatted as elegantly as he wrote and encouraged panache around the place. I thought it was great fun to meet Bert there and he fell head over heels in love with the agency and worked later and later. On our rare evenings together we talked nothing but advertising. Our combined income allowed us to live a glamorous life and we moved to 60 Sutton Place South when the building was brand new and the balconies off the apartments still enjoyed the smell of fresh sea. Nobody ever sat on their balconies, we all just opened our doors, took deep breaths of salt-air breezes and felt rich. Bert and I installed lengths of blood-orange silk draperies, painted the walls linen white, our designer wedding furniture felt at home there. It was an elegant apartment, a long way from my family's Cape Cod cottage in Poland, Ohio, but we weren't excited about it, our marriage was falling apart from lack of attention, lack of empathy, lack of any lust or love.

"Who the hell was that?" he yelled at me one evening when a friend brought me home from an agency cocktail party for a client. He knew the friend, knew he was not interested in women, knew there was nothing to be jealous about. But I hated that jealousy in him, it was so incompatible with the yawning truth of our marriage, the total lack of connection. I was bored with him.

When he blew up that evening, I left in a deadly fury, stayed with a friend and wouldn't return. After a few discussions we gave up on each other and divorced. What I remember most about that time was my restlessness, I wasn't on the right road, everything was becoming an effort. When Adolf Toigo offered me an impressive salary to join a small brain trust to do new-wave work that included television at Lennen & Newell, I accepted. When he very quickly lost the means to keep such an experiment going and gave us generous compensation, I instinctively got on a ship and went to London and Paris and Rome and Cannes. Like anyone visiting Europe for the first time, I toyed with the idea of staying there, working there. But European agencies didn't compare with New York's in the fifties, and I knew I had to return to New York to find a way to access the mysterious energy I had for the advertising business that I didn't seem to have for anything else.

When I arrived back in New York, walking down the gangplank, the first thing I saw was Ophelia, the Old English sheepdog that Bert and I had gotten before our divorce; we had joint custody of her. She was always luxuriously brushed into a huge loving flurry and her every waking thought was to stand up and hug me—or *anybody*. She had gotten loose and was wiggling her way up the gangplank offering everyone who was trying to descend a joyous kiss. Her big welcome brought the ship I'd sailed in on to a complete stop and I was so happy to see her that she made me think I was happy to see Bert, too, who was waiting, holding flowers, looking hopeful. He said that while I was away he realized how much he loved me and how much he needed me in his life. He knew his jealousies were irrational and irritating and he had thought about them, understood them better, could control them. He thought we had never really focused. We had the wrong priorities. We needed to balance our working life with something warmer and sweeter and more nurturing, we needed to have a family, to grow up, to think about someone other than ourselves. He thought we would never forgive ourselves if we didn't give ourselves another chance to have a real marriage.

Maybe it was the idea of having children—I wanted to have children, and the possibility of having children without a husband was an idea that didn't occur to one woman in a billion then. As for other men, there were a few I liked, thought about, dreamed about and could have loved, but they were even more self-involved than I was. The unvarnished truth is that I wasn't looking for the man of my dreams, I was looking for the job of my dreams, I was in love with advertising, and remarrying Bert was in a way perfect. I would be marrying a devoted friend who wouldn't get in the way of my career, and I could have children. We remarried in the Little Church Around the Corner in New York. Same maid of honor, same best man, my mother didn't say anything but I knew what she thought, it was in her eyes. I am shaking my head as I write this. "Idiot," I am saying to myself. Except—I did have children. First I had a series of tough miscarriages. Then I adopted my daughters, Katy and Pam, my babies, my loves, my angels. All the years I have had with them, and now they are the most satisfying women in the world to me. My daughters. I thank God I was stupid enough to marry Bert Wells the second time.

One night shortly after we remarried, I was half asleep and I heard a loud voice say firmly, "The End." I sat up, looked around, nobody was there, just Bert and me and he was sleeping soundly. It was the end, though, the end of one me and the beginning of another me because the next day I went to work at Doyle Dane Bernbach, where Bill opened a door for me and I could see that the advertising business offered opportunities to learn, to love, to live in ways that would make life more than I had ever imagined. Every day became a stepping-stone to my own agency, cast in my own image. Great as that was, though, it wasn't easy, and it certainly wasn't about acquiescence. Gloria Steinem had it wrong, I was no Uncle Tom. Rocky was more like it.

My daughters, Pamela and Katy.

Let's call the whole thing off

For example, take TWA (almost everybody in ad land tried to, it was considered such a plum of an advertising account). For the first four or five years we worked eye to eye and ear to ear with Blaine Cooke and chums like Frank Duffy, TWA's minister of spin, a raconteur with canny intelligence who could get anything out of an agency, and Bud Wiser, a classy man who joined TWA as president, and Brian Kennedy, a keen strategist and the astute politician of the group, who kept everyone walking to the same beat. The collective cooperation of our group was extraordinarily productive and as a result TWA did become the businessman's airline that it craved to be. There was only one small burr in our side: One of Blaine's vice-presidents, Don Casey, had a taste for power that was annoying, a managerial high-handedness that did not sit well with us. At TWA his co-workers called him the Prince of Ice because his eyes appeared to be made of one-way glass. But he was bright and, like all the others at TWA, he related well to Ted Barash, whom we hired to run the account.

We were lucky to have Ted. He was one of those choice account men who worked as devotedly for the client as for the agency. He joined TWA with his heart as well as his mind. They didn't miss that fact and trusted him as one of their own. He knew it was me who paid his salary and approved his expense accounts, though, so he would call me late at night with entrusted secrets. I would crawl out of bed to write them down. "Pssst, Mary, it's Ted, are you alone? [It's two a.m.] Guess who is on his way out at TWA. Larry Stapleton. I'll call you tomorrow with the new lineup. Sorry to wake you up but this is big news." What is it about that hour, two a.m.? Why did everyone need to read the entrails and give me auguries at two a.m.? I used to wonder where Ted was so often at that hour. He was by no means a swinger. His expense account suggested he enjoyed entertaining TWA at Manhattan's best restaurants, but at two a.m.? I never asked him. Sometimes it's better not to know everything. Anyway, he was worth it, wherever he was. He hired the absolute best, Andre van Stom, Eileen McKenna and Vince Minicucci, at top dollar, and hugged them tight so they never realized they were his slaves working 24-hour days to keep him a superstar at the agency and the airline.

TWA was one of my favorite accounts until "the troubles" began. They started with Peter Sellers. Charlie had the idea of having Peter Sellers star as a spokesman, acting as a variety of different characters who would reflect fliers' different interests in a campaign announcing TWA's new international service. As Thrifty McTravel, a bargain-hunting Scotsman, he would tell you about TWA's promotional fares. As the Honourable Jeremy Peake-Thyme, known to his British pals as "Piggy," he would tell you about the airline's gourmet meals and wines, and as Vito di Motione, the notorious Italian lover, he would croon about its Lasagne al Forno Bolognese while he made eyes at the female passengers. Peter Sellers wasn't remotely interested in making commercials, but Don Casey, who had become vice-president of advertising, liked the campaign so much he ordered Ted to "go out to Los Angeles and *don't come back without Peter Sellers.*"

Ted went to Los Angeles and found Stan, who was directing movies as well as working long-distance with Charlie. Ted asked him to find a way to persuade Peter to make the commercials. Stan and Bart MacHugh, our head of television communication, talked Peter into at least looking at a reel of Wells Rich Greene commercials. Peter loved the reel, he had worked with many of the actors in our commercials, he just didn't want to make commercials himself. But Peter's mother stepped in—so to speak. Peter's mother had left the world some years earlier but she hung around Peter to chat and give him advice. She told Peter that Stan was a great fellow who could be trusted and Peter should make the commercials. Peter told Stan about his mother and said, "OK. I will do the commercials. But you have to direct them. And listen, Stan, Mother says that if anybody wears purple on the set I must leave the set immediately and you will never see me again." Stan set up a roadblock so that anybody wearing purple couldn't get on the set. He said he knew Peter's mother was hanging around, he could feel her, and

she was some dame. (Stan is not one to see ghosts.) Peter made the commercials and we were all so aware of what a genius he was, of the Chap-
lin variety, a megastar clown, much more than just funny. Some of his
many, many, many friends have a theory that he grabbed hold of char-
acterizations with an almost diabolical intensity and after giving so
much of himself to so many of them, he eventually lost his own self and
at the end of his life became vacant.

We kept seeing that excessive streak in him, he became fanatic about
every character he created for TWA. Before we shot him as Thrifty
McTravel he studied the entire history of Scotland. He took Jerry Ranson, the senior art director on the TWA account, to Scotland to shop for
local underwear and socks; he said he couldn't go onto the set without
them because he wouldn't be real. He spent days in Scotland walking
the streets stopping people to talk to them until he had picked up the
right accent. Jerry called and told us, "If it isn't made in Scotland he
won't eat it, drink it or wear it. He *is* Thrifty now. He is reincarnated.
Oh, he's adorable, he's an adorable man." We watched Peter as he reincarnated into every character in the campaign.

While we were producing the commercials TWA went through an
executive shift and Don Casey was sent to the field, outside TWA headquarters, to a job in which he no longer supervised advertising. The
Peter Sellers campaign was completed and it was a rave at TWA headquarters. We tested it exhaustively and it exceeded every goal established for it with fliers in terms of recognition, impact, memory,
information and desire to fly TWA.

Then Bud Wiser called me and asked me to meet him privately for a
drink. "Whoa," I thought, "trouble!" Whenever a president asked me
to have a drink with him alone, it always meant trouble. Bud Wiser had
an easy, welcoming way about him, I'd never seen him irritated before.
"I've been getting reports I think you ought to hear," he began. "Some
of the men in the field who are working with Don Casey are upset about
the Sellers campaign. They're going around saying it's frivolous. I think
that's Casey's word for it." I was sure he had it wrong. "Don Casey? But
Bud, he loved the commercials! He demanded that Peter Sellers do the
commercials!" "Well"—Bud rubbed his forehead—"it must be in his
interest to disown Peter Sellers now. Anyway, this group has some let-

ters from people who think the commercials make fun of Italians, they've sent a few of them to members of the board. Blaine and I think the advertising is powerful, just what we need, and we are going to assure the board that it is working. I want you to know that we are going to stand firm about the campaign. But I want to make a presentation of all that research we did for the board meeting." Frank Duffy and Marty Stern put together a watertight presentation for him, they even telephoned every person who had written a critical letter about ethnic stereotypes and learned, to our delight, that the letter writers had never flown in an airplane, not one, and had no plans to fly in one. We wouldn't lose any sales over them.

Bud didn't have a chance to use the presentation, though, because he was fired on his way to the board meeting. Blaine was fired. Frank Duffy was fired. Blaming the deepening recession that was hurting all of the airlines at the time, the board of directors ordered a reorganization and brought in men from the field, the trenches, to toughen up management. We mourned that exodus of executives, we couldn't believe the news at first, I tried to broker some kind of pause in the plans with Charlie Tillinghast, but Charlie was moving on to the realms of the holding company and he didn't feel he had the right to alter the board's decision. When we faced the fact that the collegial atmosphere within that executive group that had been so productive for such a long run was truly gone and the board was looking to the men in the field for pragmatic solutions in a recession, we knew we were in for cloudy skies.

The Sellers campaign was killed and there was a short awkward pause as everyone at the airline and the agency waited for the other shoe to drop. Don Casey came back to direct advertising and told us that TWA should return to airline basics. TWA's on-time performance was about to become the best in the business, business fliers needed concrete reasons for flying TWA in dire times and great on-time performance was a concrete reason. We agreed that when an airline is in a position to brag about on-time performance it is a good idea to do that and we did. But on-time performance is a short-term promotion, not a long-term advertising position. Getting back to airline basics, on the other hand, was a general direction from the client for a long-term position. Our TWA group began exploring a wide variety of possibilities for Don.

I looked away for a minute because Walter Compton had given us the Alka-Seltzer account and I was driving around Central Park with Bill Bernbach and buying the Gardner agency, but one afternoon when I was doing my weekly creative review I noticed that Don Criqui was becoming the TWA spokesman. Don Criqui was a sports announcer and a Notre Dame graduate. He looked a little like Don Casey, I thought he might be a relative.

"Is he a cousin of Casey's?" I asked Ted. To which Ted replied, "Casey loves him. The field loves him. He's a jock, a sports announcer. Everything's great. Relax." I decided to ride on that positive news until we got all the other lions at the agency back into their cages.

Don Criqui or no Don Criqui, I knew there was still the need for a long-term advertising position for the airline, and pretty soon Ted made one of his two a.m. calls. "Casey says to tell you it's time for a big idea," Ted said. "He hasn't seen one he likes at the agency yet." And that was the beginning of a collective madness that gripped the agency as we slogged through a three-year search for a big idea Don could love. The problem was communication, connectedness —none of us seemed able to translate Don's thoughts or directions or to persuade him to appreciate ours. He viewed the ideas for campaigns the agency presented as if they were intended for another client and had been presented to him by mistake. After he would leave one of those presentations the creative people would feel stupid and untalented and betrayed by the rest of us, as they assumed we had not led them up the right path. Ted became more and more impatient with the creative people, and agitated, although he had no idea, either, of what was in Don's mind.

I didn't blame Ted, it was frustrating waiting for a campaign to appear that Don Casey would love. Charlie and I agreed that Don was uninterpretable. He preached to us in aphorisms so general they were meaningless, you couldn't go to work on them, they disappeared into the air like smoke. I tried to get closer to him, to find out what was going on in his mind, what ideas he was failing to make clear. But he always looked at me as if I was speaking Icelandic, which finally demoralized me, the undemoralizable.

Once, when feelings were stretched, Charlie and I created a campaign and trotted out like circus ponies determined to sell it. Don suffered us with disdain, actually with flabbergasting condescension. Charlie and I left that meeting sensing he'd enjoyed his disdain. We tried to involve Don directly in the agency creative process, but collaboration seemed to make him more irritable. When Ed Meyer came out of TWA's finance department and replaced Bud Wiser as president, he attended a few advertising meetings. After one of them he and Don left looking happy, giving us the impression we had found the answer. The next morning Ed told us that although he thought one of the campaigns was absolutely right, he couldn't convince Don. "I'm afraid you'll have to start over," he said. But now, starting over was something that was almost impossible to get anyone in the creative department to do.

Airline advertising is not only a matter of creating great television-image campaigns, it includes quantities of information-giving ads, schedules, announcements of new service and promotions of all kinds. To get talented people to work on such dry feed you have to find ways to give luster to those assignments and you have to create a cult of camaraderie in your airline group just to keep the work rolling out. When I visited our TWA creative people as they worked listlessly on the mountain of day-to-day advertising, it seemed to me that some sort of hypoxia was taking place, and I thought the entire agency could be harmed by the idea that since Blaine and his group left there had been four years of slow deterioration, that the account was not going anywhere, yet management was not willing to take a stand and go to the brink and, if necessary, give up the account. Serial rejection by a client may not be an earthshaking issue, but to manage groups of creative people, who by their very nature do more feeling than reflecting, are more intuitive than intellectual, you have to care or you'll never get their trust, so you'll never get their best work.

People kept reminding me that Bill Bernbach resigned the American Airlines account after years of a close relationship with C. R. Smith when Bob Crandall took over and Bill thought he was mistreating the agency. I remembered thinking that Bill was childish at the time and that he made Doyle Dane appear callow and spoiled. On the other hand, Bill had always threatened to fire clients who did not appreciate Doyle Dane's work, and taking that stand had done a lot to build the idea of him as the guardian of the advertising industry's soul. Wells Rich Greene didn't look to me to guard the industry's soul, I realized. I was supposed to keep the troops excited and working at their peak and I was supposed to keep the agency winning. But not at any cost.

Taking a stand and having to resign an account when a client is harmful is a call to arms that waits like a silent ghost in agency halls and whispers to chairmen to make them sweat. It isn't that it wouldn't be sweet to resign such accounts, immensely satisfying. But five minutes after the sweetness runs through your veins you have to begin firing people, often superpeople, people you will need another day, people who have done wonderful work for the agency—because agencies are never rich enough to give up large accounts without hell to pay.

I felt cornered and I was getting really angry, I was losing what little sleep I ever got and my blood pressure was rising. "Come on, Mary," I kept saying to myself, "get rid of that xxx!" I looked around very carefully but there was no one to go to at TWA who would know what I was talking about or care. Charlie Tillinghast had moved to upper reaches. Ed Meyer did not claim to be an advertising expert—at that moment he was leaning on Don, although in the not-too-distant future he, too, would find Don so difficult he would fire him. But in 1979, as I was contemplating the full price we'd pay to resign the TWA business, there was no one to appeal to at TWA.

A solution slowly eased up to me. Deregulation, which in my view ruined the quality and maybe even some of the safety of airline travel, was looming, was about to become a fact of life. Every U.S. trunk airline with the exception of United battled the idea. Almost every one of those airlines was run by a pioneer, someone who had served in World War II and after that had devoted his life to aviation. Politicians and the academics who promoted deregulation claimed the heads of the airlines had a vested interest in the status quo, but you know and I know that politicians and academics can be wrong. In fact, at that time almost every airline chief executive officer who went before Congress in the fight was nearing retirement, and if anyone had cared to look they would have seen a deeply touching group of idealists who had devoted their lives to building what was the finest air-transportation system in the world, with clean, safe planes, excellent service and fares half those in Europe.

On Harding's turn before the committees in the Senate and House of Representatives he made predictions. He said that United, the only holdout airline, was the one airline not opposing deregulation because United was so huge it was not receiving new routes from a regulated government and hadn't received any for a long time. United wanted deregulation so it could enter and leave markets at will, its dream of becoming the General Motors of the airline industry would come true. American Airlines would become the Ford and Delta would become the Chrysler. That's pretty much what happened. Today those three air-line carriers, combined, dominate the domestic and most international markets. More than 80 start-up airlines have failed. Those still operat-ing handle only dribs and drabs of the flying public. And now we just take for granted that most flights will be ugly, dirty, crowded and rude.

Realizing that medium-size carriers like Braniff would be threatened by deregulation, Harding moved to empower Braniff by taking it into major markets—the Far East, London, Germany, South America. In 1979 he was worrying that his Dallas agency, Gordon & Shortt, was not large enough, didn't have the resources to handle the scope of all Bran-iff's new services that were coming on so fast. George Gordon was a supertalent in promotional advertising. For instance, it was his idea to persuade Alexander Calder to paint a couple of Braniff planes as airmo-biles in a refreshment of Braniff's color program, to the hurrahs of busi-ness groups supporting the arts. The Calder planes were triumphs, they sparked publicity all over the world at very little cost to Braniff. Calder spent a long time in Dallas painting the planes and in the course of things he painted a number of the Braniff mechanics' toolboxes. At first the mechanics were upset, they thought their toolboxes were ruined. But when they learned that in fact their toolboxes had become works of art worth grand sums, they hid their boxes and became adoring fans of Calder's.

I had the thought, in an agency meeting about expansion, that Dal-las was one of the most logical American cities for a Wells Rich Greene branch office. Dallas and its advertising agencies were booming. We wanted to take advantage of the great migration from East to West and we had offices in Los Angeles and Seattle as well as the Gardner agency in St. Louis. That Sunday afternoon, when Harding and I were working in our dining room, stacks of papers all over the table, I told him that I was considering buying an agency in Atlanta or Dallas.

"What do you think about Wells Rich Greene making some sort of deal with George Gordon? Wells Rich Greene has a good agency in London and affiliates all over the world that could handle your expansion." Harding was deep into his papers, in another world. "Mmm," he said, "that sounds good, Tom King is the one to decide, I'll mention it to him, I suppose it would be something that would have to go to the board of directors for approval." Then he looked up and registered what I was suggesting. "What about TWA?" "Well," I said, "I think there could be problems when they notice that Braniff is flying TWA's most important routes." Harding is very gentle when he senses that I am struggling with myself about something. "I doubt that TWA cares about Braniff's routes," he said kindly. "Maybe not," I said, "but we want to set up in either Dallas or Atlanta. See if Tom likes the idea of Wells Rich Greene buying Gordon & Shortt."

While Tom King and George Gordon considered the prospect of an acquisition by Wells Rich Greene, I made my rounds and had one of my many meetings with Linda Wachner, whom I met when she became the marketing vice-president at Warner's and came to me with her small girdle-and-bra account. "Why would we take a girdle-and-bra account?" I asked her, perplexed. I could imagine all the trade ads we would have to make. No, I couldn't imagine them and I didn't want to make them. "We're a television agency," I told her. "We don't do those kinds of trade ads." She was cute, she said, "You never know, I might turn up somebody more important someday."

I've known Linda Wachner since 1974. I am asked about her all the time, as the scope of her career and personality intrigues people. I always say, "Yes, she's brilliant at what she does, she has an astute, inventive mind. Yes, she has a formidable gift for numbers. Yes, she has aggressively expressed opinions. Yes, she's tough, she doesn't fool around. Yes, she's generous, insanely generous, and loyal and sentimental, she cries at A&P openings. Yes, she likes her creature comforts. If you work relentless 24-hour days in the Mexican hills where the factories are and the marijuana grows, you prefer private planes to Range Rovers. And yes, she is a bundle of joy to work with, if she respects you. But almost nobody knows her. She unfurls so many fans, as much to confuse herself as to confuse you, that she has succeeded in creating a masterwork of confusion about who she is. I know two things for sure. Linda will see the problems that nobody else sees, and she'll be there to catch them and try to fix them long after everyone else has gone down the elevator to their other lives (a sense in her that I have an empathy for). And when she is all alone, when the fans are folded, she is not much more than a puppy who doesn't have any family to love. I know there are people who will not believe that, but I do.

We had a few wonderful years with Linda at Warner's, realizing her inventions such as "Starkers," the first stretch bra, and, with Murray Jacobs, our head of package design, her concept of taking the bra out of the drawer in the lingerie department and hanging it out for all the world to see. Murray designed bra packages as squares that could be hung and gave them great poster photographs. You could not only see them, you could see them from a mile away. That idea of Linda's transformed the industry and Warner's. Neither was ever the same. Women began to buy bras in a new way, grabbing three and four at a time, a far cry from when they were led to a fitting room so they could "try it on." With the new stretch bras you didn't need to try them on; with the new hanging packages you didn't even need a saleslady.

When she became Warner's vice-president of marketing, Phil Lamourex, her boss, said to her, "I know how aggressive you are. But remember, it took 100 years for a woman to become a vice-president of this company. So don't have bigger plans." Not many years later she returned and bought the company, I think she was the first woman to complete a hostile takeover of any company. In the meantime, however, Dave Mahoney hired her to be the president of Max Factor. When he was looking for a president, Dave, who was a good friend, asked me for a suggestion and Linda was my suggestion. We had years of feisty fun together, with Max Factor promotions like the one in which actress Jaclyn Smith says, "Part of the art of being a woman is knowing when

not to be too much of a lady"—a great, hokey line of our copywriter Joy
Goldin's.

Tom King and George Gordon decided that a Wells Rich Greene
Gordon agency in Dallas would be ideal for Braniff as the airline
became more and more international. By then I had it all planned in
my mind. We arranged to acquire a majority interest in Gordon &
Shortt's Dallas–Fort Worth office. I spoke to a few of our best TWA
executives whom we would want to move to Dallas as quickly as possible to go to work on Braniff advertising and to Bill Luceno and Chuck
Damon, whom I wanted to head up the new office as the president and
creative director. Then I got on a plane to Rome, where TWA was holding its annual international meetings. All of TWA's executives were
there, not one of them would have imagined I was coming to Rome to
resign the account. TWA was unresignable in the sense that it was such
a large and important advertising account for an agency. But it was
resignable in my eyes in 1979.

I'm gonna wash that man right outa my hair

The Rome Hilton, where the TWA meetings were being held, sits
high on one of Rome's seven hills, and that afternoon everything
that had ever been gilded in Rome was blazing in the late-day sun, a
sight of such grandeur it made me feel utterly insignificant, shattering
the aplomb I had landed with—probably because I was scared stiff. I
had a moment, standing there looking down on centuries of Rome,
thinking, "What am I doing here on this hill in Rome resigning a $30
million account? I have to be stark staring mad." I felt a blast of adrenaline and another blast of hatred for everybody at Wells Rich Greene
and TWA who had put me in that position. I was a martyr marching
into the hotel lobby, where, instead of lions, there were dozens of TWA
employees I knew having a coffee break or a cigarette. "Hi, Mary!" they
shouted, one by one. Warm smiles. Sweet fellows. "Hi, guys," I replied.

I saw Charlie Tillinghast having an argument on the other side of the lobby. He saw me and stopped and smiled his great smile and waved. I got into the elevator. "I am crazy," I thought, for by now I was dizzy, furious, weak and bordering on dementia. Then I had a vision. Sandy Meisner was on the elevator with me and he handed me a script. I had a part to play. So I reached for something mature that I knew was in me somewhere, and when I got off the elevator, where Ted Barash was waiting, hardly breathing—the poor man didn't know what to expect—I was smiling.

I had asked Ted, who was attending TWA's conference, to arrange my meeting with Don Casey and Ed Meyer, but first we met alone in a room he had reserved for me so that I could give him my prepared story. I explained to him that Braniff was becoming more and more competitive with TWA, that in the near future my relationship with Harding would put Charlie Tillinghast, Don and Ed and all the others at TWA in a terrible position, after 11 years with Wells Rich Greene they would feel they had to be honorable, but they would resent the conflict of interest. I had decided that the best thing for all concerned was to return to Braniff as its agency and at the same time take Wells Rich Greene to Dallas by acquiring a major interest in Braniff's agency, Gordon & Shortt.

Ted had leaned against the wall and then he seemed to freeze, I couldn't see him blink and he was losing color very quickly. I went to him and rubbed his face, it was ashen and cold and I thought, in a panic, that I was giving Ted Barash a heart attack. I whispered to him, "Ted, Ted, it's all right, it's going to be fine, you are going to be fine, great, wonderful, there is nothing to worry about, this is the right thing to do and I promise you, I promise you, you will be glad, you will be fine." I went on and on and on. Finally he came to, his eyes focused and he breathed big deep breaths and then he held his hands over his ears and walked around the room sobbing. I just sat down and waited. Finally, the storm let up and, still wiping his eyes with his handkerchief, he told me what a terrible mistake I was making—terrible, terrible, terrible. Then Don and Ed arrived.

They greeted me pleasantly but when they took a good look at Ted they became very quiet, mystified. I was truly shaking by then, there was no doubt about how upset I was when I told them what I had just told Ted—including the fact that we had already purchased the majority interest in Gordon & Shortt, so there was no turning back. We were not a happy group. They were nonplussed, they didn't know what in the world to say. They believed me that we had made the decision out of concern for a conflict of interest, although they protested they were not concerned about a conflict of interest. They could see that moving the agency into Dallas was a rational business decision. They resented finding out about the decision at the last minute and they certainly didn't like the idea that anybody would resign the TWA advertising account. But I think they were sad, really sad, to break up with the agency. Did I feel any glee? Oh, no. I felt sorry for everybody, especially me. I just wanted to get out of that hotel and move on.

From Rome I flew to La Fiorentina, our home in the south of France, where Harding was entertaining Bob Six and his wife, Audrey Meadows. After working together so well at Continental, Bob and Harding had deep roots, they could tell each other anything. At dinner he told Bob that I had resigned TWA and was taking Wells Rich Greene into Dallas. Bob said—prophetically, it turned out—"Well, if you ever have an opening in the future, Mary, do me a favor, call me first. Continental needs an agency like Wells Rich Greene. You people understand the airline business." I put those words into my diary.

Unforgettable

Ah, La Fiorentina. Most people who speak of it let out little sighs and look at me curiously, as if in owning it I am someone from a mysterious planet. It is so otherworldly beautiful. It is not a house, it is not real estate, it's a fantasy of what heaven might be like if things go

right. There it sits, on the tip of the peninsula of Cap Ferrat, surrounded by water on three sides. Monte Carlo twinkles a few miles to
the left, and sometimes you think you see Corsica straight ahead, way
out in the distance, in the cobalt-blue Mediterranean. Boats of all sizes
and designs sashay around La Fiorentina, staging a ballet all day long.
As you gaze out to sea, and you can gaze for hours, you understand why
Cézanne, Renoir, Monet, Signac, Matisse and Bonnard painted such
wonders in this one small part of the world and how, in a Europe that
was so often dark, they rejoiced to find year-long sun filtered so that the
living colors of the area are broken into dots and daubs or veiled so that
the sea becomes lavender, the sun pink and the moon a silvered pink or
flaming crimson, never ordinary white.

During the war the Nazi high command occupied La Fiorentina,
expecting the Allies to land nearby. When they left, as they trucked
their belongings out past the gates of the entrance courtyard with its
rows of whitewashed orange trees, they accidentally blew up the fortifi-
cations they'd built, a maze of bunkers. Years later we found their
toothbrushes and socks and books where the bunkers had been, freaks
of fate. The architecture of the villa was Florentine. When the owners
returned they rebuilt it in a Palladian style and gave it two long rows of
tall cypress trees that marched gracefully down broad grass steps to a
long pool that stretched out and spilled over into the sea. Everyone who
ever stood at the bottom of those grass steps and adjusted to the glory
of the view, startlingly wide and open, so free that you have the impression you are on the spot where you will take off from this life—everyone says the same thing. "How do you ever leave here?"

Mary Lasker knew the owners and rented the villa from them every
July: Lady Enid Kenmere, who married five men at least (three of her
husbands had mysterious deaths, adding greatly to her aura), and her
son, Rory Cameron, from whom we bought the villa. Mary invited us
to lunch when she learned that Rory had decided to sell, she knew we
were ambling about the coast looking for a pied-à-terre, three or four
rooms maybe, in St. Tropez, and she figured that if we bought La
Fiorentina she could continue to use it in July. We went to lunch,
walked down those broad, green grass steps to the sea, and midway, I

La Fiorentina, the most beautiful villa on the sea in the
south of France. I dreamt of it when I was 12, living in
Ohio.

had one of my visions, a familiar one. I'd had that vision from the time I was 12 until I was 16, living in Poland, Ohio, when I had no idea that there was such a thing as the south of France. From that vision I knew what lay ahead, I knew everything about La Fiorentina, tree after tree, room after room, as if I had seen it in a movie or in another life. "I think I'm meant to live here," I said to Harding. It wasn't exactly the pied-à-terre we had in mind, but in 1969, when we acquired La Fiorentina, villas in the south of France were not expensive and many needed sprucing up. For a decade or more after the war nobody in France had much faith in the future of the south and little interest in improving villas there.

The international set had lived a stage-set life there in the postwar years, luxurious, sometimes decadent, but without kitchens or much electricity—the cook at La Fiorentina brought fresh food from town for every meal on her bicycle and cooked it on a coal stove, and there was just enough electricity for one reading light in each room. Nevertheless, Enid Kenmere always descended to her candlelit dinners in her prewar Lucien Lelongs, Robert Piguets, and Lanvins, wearing the cabochon emeralds and rubies her devoted husbands gave her, always with a monkey or her pet hyrax sitting bright-eyed and upright on her shoulder. She was a beauty; she was also said to be a registered addict, like many in her crowd, the more colorful upper classes, many of them from the "happy valley" of Kenya, where Enid's collections of wild animals lived when they weren't with her in France. Although La Fiorentina had no real kitchen, it had cellars full of cages for the wild animals and the big, long-legged, jet-black dogs she kept and walked after midnight.

Whatever Enid Kenmere did to amuse herself in her time, her spirit welcomed us with serene joy. We acquired La Fiorentina knowing we couldn't spend much more than a few weeks a year in France until some unimaginable day when we weren't working the way we did. Mary Lasker continued her July visits, Katy and Pam and my mother grew up in La Fiorentina during the summer—my mother thought of it as her own finishing school—and many millions of dollars later, after it was restored and made hugely comfortable, it became the centerpiece of my secret weapon with clients. The men running other agencies may have been bonding with their clients while chasing little white balls around; I bonded with my clients and their wives at La Fiorentina. Most of them came for long visits, some on their honeymoons, some when Harding and I weren't there and for that time the villa was theirs, but most came for little visits with Harding and me. On hot days Harding would roar them off on the Riva to see the coast from the sea, the best way. They would come back, and at our dock they would tumble out of the boat and shriek as they hit the cool water, then they would collapse, sunburned, on the lounges at the pool. Evenings, with their French windows opened wide so they could see the lights of Monte Carlo and Italy just beyond, they would hear the tinkle of a piano as my Cole Porter pianist would try out a tune and the murmur of the waiters setting out the dinner tables in the pavilion by the sea.

Sometimes Princess Grace of Monaco would come to dinner with my clients. She would arrive as the fairy-tale princess she knew they expected. She would wear rose-petal chiffon and it would move like wings as she went about meeting people. She would smile and rest her lovely eyes on the men and they would forget everyone else. Their wives never minded, Grace was a dream, everyone was bewitched. One evening I seated her at dinner next to a client I particularly adored and watched him fall in love. Women do these little benevolences for each other. Grace knew that her performance could make my dinner party unforgettable and she would be as charming as a human can be. About midnight she would sweep a group out to the seawall, she would dance a few little steps and then sit in the center of the moon's spotlight and, with a little wave, create a magic circle around her. She teased and flirted. She would consider the possibility of skinny-dipping in the moonlit sea, she would dare my clients, and for a while such a thing seemed possible, even likely.

She never went skinny-dipping, but the spell would be cast. The night my adored client fell in love with Grace we all dallied at the steps to the sea after she left, still laughing at the possibilities. My adored client did a little samba by himself—we didn't know he could samba, it was like learning a secret. The moon laughed with us, we could feel it like a narcotic as we went back to the villa, to bed, enchanted, smiling. Then I thought of my male competitors on their golf courses and I laughed again, to myself.

We bought a small, talented company that specialized in creating and positioning new products, Doherty, Mann & Olshan, and that is when I met Ken Olshan, who eventually became the chairman of the agency. We had a glamorous screening room in the New York office—it had cashmere walls, expensive leather-and-chrome chairs that swiveled when you swiveled and allowed you to have an attitude or pose, everyone felt famous in that room. Charlie, Al Wolfe and Marty Stern interviewed Ken there and I met him for only a few minutes but I could tell immediately that he was one of those people who can bicycle and chew gum at triple speed, capable of sectioning his mind and energy so that he could operate over a broad spectrum. After he'd been at Wells Rich Greene a few months I looked at him one day, saw intelligence and ambition shining in his eyes and energy leaping out of his pores, and thought, "Ah—an apprentice!" But he was still new to us, he did not know Wells Rich Greene, he would need to learn our mercurial culture that erupted in moments of breathtaking talent, courage and improvisation as well as frustrating and feverish late nights of last-minute work, not to mention moments of depressed overload. He needed to understand why that culture achieved all it did, why it was so hot, why people who worked there felt it was the best time of their lives, how to keep that spirit alive, how to make people feel safe and appreciated and defended and still run a serious, stable, moneymaking business if he was going to become a partner with Charlie and me, who were aging fast with success. "You've got another grey hair," Charlie would say, squinting at me, but it was his hair that was greying. We made Ken the creative director, firmly under Charlie's wing, for a time, to baptize him, and later we introduced him to Procter & Gamble as the executive they dreamed of who was creative enough yet strategic enough to find the way to bridge our different cultures and enable us to have what both of our companies longed for: a mutual vision.

I was impressed with how happy Ken was with Wells Rich Greene and his various roles in it, how delighted he was with the challenges and problems and opportunities he encountered and with himself as he developed what he thought of as the new muscles he needed to wrestle with all those things. Although many graduates of Wells Rich Greene say, "Those were the happiest years of my life," you wouldn't have known it at the time. There is an ethic in superhot creative advertising agencies that says you are permitted to work yourself to death and never leave the agency, like some mad mole, so long as you don't appear to be happy about it and do your share of moaning and groaning, the agency anthem. So at first I was wary of Ken's joie de vivre and boundless enthusiasm, but I got used to it and decided it was genetic and not the sign of some impending mental problem. He was voracious about learning. In short order he absorbed the gist of every department's responsibilities and talents, something no one else ever quite did, so as the agency continued to grow, so did Ken Olshan. He was also devoted. No matter how large the problem or opportunity, I could count on him to be in my office, every ounce of his intelligence and talent on alert, with all of his impressive willpower and passion revved up for battle.

His cheerful ambition to inhale the entire agency galled many of the others. One of the reasons for the Mary cult at Wells Rich Greene was that I saw the agency as an intimate family I cherished, understood and forgave. There was an irreverence in the climate and there was candor because everyone knew that I cherished, understood and forgave. Coming into that atmosphere after it had become a creed, Ken's ambition, which sometimes seemed evangelistic, looked preposterous to the tight crew of originals, who resented that he presumed to manage and, as he was an alien, might ruin something important—maybe the agency, maybe their lives.

I don't know if Ken understood any of this then. Charlie and I ignored it, and after Ken stood tall and accepted responsibility for, first, Procter & Gamble and, later, a string of accounts, as the agency grew and changed, he duly became accepted as one of the masters of its fate.

It was on Ken's watch at Procter & Gamble that our relationship with Procter became more architectural and we finally accepted their aspirations of brand immortality and the process that required. As a result, our meetings became easier. "You have to give Ken Olshan credit," I said to Charlie, "our Procter meetings are getting positively mellow." It was also on Ken's watch that Procter gave us Pringles, although when we first got Pringles the best thing about them was the tennis-ball can they were packed in. When Pringles first appeared people viewed the can with delight and bought stacks of them and used them for storing things. Procter looked at the sales charts, rubbed its hands and said, "Oh, good, we have a hit here!" But the chips tasted like cardboard, so nobody ate them twice. Procter assigned Pringles to Wells Rich Greene just as they were about to give up on them; it was like seeing my life pass before my eyes—it was Bugles, Whistles and Daisies come back to haunt me again, cute snacks people wanted to play with, not eat. Pringles had nine lives, though. The Procter brand group and the agency were determined to make a success of Pringles; they developed into a club and used clubby expressions and hand signals too infantile to reveal, and as a group they had enough will to burn. Their death-defying tenacity, not always appreciated on Procter's top floor, got Pringles off its burial mound and reformulated into tasty, crunchy chips you could not stop eating. Bob Gill and my stepson, State Lawrence, saw such potential in Pringles chips they turned their lives over to them and pushed them into every country, every culture, every universe, stunning the Lay's potato chip mafia.

Our Pringles advertising lit the fire and got the brand going. It was one of two campaigns that survived our prodigious testing. The other campaign achieved an astronomical Burke research score, and because of that score most Procter executives and most Wells Rich Greene executives voted for it. But Procter star Steve Donovan, who was the big daddy of Pringles, agreed with Charlie and me that the other campaign, the one with the slightly lower test score, was the one with the magic. There was a lot of squabbling over the two campaigns. One morning Steve called me and suggested that I call John Smale, the new chairman of Procter, and persuade him to back our choice. John and I had worked on many campaigns together before he became chairman; he is an attractive man with a peppery personality that masks a gleam of mischief he struggles to hide. I could feel Steve Donovan smiling at me over the telephone, guessing my reluctance to call the chairman of Procter about a commercial. "If there is one thing John knows it is that you would not call him unless your convictions are enormous, he understands you." So I called John and he backed our choice and the right campaign went on the air and now every child who has ever seen a television set can sing our copywriter Larry Sokolove's tongue-twister jingle, "I've got a fever for the flavor of a Pringle."

My first board membership was of the May Company board, a frisky board that, because of its retail interests, was intent on staying as current and cool as possible. I enjoyed that board but resigned because it met all over America so frequently I found myself spending more time sitting on tarmacs waiting for planes to take off than running the agency. I was also a member of the Sun Oil board for many years while Robert Sharborough and Ted Burtis were chairmen, a board that made me conversant, temporarily, on subjects like the EPA, so that I was able to impress other heavy industry chieftains.

Hal Dean persuaded me to become a member of the Ralston Purina board, and when he was about to retire I had something to do with Bill Stiritz being chosen as his replacement. For years after the meeting I'd had in Ken Griggy's office that was so difficult for Bill and me, our relationship had been robotic. But when the Ralston board faced the challenge of replacing Hal, who had become a staunch friend of mine and helped me out of a couple of tight spots, especially once when he went over Bill Stiritz's head to stop his executives from stiffing our Los Angeles branch office, I helped Bill Stiritz to become the next chairman. Sometimes you have to take the high road.

I was familiar with the outside candidates being considered for the job, more so than most of the other board members, because sooner or later you meet or learn about everyone if you're in the advertising business. The other candidates simply didn't come up to snuff to Bill. I gave the board the distinct impression that I knew Bill Stiritz was about to be hired away into a powerful position by an important competitor and I was ominous enough to make the imminent loss of Bill a serious element in the consideration of the candidates. The truth was that I did know a competitor of Ralston's who was looking seriously at Bill for its top job and was calling me about him regularly, but the company hadn't reached the point of talking to Bill yet. So I was stretching the facts, you could say. After careful deliberation Bill Stiritz became the next chairman at Ralston, and he did an excellent job for the company and the stockholders.

Harding had an interesting board at Braniff that included a passel of politically astute businessmen from the areas of America that Braniff served, influential bankers like Gus Levy of Goldman Sachs. He also had three heroines on his board, three can-do women who left most of the male board members in the dust: Ann Chambers, the former ambassador to Britain; Mary Lasker, who was pouring money into the coffers of congressmen who voted for cancer research; and Pamela Harriman, Randolph Churchill's daughter-in-law and hostess, who had married a Washington chief, Averell Harriman.

Joe Cullman was another luminary on Harding's board. Harding met and liked him when I began working with Philip Morris. Joe was also on the Ford Motor Company board. It was that buddy sense that a board of directors spawns among its members that made Harding call Joe, pull him out of a Ford board meeting, and suggest that he tell Henry he should include Wells Rich Greene in Ford's search for an agency to handle its corporate advertising. Joe, when he was told that Harding's call was urgent, left the board meeting expecting to hear that someone had died. For years he could only sputter when he told me, as he did over and over again, that Harding had actually had the gall to pull him out of a Ford board of directors meeting just to get me an invitation to pitch for the Ford corporate advertising account. Joe did it, though; he convinced Henry, and I received a call from John Bowers, Ford's corporate advertising director, inviting Wells Rich Greene to make a presentation.

Those were the days

It was early 1979 when we made our presentation to Ford. The 1973–74 oil embargo had turned the world upside down, and by that time gasoline prices in the United States were 80 percent higher than they had been in 1970. Small, fuel-efficient foreign cars were running all over the place like ants. American cars had disappeared in California, more than 80 percent of the cars there were Japanese, the United States car market had slumped to ten and a half million, as low as anyone could remember, and it would go on slipping to barely eight million cars by 1982. Overnight, as if a wand had been waved, people decided to buy small imported cars, not big cars, and as a result 300,000 people lost their jobs with American car companies. Forty factories closed. Two thousand dealers went out of business. Nobody knew, in 1979, just how far down down would be, and Detroit had no magic to correct the situation quickly. There was a hallucinatory sign on the road near Ford's Rouge plant that clocked the cars built by the company like a thermometer, reminding Ford every day just how badly things were going. I used to imagine slipping out in the inky-black night and chopping down that awful sign.

The night before we were scheduled to interview a group of executives and factory workers at Ford who were to tell us all about the problems that Ford's corporate campaign should address, five of us flew to Detroit. We had reservations at a hotel in the Renaissance Center in downtown Detroit, an area that Henry Ford and others were trying valiantly to resuscitate but was being swamped by recession and inflation and Detroit's disappearing car market. The hotel was new, a skyscraper with heavenly heights of shining marble and glass. It had a manic grandeur in what was then an eerily abandoned downtown. We saw no porters, just one small, hungry-looking man in a grey suit who bit his nails while helping us at the check-in desk. He was glad to welcome humans and told me that the management wanted to give us their palatial penthouse apartment at a giveaway rate. It had five bedrooms, he promised, plus a variety of sitting and dining areas and 360 degrees of thrilling views. He escorted us up an elevator that rose with breakneck speed to the penthouse, where he unlocked a series of doors, waved his arms left and right to indicate the scope of the suite and suggested we choose whatever bedrooms we liked, handed us menus with long golden tassels and streamers, indicated the wraparound views of the city, and told us to call room service for anything in the world we wanted. Then he disappeared down a rabbit hole. We walked to the walls of glass and peered down. "Look," I said, "there are no lights in this hotel between us up here and the lobby down there." The hotel was nothingness for floors and floors beneath us, we were like Martians viewing earth below. We may have been the only guests. We never saw a maid, it all seemed a lark until it sunk in on us that the hotel was a metaphor for what was happening to Detroit and to the American automobile industry.

People who are depressed turn off the lights. I've seen friends do it, we saw American Motors do it and the first thing we noticed walking down the halls of the Ford Motor Company in Dearborn were the rows of dark offices. Many were empty, but some were inhabited furtively by people working only by desk lamp. Even the halls and meeting rooms had half of the lights turned off. There was a spooky, shadowy look in the building that made everyone walk close to the walls and talk just above a whisper. Charlie whispered to me, "I think they're afraid." "Well," I murmured, "when I'm afraid, the first thing I do is turn *on* the lights. All this darkness is depressing." The men we met in those dim offices told us that the buildup of recessions, inflation, gasoline shortages, rationing, harsh government regulation and the total lack of sympathy in Washington, on Wall Street and among American automobile buyers had produced a crisis that was *not their fault* and couldn't be cured in the time they had. They were as resentful as hell. "The country thinks we're dumb here in Detroit, they'd just as soon buy Japanese. They think the Japanese are the smart ones and we're the dumb ones," they said.

On top of all that, there had been a sea change in management. Henry had sent Lee Iacocca packing, some of the men we talked to were in deep mourning for Lee, and although the word was that the heroes of Ford Europe, Philip Caldwell, Red Poling and Donald Peterson, were importing their successful ideas, nobody we talked to knew what those ideas were yet. "We don't have a hot, high-tech, fuel-efficient small car ready to roll, we're just getting over the Pinto, and let's face it, there isn't a car in America that compares with the quality of the foreign cars!" They all pretty much agreed. "People don't want to buy a Ford, they don't believe in Ford, we've lost it!"

One man, sitting in the corner of his office in something like a fetal position, kept rubbing his eyes as if he feared there were tears in them. He got on my nerves, and after a while I asked him why he didn't turn his lights on and go join the grand plan. "There has to be one," I told him. "Philip Caldwell was a smash success in Europe. He'll be a smash success here." The man I'd attacked straightened his shoulders and told me crisply that I had no way of understanding the situation, and by the way, was I aware that the executives of the company had already agreed among themselves to give the corporate advertising account I craved to Ogilvie & Mather? He smiled meanly. I'd asked for that, so I had to laugh and he laughed too, and then he admitted he'd made up that bit about Ogilvie.

Luckily, before catching a flight back to New York, we were taken through a factory that had been organized for tour groups to display some of Ford's good ideas in cars and trucks. That factory tour gave us the inspiration we needed. The Ford Motor Company we witnessed in that tour was smart and confident and capable of an exciting future. It wasn't the product they had to show that was convincing—there wasn't any real product news there—it was the attitude in that factory tour that was inspirational, because it was hopeful. Hope struck us as Ford's strong suit in the immediate future. We had to make something tangible out of hope.

I told Marty Stern and our research department to find out what automobile buyers really thought about buying a Ford at that moment and what they really felt about the Ford Motor Company. "We have to look into their hearts, where their loyalty is, where their patriotism is— somewhere in those hearts there has to be some negative feelings about the Japanese and Germans, don't you think? Schmooze them about the Lincoln Town Car, the Thunderbird and the Mustang, even the Model T, and see what comes up—what do they feel? Tell them Ford is just about to roll out the highest-quality, most gas-efficient cars in the world—small cars that are roomy and luxurious inside and oh so beautiful, slippery and aerodynamic outside—cars that are going to look like a million dollars but are going to cost less than a Toyota. See if you can make them hungry for those cars." Marty was impressed. "They sound great, when will they roll out?" I crossed my eyes at him. "Marty, use your head, we need serious ammunition to present a campaign about love to those people at Ford or they'll laugh us out of town. We'll worry about the new cars later." We agreed to spend whatever it took for first-class psychological research and to reach significant numbers of people quickly. Our experience with American Motors had taught us to stand on respectable information when we were controversial.

We knew absolutely nothing about Ford's product plans. We had not met Philip Caldwell, let alone Henry Ford, we hadn't met anyone who knew very much about the revolution that was being plotted at the top of Ford that would eventually reinvent the company, we knew nothing about Ford's aerodynamics, the "aero look" or anything else about the smart cars in their master plan. We'd been invited into the arena at the last minute merely as a favor to Joe Cullman, there was barely time to blink. We wanted to win the account, so we just stepped out into the cold thin air and flew on faith that management was fully aware that time was precious, that it would take scary amounts of time for Ford to create a complete turnaround in the United States. We thought the only meaningful contribution that corporate advertising could make at that critical hour would be to produce a wave of fresh confidence in Ford among Ford owners, new car buyers, Washington critics, the press and, most important of all, among those downtrodden souls who were sitting in those dark offices at Ford. We had to get them to turn their lights on.

It's all there!" Marty Stern came charging into my office all smiles. "There's a gold mine of good feelings out there—you can count on it!" Marty was very excited. He staggered into our boardroom with stacks of papers and booklets followed by a tired army of research consultants and their assistants. "It's deep-rooted, but when you touch a nerve it glows, it's palpable, and when you pump you get fireworks!" Oh, that made me feel good. I'd counted on a reservoir of goodwill towards Ford. I had suggested "Ford, That's Incredible" to Charlie as an exuberant shout of confidence and he had gone ahead and written commercials and Steve Karmen had already created an "Incredible" marching song we were crazy about, the kind that makes people salute.

[*Music:*] *If we could take you through the plant*
   To show you what is new
   And let you see what's going on
   And watch the things we do,
   If you could see the cars and trucks
   We're working on for you,
   You'd say, INCREDIBLE, FORD, THAT'S INCREDIBLE.
   If you knew how much money
   We're spending every day
   To help us find the way,
   If you could see tomorrow
   The way it looks to us today,
   You'd say, INCREDIBLE, FORD, THAT'S INCREDIBLE.

NARRATOR: Introducing the incredible Ford factory tour. Come
and see the things we're doing to rethink, redesign, reshape the
automobile, incredible things to produce a new generation of
more fuel-efficient cars and trucks.

[Music:] *If you could see tomorrow*
   How it looks to us today,
   You'd say, INCREDIBLE, FORD, THAT'S INCREDIBLE.

We made our first presentation to the executives of the Ford Motor
Company about a week before I went to Rome to resign the TWA
account.

Sometimes getting your arms around an advertising agency is like
reassembling Saint Teresa—important parts are to be found all over the
place. One minute I was in Rome, the next I was walking through real
estate in downtown Dallas looking for a site for our new branch office
and the next I was eyeing a building in Newport Beach to house the
Century 21 account. Then, suddenly, there I was trying to transform a
small, nondescript meeting room at Ford World Headquarters into a
theatre capable of a major moment in Ford history. It had a murky little screening room; I was told that Henry sometimes watched presenta-

tions unannounced there. Well, I thought, as we stacked our story-boards on the floor against the wall and set up a music player—bare bones—sometimes that's the best background you can have if you're going to present a surprise.

Charlie was giving the "Ford, That's Incredible" music a trial run when the door opened and everybody arrived at once, a roomful of Ford executives who looked alert and curious and amused and bemused. There were about 12 of them and just a few of us from the agency. I loved moments like that when I was the only woman in the group. I knew that once everyone was seated I could count to five and every head would turn to me for the show to begin. I didn't have to be told who Philip Caldwell was, he was the man who came in wearing the title and the responsibility, immaculate in a fine suit—an orderly, disciplined man, but you could tell he had deep rivers of passion for success, he wouldn't tire until he achieved it. I adored him from the first second and he proved to be up to the enormous task ahead. He came into the room that day with his eyes dancing to our marching music, he said later that it had slipped in under the door of his office and had been a very happy experience. He was followed by a beguiling gentleman with an English actor's haircut, eyeglasses that he must have trained to drop low on his nose so that he could peer at things incognito, casual sloping shoulders—he was obviously more a playwright than a Detroit executive. He was Walter Hayes, the vice-president of public affairs, and he would turn out to be a godsend. The charmer in the room, the good-looking, witty one, just a tad world-weary, who I guessed was vice-president of marketing or sales, Ben Bidwell, was welcoming enough, but he was so obviously amused I knew he thought we didn't stand a chance of getting the account.

We got the account. Our conviction and our proof that there was a deep abiding love for Ford in the hearts and minds of Americans, a love that we advised them to lift heaven and earth to bring to the surface because it was priceless and magical and would buy them the time they needed, convinced Philip Caldwell and most of the others. They did indeed know they needed time to keep their captive car buyers from buying Japanese cars until the new high-tech Fords rolled around, and to keep their dealers in place and make them believe. They needed time to change the bad press they were getting into positive press and to change the perplexing, scolding attitude towards Detroit in Washington. Their grand plan—one of the biggest industrial revolutions in history when you consider everything Detroit finally accomplished in the early eighties—had just begun and we wouldn't see the proof of the pudding for a while. They were deeply worried at Ford about their customers, their dealers, their employees. Love sounded good to them.

I gave them a motherly lecture on confidence, the need to demonstrate confidence flat out. The world needed to see and to smell a confident Ford Motor Company at that very moment when things were at their worst. People buy from winners, not losers. "For God's sake, turn on the lights in this building," I told them, "it looks like you're getting ready to die here."

Ben Bidwell told me that when I began talking about how much America loved Ford and how important that love was he thought to himself, "Oh, come on, nobody here is going to buy that sappy love stuff." And then he looked around the table and thought, "Holy shit, they *are* buying it." Philip Caldwell and Walter Hayes understood all about love. They understood why our first commercials focused on the local factory tour and the supremely confident marching music. They understood turning on the lights as a metaphor for lighting up the company and giving it confidence and energy and belief in the future. They called me soon after the meeting to give us the good news. We went to work on the Incredible Factory Tour and a few of us moved into Ford World Headquarters for a spell to learn all we could about Ford's grand plan.

A couple of months later I got a call asking Charlie and me to fly to Detroit the following morning to make a private presentation of our thinking and the advertising to Henry Ford. Charlie had taken the day off, it was July and he was in the Hamptons and he had only a white suit there. "I can't make a presentation to Henry Ford in a white suit!" he complained over the phone. "You don't have time to get another suit. Henry Ford is a sophisticated man. He'll think it's the latest thing, especially when he sees your new electrified haircut."

Ford's World Headquarters in Dearborn had a penthouse with bedrooms for board members, dining rooms, a small gymnasium. It wasn't a lavish place, but it was a formal place where you wouldn't laugh very loud. Charlie and I were taken to a board of directors room so big the Detroit Lions could have played a game there. The board table, another vast tree, was the shape of a U and Henry's chair was at the saddle of it. He hadn't arrived, so Charlie and I tried out different places to stand to make our presentation to him, but most of the room required a microphone. All alone in that gargantuan room waiting for the real Henry Ford to appear, we developed terrible stage fright. I was sure my voice would shake. The neurons in my neocortex must have frozen, my mind was out of my control. Charlie said later that he felt like Quasimodo in a white suit about to take a great fall. I am not exaggerating these feelings—every once in a while in ad biz you are overwhelmed by your own presumptuousness. Then some trick entrance behind Henry's chair stirred and Henry appeared out of nowhere. After looking at the two of us with some astonishment, I thought, he smiled at us warmly, shook my hand, almost bowed and looked fondly at Charlie. "Please," he said, "I have heard about your good ideas and I am eager to see your presentation."

Charlie and I stood opposite Henry, inside the saddle of the table; we were pretty well joined at the hip, me expounding on America's love for Ford and Charlie singing and dancing to demonstrate the commercials. I was in charge of the music player, and our anthem, "Ford, That's Incredible," had just begun with all its bravado when the trick door behind Henry stirred again and an arm shot out with a telegram in its hand and waved wildly at Henry.

He took the telegram, excused himself and read it. I turned off the music and Charlie stopped dancing. Henry absorbed his news and then shared it. "Carter's sacked his entire cabinet and the White House staff, he's asked them to resign thanks to their idiotic handling of the fuel crisis. You know his ratings are up since his last speech, I think it was because he wore a sweater, made him look real for some reason, but I think he's blown his future. Depends on who he replaces them all with." Henry looked at Charlie expectantly and Charlie happily started to discuss Carter with him but I nudged him. "Charlie, the cars," I said, and we picked up where we'd left off, singing and dancing. I'd give anything for a film of it.

Henry liked the whole thing. He asked us to go through it all twice. "I like that music, can you leave it with me? I think we should play it in the halls." And they did play it in the halls. They played it all over the place. It was cheering. And they turned on the lights.

Charlie won every award there was for the Incredible Factory Tour commercials, even from the Japanese, and to everyone's amazement thousands of people lined up to take the tour. We hadn't counted on that. Ford wasn't in the tour business, the factory tour was a local pleasantry, but the goodwill towards Ford that I had become messianic about turned out to be easy to trigger. I think people love to love, given a chance. At first all those people standing in lines to take the tour seemed a euphoric success, many of them came from long distances, Montana and Wyoming. But after six weeks of traffic jams and parking tickets and exhausted tour directors at the factory who were not really equipped for that scenario we stopped advertising the tour and moved on in the campaign.

There was an acute sense of emergency in the air all during this time. Ford's stock had dropped to a low of 17 and Wall Street was full of gloom and doom and predictions that Ford would be looking for a bailout like Chrysler's. To convince Wall Street, Washington and everybody else that the Ford Motor Company was alive and well we created a "confidence" campaign about the success Ford was having with its small, high-tech cars in Europe, with satellites, aerospace, electronics, aerodynamics, with tractors and with racing. It is difficult to assess the effect of any corporate campaign, but at a make-or-break time this one turned the thinking of a number of influentials in powerful places, and it definitely made a difference at Ford. After a couple of years of the campaign the *Wall Street Journal* gave us a special award and a fancy lunch for beating their Starch readership records religiously, year after year.

We were the agency for attitudes towards Ford, but not for the automobiles themselves. Ford was unyieldingly territorial about its agencies. Ford cars and trucks were tenured at J. Walter Thompson.

Mercury was tenured at Young & Rubicam. When we would try to use a Ford or Mercury in a corporate ad to make a point, we were seen as sharks trying to slip into the feeding pens of J. Walter Thompson or Young & Rubicam. Some of this loyalty came about because of the maze of complications when a corporation is in partnership with dealerships. But much of it was a high-church belief that automobiles actually sold themselves with their sheet metal and chrome and their bells and whistles. Historically, the unveiling of a new year's car models was a theatrical event in every small town in America. The local dealers' glass windows were stages and everybody came to town to see the red velvet cover removed from the new model, as thrilling an act as the lowering of Andrew Lloyd Webber's wondrous chandelier. So for a very long time advertising was seen as a necessary competitive action but not as an ultimately decisive one.

Our position, as the agency for corporate advertising, would have been unnervingly fragile except that Americans had fallen in love with Japanese automobile workers and were seeing the American autoworkers as inept slouches who were foisting off cars low in quality, durability and reliability on them. Henry and Philip Caldwell had been visionary enough to see that quality was the issue coming to haunt all of the industrial areas of the United States and they intended to reinvent Ford as the manufacturer that would set the ultimate standards in automobile durability, quality and reliability as well as in design, beauty and comfort. Such ambition required not only hoards of financial resources but also courage and conviction.

An intrinsic part of the puzzle would be the Ford autoworker, who was frightened like everybody else in Detroit. Red Poling had joined Philip Caldwell in the move from Ford Europe to Detroit, he was the inside production man. Somebody said he was an ice-water kind of guy, but I thought he was simply clearheaded and direct, you always knew what he really thought. I loved the fact that he cared so deeply about the workers, their understanding of the grand plan, their willingness to believe in it and to do their part.

We had a couple of discussions with him about what our campaign could do to enlist the workers in Ford's drive to improve durability, quality and reliability. Charlie and Bob Cox carved out the bones of a campaign in which Ford's workers became the spokesmen for Ford corporate and we took it back to Red for his reactions. He was pleased that the campaign starred the Ford workers, but then he discovered Bob planned to use actors, not the workers themselves, in the commercials. "Why would you use actors when you can have the real thing, the real workers?" He was pacing in an Indian circle around us. We tried to explain that actors make better workers in commercials than real workers, but that just made him furious, so Charlie jumped to his feet and began to hire all the workers at the Ford Motor Company right then and there on the spot. As he described each man in detail as a potential Paul Newman I could see Red lighten up, yes, he liked it, he liked it, and he not only approved the campaign, he took ownership of it, guaranteeing it and Wells Rich Greene a long life.

Charlie and I were not satisfied with the theme line of that advertising and we tussled over it for a few days. I was also caught up in a major disagreement with Philip Morris at the time, so I pushed the Ford campaign to the suburbs of my mind. Then, in the middle of one night (it was always the middle of the night), Charlie called. "I've got it," he purred. Charlie purrs, he puts his lips together and makes a cat's purr. There is no doubting his pleasure with himself when he purrs. I had not slept, I was imagining that I was axing an executive at Philip Morris. I was in a murderous mood. "Charlie, it's three a.m. *What* have you got?" "The line for Ford," he purred. "It was a nocturnal emission." He laughed gaily. "Are you ready?" Long dramatic pause. "Quality is Job One." Long dramatic pause. I didn't get it. "What does 'Job One' mean?" "It's auto-production slang, it means number one in importance," he said. "I am a genius, you know. This is iconic. It will be one of those automotive themes that are recalled by television viewers for years to come." "Try it on Red Poling," I said. "If he understands it, great." Red understood it perfectly. Everybody at Ford understood it, especially the workers, who did in fact become local TV stars, saying "Quality is Job One" on television for years and years.

Burt Manning, the Houdini of J. Walter Thompson, who gave that agency some magnificent moments through the years and who looked over their Ford business, had advised Philip Caldwell that quality was the big issue Ford's corporate advertising should address. Machiavellian Manning. The truth was that Burt thought quality was such a boring, humdrum subject that Wells Rich Greene would impale itself on it and then J. Walter Thompson could waltz along and pick up the account. But one morning he turned on his television and saw our first "Quality is Job One" commercial, starring a member of Red Poling's very talented Ford production line. He says he looked at that production-line worker and swore and told his startled writers that he had no doubt now that Wells Rich Greene would be keeping the Ford corporate account. He saw the whole picture. The impact the advertising would have on the Ford workers themselves would ensure its success.

And it did. Every single time we filmed a worker in his home plant the quality of workmanship at that plant shot up. It was a wonderful thing to see happen. It was as if the whole plant had gone on stage and declared it was personally responsible for the quality coming out of the Ford Motor Company. Plant managers fought to have commercials made in their plants starring their workers. The agency made a drama out of scheduling and orchestrating the filming of the workers, plant by plant. Many workers turned out to be talented spokesmen; their unquestionable sincerity did a lot to shine up the image of the American autoworker in that wintry period.

By the time Henry retired, and later, when Phil Caldwell retired, Ford's grand plan was in high gear and the company was roaring once again, earning record profits, more than General Motors for the first time since 1926. Don Peterson followed Philip as chairman, he loved cars, you could watch him slide his hand over one and get a sense of the way he felt, and he was followed by Red Poling. They weren't exactly buddies, those four fellows, Henry, Philip, Don and Red, they weren't always cozy together, but they were all leaders. My stepson, Jim, became the head of our Detroit office, and we hired Bill Benton, who had been our guide at Ford, to become a sort of supernanny for us. All in all I remember our years at Ford with a warm inner smile.

But the best was knowing Henry.

Harding and Henry met and clicked. They looked at the world

through the same glasses. They were men's men, down to earth, they liked to have a good time but they were serious men and they were worldly, they knew what was going on everywhere and why. Henry had many friends. Some he had been in cahoots with for a long time, like Max Fisher in Detroit; some helped him with his life, like Walter Hayes and his chief lawyer, Frank Chopin, who became a dear friend of Henry's wife Kate's, too, and of Harding's and mine. Henry described Frank to me as "a genius of sorts and a man with a natural inclination to protect you from mischief, bully attacks and warmongers. There are a lot of those people around, you know, Mary," he told me.

Henry and Harding had a lot in common. They were Democrats close to Lyndon Johnson; they were fiercely capable men; they loved to look out for themselves, create their own lifestyles, drive their own cars, make their own plans. Both loved their business lives but had been captive to them long enough to relish the idea of pulling back, and by the time they became friends they were both itching to have more freedom and fun, to feel good. We only began spending prime time with Henry after he married Kate in 1980, and we could see that Kate was going to become an important friend. After they bought a yacht and a plane we would go play with them when we could and they would hang out with us in Mustique and in the south of France.

Henry was crazy about Kate, he loved the straightforward way she loved him. He loved her independence of him, too, her irreverence and humor, the vivid sparkle in her; she would dance for him, stretch and slither her long legs, toss her red mane of hair and grin with devilish eyes. Once, the summer of 1986, Henry and I were paddling about, almost alone in the bay at La Fiorentina, late in the afternoon towards evening when the light was lavender and the sea looked oily in the sun that had dipped below. I was making little lazy swirls in the water and sending them towards Henry and he swirled them back to me. He had gotten a haircut and the barber had given him his money's worth, I told him he looked like one of the Nazis who had occupied La Fiorentina during the war. He laughed and told me to have respect for my elders and reminded me that his previous wife wouldn't even allow me to attend a dinner given for them at a house just a ripple away from where we were floating. He looked up at Kate dozing on our port, a lovely sight with her red hair tangled up into a knot on the top of her head, and then he looked back at me with eyes that smiled deep from his soul. "Oh, Mary, I am a happy man, I am finally a happy man," he beamed at me and sent more little sea swirls at me.

Come fly with me

Harding loved aviation. It had been his vocation and his avocation for 40 years, he loved all it taught him, all the adventures and challenges that were a part of it. But he had flown 300,000 miles a year for a long time, he always had a packed suitcase in his office ready to go. Living like that, ready for anything on a moment's notice, sleeping with one eye half-open expecting the telephone to ring with God knows what, he was tired. When deregulation became a serious issue, he thought it was time for a change, time to spend more time with me and the children, time to enjoy our ranch in Arizona. When Harding daydreamed it was about that ranch and its big blue sky, about never wearing a tie, and living in those jeans of his that were so old it was a miracle they hung on, and about Kimlar, his stallion, a magnificent, intimidating creature with wild eyes. They identified, Kimlar and Harding, they moved as if they were one animal and on those Arizona hills covered with slippery dry stones that gave me palpitations, they were always poised to fly as if *they* were a plane.

"The airline business is a young man's business," Harding said when he told me he was going to leave Braniff. He'd grown up in oil country, so he thought that to satisfy his need for at least some risk in his life he would join Joe Elsbury, a friend in Louisiana, and Doug Faulkner, a friend in Oklahoma, to explore for oil and gas. After he left the airline Wells Rich Greene continued to handle Braniff's advertising for a while, but it was an uncomfortable arrangement for the new management and for us. We parted company, although the agency went on handling Braniff's international business. Harding suggested I call Bob Six, who was still the chairman at Continental, and remind him that he told me to call him when I was free to handle his advertising. I invited Bob and Audrey to meet us at La Fiorentina to discuss possibilities. Bob and Audrey never ever refused an invitation to La Fiorentina, they loved it the way we loved it, and I could tell that Bob was accepting more than the invitation to France, he was rearranging his future to include Wells Rich Greene. I had a date with Tom Labrecque, the president of Chase and one of my all-time favorite clients. He was deeply involved with Marymount College and had asked me to make its commencement address. When I left the school I flew to Nice with Harding to greet the Sixes. We spent that weekend sitting at a table looking over the sunny seas to Italy, working out the details of Wells Rich Greene handling Continental.

It wasn't silky going. Frank Lorenzo had begun a tenacious hostile takeover that, along with the death of his wife, apparently caused Al Feldman, the president of Continental, to lie on the sofa in his office and shoot himself. There were other problems; Continental had the same cash shortages many airlines had in the hurlyburly of deregulation. But Bob was confident, his employees were loyal, the agency knew the business and we knew each other. So we arranged for Wells Rich Greene to make a presentation to George Warde, who was about to become Bob's new president. I called Andre van Stom, who had been a smashing success in our years with TWA, and persuaded him to fly to Wells Rich Greene's Los Angeles office from Australia, where he was living, to help us make the presentation. Howie Cohen and Bob Pasqualina, who had created the "I Can't Believe I Ate the Whole Thing" commercial for Alka-Seltzer, were now the creative executives in our Los Angeles office. They produced an advertising position we all liked, "The Return of the Proud Bird," playing off a campaign from the days when Harding and Bob were running Continental as a team and they called their fleet "the Proud Birds with the Golden Tails."

On the 14th of October Continental announced Wells Rich Greene as their new agency. In November Mike Levine, who had been at the

Civil Aeronautics Board, joined Continental as senior vice-president of marketing. He was an academic, a theorist, but he jumped right into the pot with us. And although at lower levels at Continental there was some irritation at the sudden change of agencies, at the top levels we were an effervescent group—it is exhilarating to work with friends, particularly friends who have courage, intelligence and style. Which is why I was thrilled and not as nervous as I probably should have been when Ed Acker called me only a month later to ask if Wells Rich Greene would handle the Pan Am account and said he saw no problem at all if we continued to work for Continental. "I know you can manage both accounts without a problem," he said. Considering the natures of Bob Six and Ed Acker, I was sure we could, although I knew we would face a Wagnerian uproar on Madison Avenue.

Ed Acker and I had worked together swimmingly when he was the president of Braniff. He is the kind of man who relishes big ideas, not only because he is courageous, although he is one of the most unflappable men I ever worked with, but because he understands the results a good idea will produce. He had understood every step Harding and I had taken in the color program at Braniff and our reasoning. He had left Braniff and gone to Air Florida as the chief executive officer and had a success there, but he couldn't resist when he was asked to be the chairman of the failing Pan Am in the fall of 1981—although he said it was a little like becoming the chairman of the *Titanic* after it hit the ice.

After resigning the American Airlines business, Bill Bernbach had been happy to replace it with Pan Am. Ed told me that he had gone to Doyle Dane Bernbach excited about working with such talented people but when he got there he found a desert. As far as he could see there was nobody there working on Pan Am. His executives told him that there had been a vacuum since the first day with the agency; very little was ever done or produced, and there was barely anything ready to run now. Ed said he wasn't even sure who was in charge of the account. Pan Am was in a plunging descent and needed cash revenues delivered by advertising immediately, but he had no one to turn to. Bill Bernbach wasn't around, he said, and if he'd met Joe Daly he didn't remember him. "I know it is a legendary agency, Mary, it is a mystery to all of us here at

Pan Am, but we don't seem to mean a thing to them. That agency's gone south, or somewhere, but I don't have time to search for it. I need an agency this second. I know you. I know what you do. I need you to do what you do. What do you think?"

"Yes, I know what to do," I told him, my mind was going clackety-clack, picking up speed at the thought of yet another airline. We still had the core of our TWA group working in our New York office. If there was one industry in my bones, it was the airline industry. We could get a campaign together in miraculous time. Ed needed a miracle. Pan Am needed a miracle to survive, and I was a sucker for anyone looking for a miracle. Ed was my friend, I knew it was possible to make miracles with Ed Acker. I wanted the account.

It was greedy to want to handle both accounts, but I had never believed in the age-old conflict theory, so I called Bob Six to see how he felt about it, the decision had to be his. I knew Bob was big-minded, loved Harding, loved me, loved the new client agency relationship we were developing in Los Angeles and loved his new advertising, but like all airlines at the time Continental had problems; he might not want to share Wells Rich Greene.

Conflicts in advertising are taboos as religious as any you would find in the Middle Ages. They are based on the notion of creative corruption; the theory is that an agency can't be trusted to work evenhandedly and honestly with competitive clients. Someone might leak marketing secrets. And then there is the big question: Which client would get the best ideas? Even though advertising ideas are created for clients as individually as custom-made clothing, and even though a great idea for United Airlines would not be the best idea for Delta. In the future, perhaps Internet advertising will be too democratic to allow an advertiser to keep an agency from working for competitors, but in November 1981 there was a golden rule that prohibited most competitive advertising, and, amazingly, there pretty much still is.

Bob answered the phone and said, in his lilting rasp, "You want to handle us both, is that what you're saying? You think you can do that? Great thinking, great advertising, great planning for us both? Well, we only compete with Pan Am over 10 percent of our routes, Houston really, most of the rest is dregs. I don't know what George will say but I don't think he'll care, he likes your agency out here a lot and so do I. You'd handle Pan Am in New York, wouldn't you? With different people. It's OK with me. I wish Ed luck with Pan Am, it won't be easy going."

I had no sooner given Charlie and Ken this news than the press got word of it and started beating drums. Before Pan Am's official resignation could reach Doyle Dane Bernbach—before Bob Six and George Warde had a chance to present the idea to their managers—before Charlie and Ken were able to explain the situation to Wells Rich Greene—the news was on the street.

There was another one of those uproars. Bill Bernbach was so livid he was rude to Ed Acker when the two men finally did meet, unexpectedly, in a restaurant. Most of the advertising world assumed Continental would resign Wells Rich Greene. Bob did begin to get some flak from below at the airline. Ken Olshan and I flew to Los Angeles to meet with Continental's management group at the airline. We offered to set up our Los Angeles office as a subsidiary totally independent of Wells Rich Greene U.S.A. We renamed it Johns, Cohen and Pasqualina, Inc., and announced that it was a subsidiary of Gardner Advertising, which was a subsidiary of Wells Rich Greene. It was convincing on paper. Continental bought the new structure and, mollified, one of Continental's advertising managers told *Adweek* that "Wells Rich Greene does marvelous stuff; we think they can help us a lot. We need that kind of advertising to make some headway in the marketplace." For a while everyone concerned was so titillated and so engrossed in producing new advertising we forgot all about Frank Lorenzo.

January seventh Pan Am fired Doyle Dane Bernbach and announced Wells Rich Greene as its worldwide agency. Doyle Dane threw a tantrum and refused to do any work at all for the three months it was obligated to by contract. That didn't make a whole lot of difference to Pan Am, as they hadn't been getting much advertising anyway—no one ever explained why—but as the airline was in dire need of the revenues that would be produced by advertising we jumped to put together an organization that could get advertising out overnight. It had to be good—no, it had to be *great*—advertising. I was not about to be burned at the stake for breaking the rules and then fail.

We regrouped our TWA team, reassembled our TWA affiliate agencies all over Pan Am's international system (they just changed the signs over their doors and went to work for Pan Am) and worldwide we began turning out work. One week later we had our first ads running in newspapers and on radio throughout the country and in all the major markets in Europe.

I had long meetings with Ed to talk about the opportunities for Pan Am in an era of deregulation. All hell was breaking loose. Without government regulation all the airlines were grabbing the same profitable routes, eliminating the same unprofitable routes, abandoning cities right and left, changing their minds and then changing their minds again. As a result advertising was being created too quickly and changed in midair, and that's just the way it looked—like advertising accidents. All-type ads were thrown together and run without any thought to the intelligence of the information, the style or readability of the typeface, the imagery or, all too often, the accuracy. The cumulative impression of that advertising was that the airlines were all alike, they were out of control, they would give you bad service, they might be messy about their maintenance, they were even confused from day to day about where the planes were flying—destinations were always changing.

Ed and I thought we saw an opportunity in that disarray for an airline that was as experienced and respected as Pan Am. There is a natural, human, deep-down fear of flying and the schlocky advertising coming out of the industry at that time was not reassuring. We decided to create a style for Pan Am advertising that would remind fliers of how experienced Pan Am was, how long and how far it had flown, what great international service it stood for and, in a subliminal way, the heroic experience it had in emergencies and also in operating in difficult parts of the world. The thrust of our image campaign would be to establish authority and leadership in an industry in chaos. We would make people feel safe on Pan Am. And we would also make them expect to get more for their money on Pan Am.

We also needed to produce a separate, cash-generating campaign of ideas and promotions designed to raise revenues quickly in specific markets during specific seasons to raise the cash Pan Am was going to need to operate through the difficult year ahead.

At the agency, after my meetings with Ed, I talked about the importance of the style, that the type and the pictures should look as if they were solidly on the page, almost engraved, not thrown on it carelessly as it seemed to be in most airline advertising. The ads should look as if we had spent more money to produce them than other airlines spent, they should give the impression that Pan Am was experienced, confident, in control of itself and was not losing its head while others were losing theirs. I wanted the ads to remind fliers of Pan Am's greatest days, there should be an elegance about them because elegance reeks confidence. We would rename coach, we would call it cabin class like in the great ocean liners. "Cabin class is where all the fun is," I rhapsodized. "That's where the young and the hip fly. It isn't just cheap." Our Pan Am group never let me forget that line, they reminded me of it every time they returned from a 12-hour trip in cabin class, "where all the fun is."

Charlie and I thought that the sort of promotion advertising that could bring in revenues quickly needed to have branding ideas that were just a little bit corny, fun and catchy enough to remember. They would get the fastest results and they would play well against the big image campaign. Timing was tough. We needed both the image campaign and the first promotions to present to Ed and his managers in a few weeks. I gave everybody anxiety attacks reminding them over and over that the advertising had to be great, not good. I myself had an anxiety attack once, in New Orleans, at a Midas muffler convention, when Charlie and Bob Wilvers and Paul Margulies brought the first roughs of the Pan Am image campaign for me to see. I sneaked out of the convention and met them in a hotel room. I was so appalled at what they showed me, at the ordinariness of it, that I yelled and I repeated, word for word, all the directions I had given them at our earlier meeting. I sobbed real tears and I ripped off my gold watch and threw it at them because there was no more time and I squeezed them into a corner where they stood, stunned. "You let me down, how could you let me down, this is the most important time in our lives, I cannot bear this, my God I don't know what to do!"—and I left them to commit suicide. I was magnificent. The next work they showed me was magnificent.

When we stood up to make our presentation to Pan Am they didn't expect a hit show—after all, they hadn't had much advertising for six months and we had been working for them for only two weeks, but no one had slept at Wells Rich Greene, we used every psychological trick we knew to keep the agency awake and on an inspirational high and every financial incentive we could afford to keep everybody at work. Advertising rolled out of our offices into the hands of Wells Rich Greene's suppliers, who stood in line, day and night, to take it and turn it into gold. We had threatened to pull the nails off any supplier who let us down. When the day arrived we had stunning examples of the image campaign and promotional, cash-generation advertising ready to run in every country in the world. Paul Schulman, our advertising manager, had every step organized, ready to go, the type houses worked 24-hour shifts. Blessed Howard Zieff canceled a big shoot for a beer company and was standing by a phone with his airline ticket in his pocket ready to fly to San Diego to re-create one of Pan Am's famous flying boats in one of our image commercials. Steve Karmen had created one of his stirring anthems and had a date with an orchestra to record it, that anthem made everybody cry, a sure sign of success. Our production world was focused, poised, ready to take the orders and roll.

When we finished presenting the two campaigns Ed asked, "What do we have to do to get it going?" Eileen McKenna, the account supervisor we had stolen from TWA for this challenge, slid an estimate under his nose and said, "Just sign on this dotted line and we'll be out of here and on our way." Applause. But also shimmering relief at all the action. I remember one of Ed's executives, Steve Wolf, in red suspenders, with mustache, holding a plate of cheesecake at the buffet we set up after the meeting. "Excellent," he kept saying over and over. I think he meant the advertising, although it was good cheesecake.

We had dinner to be happy together, Bob and Audrey, Harding and I, and Ed brought Sandy Faulkner. He was eager to marry her, a stunning young woman who welcomed life with a myriad of energies that even impressed Audrey, who was no slouch in that department. We had a lot in common, Sandy and I, she was an only child, had gone to Carnegie's drama school and if necessary could turn a deadly dull scene into a breakout song, she was a fashion expert in a department store and was about to become the wife of the chairman of an airline—we connected right away. She has a Capra-movie kind of sweetness, you don't see a lot of it, Charlie has it, too. Neither of them would admit to it, they would prefer to be cool cats. That evening we went to Doubles, a restaurant club in the Sherry-Netherland Hotel. We were feeling daring, here we were out in public, the agency with its two airline accounts, ye gods and little fishes! At that time we were still handling Braniff's advertising in Europe, the advertising press never grasped the fact that Wells Rich Greene actually had *three* airline accounts, not just two. I remember the sounds of that evening, it was full of Audrey's riproaring laughter and the balmy feeling that the world was as it should be and it was good.

But only one year later Frank Lorenzo finally gained control of Continental, merged it with Texas International and fired George Warde and Mike Levine and Wells Rich Greene. After he offered Continental's employees 35 percent of the common stock in exchange for $150 million in salary givebacks and was rejected by employees who were horrified at the prospect of working for Frank Lorenzo, he put Continental into Chapter 11 and shut down the airline kerplunk. That brought everybody to their knees! Somewhere in those concussive months Bob Six was slipped into retirement, he and Audrey were inconsolable at the manner and the means. For example, for many years it had been taken for granted that the art collected for Bob's office from their many trips online to Hawaii and Micronesia and Japan would pass to Bob on his retirement as a rightful gift, it was his, theirs, the fruits of developing a part of the world for tourism that might not have occurred without the charisma and virtuosity of Bob and Audrey—but they didn't receive one painting or object. There were other, more serious indignities, but the loss of the art rankled most. Sharon and Frank

Lorenzo were not aware of how abused the Sixes felt about the art; the Sixes thought of it as having been stolen from them. Bob and Audrey had the kind of pride people used to have in the good old days and it was only because Bob felt so close to Harding that he would reveal how much pain the two of them felt, after 45 years, at the loss of Continental in their lives. At some point the art became a metaphor for the airline; somehow it was easier for us all to mourn the art.

The loss of Continental was a blow to our Los Angeles office, too, but most of the Los Angeles branches of New York agencies operated in a state of disbelief, always expecting the worst. Most of them were agencies for motion-picture companies handling specific movie assignments, and those were precarious client relationships to say the least. It wasn't easy to get the country's top advertising talents to work in a Los Angeles agency. The relentless obsession with a movie's first weekend results, the humpty-dumpty quality of life working for movie producers who were always on the edge and the humiliation of having to sell yourself so hard made it impossible to have a real life doing advertising for movies—most big advertising stars preferred the strong, stable agencies in New York. But we managed to keep a high level of creative talent there; Bob Kuperman and Pacy Markman, Howie Cohen and Bob Pasqualina, worked their way through the Columbia power brokers, Norman Levy, Bob Cort, Stanley Schneider, Alan Herschfield, Peter Allen.

We had a few normal accounts. For one of them, Jack in the Box, a fast-food chain on the West Coast, Howie created a commercial I absolutely adored. To announce a new, improved Jack in the Box menu, a little old lady blew up the clown that stood at the entrance to every Jack in the Box restaurant. "Waste 'em!" she yelled, and the clown blew to high heaven. The commercial was a rousing hit, but it outraged a group who were protesting the use of explosives on television. "Look at these letters," the manager said to me, indicating stacks of mail in his mailroom. Talk about explosives! I have never read more threatening, frenzied, slasher letters. There is a psycho element watching television that terrifies me, because, although it is a very small element judging by the number of letters received, it has a profound effect on major corporations. The letters attacked the Ralston Purina Company, the owners of Jack in the Box, and its directors with such threatening hysteria that although we also received many more complimentary letters and customers were standing in lines at the restaurants, we stopped blowing up the clowns. One of the executives at the company said, "Mary, I can't sleep, I keep worrying that our advertising, funny and sweet as it is, could stimulate an act of real violence. These people are vile."

The other coveted account on the West Coast was Gallo, and Ernest and Julio Gallo were agency flirts, always making eyes at different agencies, always threatening to divorce the ones they had. They were eager to change their reputation from a company that sold jugs of junk wine to winos to a company that made fine, serious wines for the up-and-coming. The brothers were notorious at cuckolding their agencies and bruising their feelings, but as there were few accounts to be had outside the movie business there was always an agency with eyes for Gallo. I myself strolled down the garden path with Ernest at his home, where we whispered sweet nothings to one another, and followed up that charade with a series of meetings at Gallo's offices presenting advertising that turned out to be sweet nothing too.

Atari was the best California account we ever had but we handled it mostly from New York. Atari was owned by Warner Brothers. It made the simple computer and video games we played before the world turned into a collection of technology buffs and computer nerds. Ray Kassar ran Atari at its zenith; he understood the good life. I served him a 1947 Cheval Blanc once and I always thought that bottle of wine got us the account—or maybe it was the Petrus. Anyway, we liked each other. He hired Ted Voss from Polaroid to oversee his advertising, a smart move. And Wells Rich Greene's creative work selling Atari's video games to children was good enough to earn us the computer-game account away from Young & Rubicam just about the time Steve Ross hired Alan Alda to be the spokesman for it. Alan Alda had a ferocious agent-manager, Marty Bregman, you couldn't help loving him for Alan Alda's sake. He always demanded a fortune for Alan in a big growly voice. One evening Charlie and I had dinner with Ray and Ted and Marty and Alan and Steve to discuss the advertising. Alan arrived as if he was stepping out of *M*A*S*H*, the same funny-wry personality. But it was Steve Ross who left a lasting impression on me as a man so intuitive about managing and manipulating people that he breathed through their pores and thought through their brains and understood precisely what keys to play and could be counted on to be a master general who would lead his group to success with supreme civility.

The dislocations caused by deregulation gave most airlines cash emergencies in the early eighties, not just Continental. Ed Acker had an idea a minute about promotions that could raise cash, I interpreted them to Charlie, Andre and Eileen and we would then sit down and salt-and-pepper them in some memorable way. For example, when Ed told me Pan Am didn't have the money to get through the winter, which was the airline's slow season, and needed a major infusion fast, he thought a $99 ticket to anywhere Pan Am flew in the United States might do the trick and a line popped out of Charlie's mouth that helped ensure it would. "Get me on a Pan Am $99er!" he said. All sorts of people said that line in some memorable way in the advertising, but the best was an old-geezer character who, when he said "Get me on a Pan Am $99er!" in a wheezer-geezer voice made the telephones at Pan Am fall off their hooks. It was a great offer, $99 to everywhere Pan Am flew in the United States—at that price you *had* to fly someplace. But the advertising was just simple and catchy and corny enough to stay fixed, enticingly, in your mind, it wouldn't let go of you. That's what branding is supposed to do. We branded that $99 fare as a Pan Am fare, and even though other airlines copied it, it was remembered as Pan Am's fare, it was Pan Am's success, and the cash poured in to carry Pan Am through the winter.

The coup de théâtre, the Pan Am Shuttle, was Ed's idea. The Eastern Shuttle had been operating without competition for 25 years. When Ed came up with the idea, scrawled on his yellow pad, and took it into one of Pan Am's weekly marketing meetings, his fellows said, "Ed, that'll never work! Eastern owns the shuttle business." For a few weeks there was complete rejection. Finally, exasperated, Ed called a meeting and announced, "The Pan Am Shuttle is going to start October 15th. Anyone not on board should leave the room now." Every man became an enthusiast.

Ed found a terminal conveniently next to La Guardia, the Marine Terminal, a ramshackle art deco masterpiece with bona fide WPA murals on the walls. I always hated those murals, all those stern faces, but the gods must have loved them, because between June and October 1986, a very short time, Ed's builders managed to transform the Marine Terminal into a really handsome pavilion, ready to take on Pan Am's duel with the Eastern Shuttle. Pan Am's problem then was that nobody knew where the Marine Terminal was. New York taxi drivers certainly didn't, and although there were big signs directing traffic to the Eastern Shuttle exit on the highway to La Guardia, there wasn't one sign directing traffic to the Marine Terminal. To obtain permission for such signage in the state of New York could require years of meetings with a wide assortment of powerful and protective commissioners from the Port Authority of New York and New Jersey, maybe even governor's committees pulled together for political reasons, city councilmen, ecologists, and there would have to be prayers to Robert Moses. All those good people could be counted on to denounce anything new at La Guardia. What to do? We brought in Phyllis Wagner. She hadn't been married to Bob Wagner all those years while he was the mayor of New York for nothing, she probably knew the ins and outs of New York better than anyone else. I didn't hire her with the idea that she would be our New York wizard but she certainly turned out to be. She always knew where to go, what to say and just whose back to scratch, and voilà, Pan Am received wonderful signs so big and commanding they yanked drivers off the highway into the Marine Terminal.

Pan Am put fresh bagels on board the flights and a choice of beverages and the Eastern Shuttle folks said, "There goes the neighborhood!" They had been getting away with murder for years and were appalled to see Pan Am's extra legroom, free *Wall Street Journal*s and *New York Times*, free snacks, spruced-up planes and, horror of horrors, automated ticketing machines for super-fast boarding. People were used to sprinting to the shuttle gate at the last minute; they discovered quickly they could be even later and still make the Pan Am Shuttle.

That shuttle was a dream to advertise. It made sense to compete with the Eastern Shuttle head-on to capitalize on the universal familiarity of it; people understood immediately what the Pan Am Shuttle was and what it did and where it flew if it was competing with the Eastern Shuttle. Then all we had to do was dramatize the small improvements Pan Am offered, because they seemed magnificent to the regular shuttle flier, who had gone 25 years without any improvements whatsoever. We expected them to appreciate the faster boarding in the Marine Terminal, but what bowled them over were the bagels. I wouldn't have believed so many people could carry on with such passion about a bagel.

Our shuttle advertising, written by Bill Lower, was hip, sly, a spoof on the Eastern Shuttle, it was very "insider New York" and New Yorkers loved it. After only a couple of months of advertising the Pan Am Shuttle achieved an awareness level of 88 percent and after only a year of operation it owned a large share of the market. Ed Acker's shuttle became such a valuable asset that Donald Trump bought the Eastern Shuttle to compete with it, imagining hosannas. And, sad to tell, the day would come, much later, when Pan Am would sell its shuttle for a big price to solve big problems.

How do you keep the music playing?

I worry that sometimes when I am telling you about the world of advertising I appear to be describing a garden of bagels and Calders and Alka-Seltzer delights. But the advertising business is not a cute business. Your warmest clients can be the ones that give you the coldest chills. In 1981, the year Harding left Braniff and Wells Rich Greene went to work for Bob Six at Continental, that summer I was so tired I felt I was losing my sense of wonder, and I figured that was a warning. Maybe it was because we had crammed 20 years of nonstop work into

15. Maybe we got too many new clients in too short a time or had too many surprises. Maybe I'd seen too many faces turned to me over the conference table expecting me to pull the rabbit out. The fact was that I'd lost my magic wand someplace and I was seriously concerned about it. I'd looked around the agency and hadn't seen any emergencies so I ran away to La Fiorentina. Ken Olshan and his wife, Patsy, Kathie Durham and my daughter Katy had gone with Harding and me. As soon as we arrived, while the suitcases were being unpacked, I headed for the long saltwater pool at the bottom of the grass steps and went under.

Wherever I'd lost my magic, I'd also lost my sex appeal. Kathie and I had looked each other over on the way to the pool the way only major friends dare to do, and on that last long run seeing clients from St. Louis to Cincinnati to Los Angeles to Elkhart, Indiana, my body had turned old, like pale cheese, like it was somebody else's, so discouraging. In the pool, down under, hearing nothing, seeing nothing, feeling only the slippery cool saltwater for a while, though, I decided I'd live. I thought about sitting on the edge of the pool, enjoying that amazing view down the sea to Italy, and I felt a tiny flicker of joy light up in the center of my heart. It felt so good. The pool was 100 feet long. I was at the far end when I saw Ken's face above me, wavy through the water. My joy went *phhht.* I came up and took the telephone. It was Charlie. His voice was so flat that I knew there was big trouble.

"Mary, I just had lunch with Jimmy Morgan after a meeting at Philip Morris and he fired us. He fired the agency. He invited me to lunch and I figured something was wrong—for him to invite me like that. I was shocked. I said maybe he ought to wait and talk to you. But he said no, he's made the decision. He went on and on about how hopeless the campaign is and the organization—I don't know—he seemed so angry. I said everything I could think of. Believe me, I tried to talk him out of it. I begged him to at least wait until you get back. But he is determined. God. He walked out on me, he just left me there at the restaurant. I could hardly stand up. I'm shaking."

Go away, Charlie. I want to do laps in my pool. I want to look at my view. I want my mother—anybody—to take Jimmy Morgan and chuck him. I don't care about Philip Morris. I don't care about Wells Rich Greene. I want to go to my pal Lynn Wyatt's birthday bash. I want to dance. I want to giggle. "Charlie," I said, "it's not possible. After 14 years—without any warning? He approved a bunch of ads a few days ago. So why? What happened? Why today?" Just words, just dust. Ken, everybody, was dripping around me, worried.

"Mary, it's over. I promise you."

The account was gone. There was no hope. Nothing to do. But that's not how this game is played. In this game you have to win. The consequences are too big. Somehow or other you have to get everybody back to the playing field again and win. We waddled back to the villa, pathetic seals in damp towels. Kathie and Katy started to cry. That's all I needed. Ken was quiet. Harding kept looking at me expectantly. He knew what *he* would do, he was born a wagon driver.

Philip Morris and Benson & Hedges were important symbols of our success, symbols of the exciting young agency we were, so in tune with its time. They were symbols of *my* success, too. The very idea that Philip Morris would leave Wells Rich Greene was cosmic. It was a sign from the universe saying we had had our day, we weren't shamans anymore. The news would make our other clients uneasy and restless, it would be very hard to explain to new business. We simply couldn't afford to lose the Benson & Hedges account then.

If that wasn't enough, I felt betrayed. They hadn't warned me and they were my friends at Philip Morris. No one at the agency had a clue that such a thing could happen. No one in the rank and file at Philip Morris had, either, they said. Jimmy Morgan had been promoted and had the authority. He was a smart young marketing man with strong opinions. Apparently one of them was that he needed a new agency to work with. That's ad biz. Joe Cullman and Jack Landry, who had given us the account in 1966, had moved up and now, in 1981, they were out of the day-to-day operation. George Weissman was chairman. Jimmy had taken over marketing and he was our new boss.

In the villa I started to make calls to Philip Morris. I dreaded the calls. I do not like to be on my stomach saying please. Jimmy wasn't in. I reached Joe, he didn't know what he could do about it. A friend and a sweetheart, he promised to do what he could. I tried George but he was out, too. I called Jack. He'd been waiting for my call. We had worked together on the account for so long he knew how hard it would be for me. He said he would try to set up a meeting for me with Jimmy on Monday and he would talk to George for me. Then Jimmy called. He was angry—I suppose he needed to be to rev up his engines to fire us. He was tight, grim, and as Charlie said, he'd made up his mind. But he agreed to see me Monday morning at ten.

We repacked the bags and sat up most of the night, a miserable group. We couldn't talk, we just sat and felt the weight of it. There wasn't enough air. I whined to myself. I hated Jimmy Morgan. But what good would that do? The advertising business is a dangerous business, there are no guarantees. It's not for sissies. It's a business about creating miracles, I told myself. Since the beginning of time it has been the fanatics who have created the miracles and I was nothing if not a fanatic. I knew I had to find out from Jimmy exactly how to turn Wells Rich Greene into a new agency that would bring his ideas to life. Then I had to persuade him to let us do that.

He was waiting for me Monday at ten. He was ice. He has Irish blue eyes but they were white, he was so unhappy having to deal with me. I arrived with a steno pad and a very good attitude. I begged him to tell me—no holds barred—everything that was wrong with Wells Rich Greene and our advertising from his point of view. Then I opened my steno pad.

He erupted criticisms and insults for one hour, two hours, three hours, four hours, without a pause or a sip of water, it was a scalding filibuster and I wrote down every blessed word he said while indigestion was making me sick. We must have been some sight: Jimmy stomping around me, pouring out everything that had built up in him to say, and me, shrunk, hunched over my steno pad, rapt, taking dictation.

He wasn't fair—wasn't in the mood to be fair. This is the story. In the beginning there was only one other cigarette longer than king-size and it wasn't advertising its length, so there was no consciousness of a longer cigarette in the market. We had that whole playing field to ourselves. It was as if we and we alone had a product superiority—extra length at no extra cost. We advertised it with the style of the sixties, irreverence. People smoking the new longer Benson & Hedges in our television commercials weren't used to the extra length, so they kept breaking them in outlandish ways. Nobody had ever mutilated a cigarette before in American advertising—cigarettes, like automobiles, had always been treated with reverent respect by their manufacturers. Then we came along, the TV terrorists of the sixties, and actually broke those little devils. It was truly shocking. Anything anti-establishment seemed smart in the mid-sixties, so our advertising made Benson & Hedges wildly hip and cool and the cigarette to be seen with. But the main reason our irreverent advertising sold so many cigarettes was because the irreverence was about a product advantage—you got extra cigarette length at no extra cost.

First we lost the product advantage, because the other cigarette companies saw our success and rushed to introduce their own longer cigarettes; the market became flooded with them, all at the same price. Then we lost television and we discovered that a cigarette broken in print, with no movement, is not the dramatic surprise that a cigarette broken on television is. It is not as shocking, so it is not as stylish. When Jack Landry dragged me off for a drink to tell me that he feared the Benson & Hedges television campaign wouldn't translate to print with the same thunder, he was absolutely right. Charlie's new campaign, "America's Favorite Cigarette Break," an assemblage of still photographs of smokers having accidents with their longer cigarettes, although clever, couldn't keep Benson & Hedges in the style to which it had become accustomed. After a while we started to lose some of our hip image.

Wells Rich Greene should have found a completely new way to keep Benson & Hedges hip. We didn't because we lost control of the advertising. We started out creating the advertising our way and we had fantastic focus. But the Philip Morris Company was crazy about advertising, almost everybody in the place was the advertising director. Little by little, after the Benson & Hedges campaign went from television to print, the Philip Morris marketing department insisted on taking back the control it was used to having over agencies. We wouldn't have kept the account 15 years if we had stamped our foot and insisted on keeping control. So a committee of them and us evolved and began to create the Benson & Hedges advertising together.

Committees can develop a campaign about a thing like the Marlboro cowboy, you can fine-tune cowboys for years by paying close attention to the photographs and the use of type. But committees have trouble creating a new style, because the essence of style is an intuition that is perpetually changing. Committees are ponderous, and it don't mean a thing if it ain't got that swing. By the time a committee would get around to creating a new style it would seem prehistoric.

Philip Morris made the mistake of insisting that we continue to search for different ways to break Benson & Hedges cigarettes in photographs or find other ways to dramatize length—long after its length was moot. We should have been inventing radical new ways to keep the cigarette stylish. But Philip Morris didn't think like a fashion business, and Wells Rich Greene didn't want to lose the account, so the agency went along and tried its best to invent hip photographs of broken cigarettes. I went along, too, I was too busy getting other new accounts and putting out other fires. I had only recently resigned TWA, I couldn't resign every account that didn't give us free rein. Anyway, as the agency grew large I started seeing at least a few shades of grey, not just black and white. The brand was selling fairly well and we liked the people at Philip Morris, they had become good friends, why rock a smooth-sailing account? Jimmy exploded to me about a lot of things that day in his office, but what he really wanted was to get Benson & Hedges out of the committee's hands and into his own—he thought he was the intuitive, the alchemist who could turn it into a hot, firecracker brand again.

I wanted to have an honest talk with Jimmy about intuitive advertising and style, but I knew that was not the day. I kept my head down and wrote. When he finished, when he ran out of steam and accusations, when he was absolutely drained, he says, he started to feel sorry for me. I think he was afraid I would try to kiss his feet.

I asked him, very carefully, if he would give Wells Rich Greene another chance if we corrected every mistake he had described to me—

in 24 hours. "You can't do it in 24 hours, Mary," he said, exasperated. I repeated: Would he give Wells Rich Greene another chance if we corrected every mistake in 24 hours? He winced. What could he do? He gave us 24 hours.

In 24 hours Wells Rich Greene redesigned the Philip Morris group to give Jimmy an agency he would want to work with. It's amazing what you can do when you are hanging by a hair. Ken and Charlie and I X-rayed the agency and found people who had an eye for trends and pulled them into a new group for Jimmy. We would have to bring in some young avant-garde print talent for him, too. We called a superstar we admired at another agency, hired him over the phone with amoral amounts of money and big promises, gambling outrageously, but we knew he had what it would take with Jimmy. Very late that night we talked our way through a new attitude towards Philip Morris and towards Jimmy—we regeared the account towards him, of course, and created an organizational mechanism that would keep us charged with current ideas for him. All this would make the account more expensive to operate, perhaps unprofitable for a while, but we agreed to the investment, then kept the art production department up the rest of the night making our plans look hot and tasty on presentation boards.

The following morning, blowing my trumpets, I marched to Jimmy's office with a new agency for him as well as my new personal commitment, my new personal state of thrall and my new personal humbleness. When he saw me marching down the hall towards his office he heard my trumpets loud and clear and he sighed and sat down. He was big about it, bless his heart. He tilted his chair back, stretched his hands up behind his head, rocked, grinned at me and agreed to give Wells Rich Greene another chance.

That's when the excruciating work began for Philip Morris, and that's when Ed Acker called me about taking on Pan Am. I never did get back to France for that swim, that view, that summer. But I did learn to love Jimmy Morgan dearly, and we went on to have a rollicking future.

So the story had a happy ending, no? Not exactly.

In 1986 Jimmy left Philip Morris to run Atari and we had happy times with him there, too. Bill Campbell became the new head of marketing at Philip Morris. He had been running Philip Morris business in the Far East out of Hong Kong. He had that appealing manner people get who live abroad in exotic, international towns—pragmatic, smiling, careful.

His first complaint was that Wells Rich Greene should pay more attention to detail. I was going to defend us but when I looked at Charlie I noticed that for some reason that day he was wearing the pants from one suit and the jacket from another, so I let it pass. Then Bill said he thought all the advertising at Philip Morris needed refreshing. He observed that Philip Morris was a master at branding but even the biggest brands became stale and lost their meaning if you looked away from them. "You have to stay alert," he said, "you can't get comfortable with successful brands." I agreed with him. I talked to Charlie about looking at Benson & Hedges like a revolutionary. Charlie and I started looking around at people who were doing work that was advanced hip. He went to Italy to investigate a few controversial talents there. I should point out that by 1986 Wells Rich Greene was a very big agency with a lot of major clients who wanted fabulous work. It was hard for Charlie or Ken or me to spend nonstop time on any one account. But I had learned something from Jimmy Morgan. I figured that Bill Campbell didn't hold us holy, either, just because of our many years with Philip Morris. I started to feel his intentions like a heat rash and I knew I had to take Benson & Hedges out into deep blue waters again.

I got all excited, the way that I do, and decided that Wells Rich Greene needed a special group that adored print advertising. We tended to hire movie talent; I wanted people who had hothouse editorial backgrounds or who came out of the art world or MTV—people who were trendy personally, obsessed with the new. *Branché* is the word in France—it means being connected in the coolest way. I wanted a *branché* group to handle Benson & Hedges. I zeroed in on Ron Albrecht, an art director who was beginning to shake up women's magazines with his very new-looking *Elle.* He joined us as the guru of what we called our new Image Group.

Then Harding and I went to see Woody Allen's movie *Hannah and Her Sisters*. There was a scene in the movie where Hannah, her sisters and their husbands sat around a Sunday dinner table talking and smoking. It was the quintessence of an eighties smoking moment. How could I capture the feeling of that scene and others like it in ordinary lifeless print? Life in the movies always seems so much more alive than life in print.

Bob Ciano, who was at Time-Life, helped me first, we designed the architecture of a storytelling campaign about smoking moments. Then Ron Albrecht arrived at the agency and he and I put together what I called the Hannah campaign. It had arresting pictures of people who were smoking that looked more like stills pulled from a movie than most pictures. There was something pulsing, up-above-the-page about those pictures. Pictures like that were hard to find, so we talked to Bruce Weber, who created so many images for Ralph Lauren and Calvin Klein. And we talked to Dennis Peal, a photographer so cinematic he knew exactly what to shoot for. Both men went off and produced extraordinary, restless, moving pictures that had some kind of unusual inner human life.

I was so pleased with our new, exploratory work for Benson & Hedges I took a few days to fly to Russia with Ed and Sandy Acker and Harding on an important trip Pan Am had arranged with Aeroflot. Returning from Russia, we stopped in France for a weekend at La Fiorentina.

We had just arrived. We were at the pool. It was July. The phone rang.

Yes—it was Charlie. He said that Bill Campbell had decided to put the Benson & Hedges account up for review—to see what other agencies might do with the cigarette. We had been invited to make a presentation to try to keep the account. But insiders told us Bill had fallen in love with another agency and we were dead in the water.

"Oh no, please no, please," I prayed to something in myself. I finally spoke to him. "Oh, Charlie, I've got great work going on, I've spent a lot of money on that work!" This time I didn't telephone anybody. I just got on a plane. I walked into Wells Rich Greene the next morning, a blistering Sunday, and the first thing that struck me was that the air-conditioning wasn't working. It took special, expensive arrangements to have air-conditioning weekends. After all, nobody works weekends in a hot New York summer. Just me and a fraternity of art directors and Harold Singer, our indefatigable head of print production, crawling on the floor outside John Mari's art studio, layout to layout. (You do this by computer now, elegantly.) I was obsessed. When he could, Charlie would join me there on the floor, refining, refining, refining our work on Benson & Hedges. We spent long, bleary hours staring at type—a good picture was important to Philip Morris, but handling type well was a fetish.

They were surprised at our presentation at Philip Morris, maybe even a bit dismayed. They hadn't expected to like it. At the end Bill Campbell shook his head, laughed, sighed, said, "You people have guts." He showed our Hannah campaign to Hamish Maxwell, who was the chairman, and to others and pretty soon we were back in business at Philip Morris.

For a while. As I said, advertising is not for sissies. But advertising is one of the world's most educational businesses. Many of our clients and friends wanted their children to experience the panorama of business that you view in advertising while they were college age and about to choose their futures. Some agencies will not hire children of clients, friends or employees, but I thought those students were great trainees and useful, they all had good genes and they had monkeys on their backs to do well at the agency. One or two of them went home to Daddy and whined about the agency because we didn't give them our expensive television commercials to train on or they thought they could run the agency better than I did, but most of them were chips off the old blocks and we were happy to have them. I insisted that my own children work at Wells Rich Greene for the enlightenment because agency experience almost always stimulates you to think big.

Prince Albert of Monaco came to work for a short time to learn something about American marketing. We introduced him as Albert Grimaldi from Brooklyn so that he wouldn't be treated as if he were a leper or, worse, a prince. Princess Grace had asked me to set up a train-

ing program for him and he was eager to learn about American marketing and advertising. He was a serious and talented marketing student,
he absorbed it all. He fit right in. I told Princess Grace that he would
make a knockout advertising executive. "Well, if he ever needs a
job . . . ," she said, looking at me over her glasses.

I haven't got time for the pain

The first cancer arrived unannounced. Late June 1980, I was on my
way to Detroit and I popped into New York Hospital for a D&C
because my gynecologist believed in regular D&Cs, Dr. Bill Davis was
the worrying kind. I was feeling ridiculously pleased to hide out one
night in New York Hospital with *Vogue* under my arm; nobody in the
world would call me there and I could spend a secret evening fantasizing about clothes.

Kathie arrived in the morning, as she did wherever I was, I know
that when I immigrate to the moon she will arrive at seven a.m. with
the mail. I had a reservation on a noon flight, we scanned my mail and
planned July while we waited for Dr. Davis to appear with the test
results. When the morning grew late and he didn't appear, I got
dressed and was about to head for the airport, but then he walked in the
door with the head of gynecological surgery, Dr. Stanley Birnbaum. He
looked doleful, apologetic. "You have a small tumor in your uterus,
Mrs. Lawrence—now please don't be frightened, it is a very early
tumor, so even if it is malignant it looks to be well contained."

Tumor? Uterus? Malignant? Contained? As the song says, it never
entered my mind. I was never sick. This little meeting couldn't be
about me.

Dr. Davis explained that I was in luck, Dr. Birnbaum was New
York's most respected gynecological surgeon, the one who was most in
demand, he was a good friend of Bill Davis's and would adapt his

schedule to operate first thing in the morning. Operate? Operate? I know what they mean by dumbstruck. I was dumbstruck. I was on my way to a Ford meeting in Detroit. I absolutely had to be there. What were they talking about? It finally sunk in that those gentlemen in white coats planned to remove my uterus the following morning. Over my dead body, I thought, I am going to Detroit. "What"—I looked at Dr. Birnbaum, the surgeon of choice—"what if I don't do anything?" Dr. Birnbaum is a warm and kind man. He took a step towards me, I think he wanted to give me a little pat. "If you don't do anything it will kill you," he said.

I looked at Kathie. We identify like mirrors. She looked as if she was going to have a tumor removed in the morning and then probably die. That was the moment I chose denial. "Sit down, Kath. It's OK. I'll be fine." I smiled sweetly at her and then at Dr. Birnbaum. "Tell me about it," I said genially, conversationally. He sat on the little stool at the foot of the bed. "If the tumor is malignant, as small as it looks, contained as I think it is, we should have no trouble removing it all. We'll remove your ovaries, too, that would be wise. This may be an odd thing to say, Mrs. Lawrence, but if you have to have a cancer this is the one to have. The percentages of success are high." I was floating, cool, serene, above it all. "That's good news," I said. "How soon will I be able to leave for Detroit?" "Well, if it is malignant," Dr. Birnbaum said, looking at the calendar flopped open on Kathie's lap, "it will take you a few days to be up and about, then you'll need ten days or a couple of weeks to heal well enough to begin the treatments. You will want to have a short course of radiation treatments over at Memorial—prophylactically—because those radiation treatments bring the success statistics of these operations up to the top nineties. So you're lucky, Mrs. Lawrence."

They all left, the doctors to set up my operation, Kathie to make the million and one adjustments at the agency. "Kath, this is nothing. Please don't get dramatic. We do not want anyone to know about this, no friends, no clients, no press, nobody. I'll call Harding now and I'll tell the girls and Mother. But that's it. We don't want other agencies making a deal out of this. Tell Charlie, Ken, anyone important who asks that I am having one of those little female operations—that will stop them in their tracks. If you are casual they will be casual. That's what we want—we want all of this to be casual. This is going to pass very quickly, we must not make more of it than it is." We hugged. Kathie looked as if she knew a secret, I was dying. She didn't want to leave me there alone. She wanted to stay and have an operation too. But she knew I was right, it was best to be casual for Wells Rich Greene's sake. So she left, cranking up her sunny self, chirping at the nurses.

From an early time I have been aware of an alternate me somewhere deep inside, "the Watcher" is how I thought of it, something egoless, emotionless, judgement-less, disinterested but not uninterested, something that simply sees. When Kathie left, when she closed the door behind her, the Watcher moved into position and took over.

Harding wanted to take the next flight but I grappled with him and after a long and intense telephone discussion persuaded him that I just wanted to get the operation over with and get on with things, I couldn't bear a lot of drama, he should let me do such a personal thing my own way, he should wait and come up for the weekend, we could discuss the treatments they were scheduling for me then—and would he please talk to the kids (Katy had a summer job at Braniff and Pam was at school in Dallas), and would he call my mother—I needed some time to think about the tumor quietly, by myself. But I didn't think about it. I wasn't introspective. I didn't know how to be introspective. I didn't know how to think my way through fear. My way was to deny that there was anything to fear, to whistle in the dark. I lay on the bed waiting for morning, waiting for this to pass, waiting to take the first possible plane to Detroit to continue living my life.

The Watcher saw it all though. First, through fuzz, a smiling Dr Birnbaum: "It was malignant, Mrs. Lawrence, but I got it all, I'm certain of that, and I would bet a lot on the ovaries, you are going to be fine." I would have left New York Hospital immediately except that any operation in stomach territory leaves you bent over with pain, and for a few days you can't stand up straight, let alone trot off to an airport. Slouching back from my first attempt to walk the halls, I looked up into a pair of burning eyes—a nurse I hadn't seen before was watching me struggle to stand straight. "You are a lucky woman, Mrs. Lawrence," she said. "Her patient has ovarian cancer," my nurse told me later, "and that's really hard."

Harding ignored me, caught a plane and appeared minutes after the operation. He thought I should allow myself a catharsis, I should refuel my enthusiasms at La Fiorentina before going to the office and before I began the radiation treatments. I have a photograph of me, my mother, Katy, Pam and Kathie looking intoxicated, serenaded by a violinist at dinner on that blissful little trip to France.

Checking into Memorial Hospital for the treatments when I returned was a ceremony of a special, irritating kind, it took all day, but finally I was shown to the locker room and given a key and one of those pea-green cotton hospital robes that have been sterilized and pulverized and boiled in lye. I was the kind that refused to put it on, I always carried it folded into a stiff little square down to the basement, where the machines were installed because they were so heavy.

The first machine I was introduced to would attempt to locate the exact target for radiation, the site of the tumor and its neighborhood where a dangerous cell could lurk. One doctor was the site detective, charged with protecting me from unnecessary radiation damage; I was told his collaborator was the world's specialist at creating sculptures that were small cradles. My cradle would hold my body motionless in a position that offered up my perfect spot to the radiation machine. I felt no shame naked with those doctors. They threw their arms around my hips to make their adjustments as though I was a side of beef. Cooperating with them, I could see my hip as a haunch, my thigh as a mound, my arms as a nuisance, always in the way. They were wizards, virtuosos, connoisseurs of a new art form. Radiation was a merciful breakthrough, and the first doctors privileged to work with the machines were groping their way towards the cure of cancer. They looked at us all calmly, the naked fat ones and the naked skinny ones, the naked ones too sick to hoist themselves up into the cradle, the naked ones in acute pain, the naked ones dizzy from chemotherapy, the naked children—and we looked back at them, grateful. We were all given tattoos to guide the operators of the radiation machines, flecks like black ants.

When my cradle was ready I was surprised at how small it was; after much editing a large apparatus had been carved into something like a saucer that I could slip in and out of easily. I was ready, they said, to begin the treatments, I would be given a schedule each week at the desk in the waiting room outside the rooms with the machines. "The machines are relatively new technology," my radiation supervisor told me. "They are prima donnas. They are always down for repairs and that creates scheduling nightmares for us and for all of you, too. Many patients catch buses early in the morning and spend hours getting here and then their machine goes down, maybe for twenty-four hours, and they have to bus all the way back home, turn around and repeat the trip. The worst of it is that we know for certain that the closer you stick to the schedule that is designed for you, the closer you get to those high-nineties statistics of cure. You will see a lot of people desperate to stick to their schedules, sitting tight, right in this waiting room, half the night if need be, until their machine is working again, so they won't lose their slot."

I saw them. The waiting room was small and ribbed with narrow rows of seats. The important space was given to the machines. No thought had been given to ambiance, to cheer. Nobody would have noticed. The patients were tuned to the women at the desk who would call their name or announce a machine failure. In every other conscious way the patients were switched off. They didn't look at each other. Most of them wore their boiled green robes without a thought. A man with a tumor on the side of his head as large as a grapefruit sat and stared at his thumbs. An older woman so thin her bones were piercing her skin, who was violently nauseated every single day, was led back and forth, back and forth by her daughter to one of the minuscule bathrooms immediately off the waiting room. A bald black man with a stomach swollen twice its normal size so that he couldn't quite close his green robe, who never seemed to breathe, kept mashing his wife's hand, and she seemed glad he did. The babies, the children, the teenagers who could not walk were held in their beds, waiting, all together in an area that was not a room, just a space large enough to hold the beds,

People came from every corner of the world to sit stone quiet in the waiting room until it was their turn with the machines. Most of the world did not have the machines yet, they were new and they were astronomically expensive. So, rich or poor, whatever your nationality or ethnic background, whatever your religion, all you cared about was being in that room. It wasn't a democratic experience. You didn't know anyone else was there. You cared only about the machines.

In 1980 they were universes of hope and dreams, symphonies that seemed able to take you to heights of rapture, sacred opportunities at another crack at life, metallic sculptures of survival, I heard them described all those ways. But the first time I saw one I thought it was the ugliest thing I had ever seen. Each machine had been given a room that appeared to be made of lead. It crawled on the ceiling and hung there waiting for you and when you were ready, when you were lying on the narrow sacrificial slab that had been covered with a sheet for you, when the operator had checked to be sure you were positioned correctly in your cradle, after he had left, shutting the heavy metal door with a polarizing *kathunk* and you were alone, when a voice from nowhere told you not to move, ready or not, your machine sleekly lowered itself down to you, aiming its killing rays at your tattoo, your site. At the planned distance, it stopped and made an unearthly and ungodly sound for an unbearable time.

I kept thinking I was falling off the slab, it seemed so narrow and high. I tried to be funny, I told myself I was testing for a part in Stanley Kubrick's new film. I tried thinking of beautiful, peaceful things— Vermeer, for example. At last I tried meditation, I imagined diving into the cool pool at La Fiorentina and swimming laps, and those laps helped, I finally learned exactly how many laps it took to get me through my times under the machine.

The men and women who operated the machines were pleasant but disinterested; they had been doing that work long enough to build up protection from heartbreak—except when they were working with children, they were so sweet with children, they were clever with them.

They didn't care that I entered the room dressed, that I undressed and redressed in the corner and never seemed to have a green robe. I left sneaking out the back corridor that wound its way through small offices assigned to nurses and doctors and people handling paperwork stacked into towers so that I could avoid walking through the waiting room again. I was not heroic. I learned early on that I could wait for my turn on the machine in the outer hall talking to the office on the wall phone instead of sitting in the waiting room with my fellow humans, and when my name was called I walked through the waiting room with blinders.

But I couldn't ignore the nausea and the diarrhea. Radiation to the stomach area can give you squalls of nausea, battering waves of sickness so awful you cannot move, you cannot breathe, you must lie absolutely still for hours, anything else is unthinkable. I had a long sofa at the office and I spent a lot of time on it, helpless. Treatments were scheduled to give you free weekends for rest and relief. One weekend I tried flying to Dallas and then on to our ranch in Arizona with Harding and Katy, the house had been redecorated and I was longing to see it, I must have been out of my mind. The dispensary at Memorial gave me a large bottle of paregoric, a strong potion of opium and camphor that is reputed to be able to bring Niagara Falls to a halt. It did nothing for me. For me, the side effects of the treatments were pitiless. But I never cried, because I saw just how lucky I was.

When the series of treatments was completed it took only a few days to pull myself together. "You'll be fine now," the radiation supervisor told me. "You may get something else one day, but not this." Whereupon the Watcher slipped back into its normal position, Mary Wells returned, flew off to Detroit to see Henry, worked with Jimmy Morgan and began trying to balance three airlines' advertising accounts.

The second cancer announced its arrival in my dreams. 1986 was a pressure-cooker year. In 1984 the agency had run out of room at the General Motors Building and moved to a sleek building that looked like a surfer wave in Hawaii, everybody called it the Avon building until Sheldon Solow, the developer, had Ivan Chermayeff erect a Mondrianish red-and-black sculpture that read "9" so fervently everybody forgot Avon. The agency continued to grow beyond anybody's expectations, and by 1986 we were short of space again and I was tramping around the area looking for more. We kept the Benson & Hedges account, the Pan Am Shuttle took off to cheers and Ken beautifully orchestrated the agency's presentations to Oil of Olay and Cadbury Schweppes, winning those large and complicated accounts. In 1986 Charlie and Ken and I spent so much time sitting side by side on airlines we stopped talking to one another and just grunted, we walked the aisles for exercise and closed our eyes when we saw trays coming.

Charlie began to fantasize that we should sell the agency for enough money so that he could move to the Hamptons and write books or plays. Ever since he married lovely Susan, a television producer at Doyle Dane Bernbach, and ever since they adopted Mary and Sam, my long-distance godchildren, he had been fantasizing about ways to work at home. "Are we having fun now?" he would ask me in a loud whisper, squeezed into his 727 seat, staring down at something that usually looked like a plate of dog food. "I'm tired of bringing out the best in other people," he would tell me as if confiding a secret. Ken would roll his eyes at me and grin. He was never tired. And I would never admit that I was.

Once, on our way back from Chicago, between laps up and down the aisle, I leaned against the bulkhead and looked back at the seedy, dirty, airless plane, at the pale, comatose passengers and at Charlie and Ken, aging before my eyes, and thought for the first time since the first day of Wells Rich Greene, "This is ugly, this is boring—is this it?" The trouble was that the three of us were entrepreneurs, very good at producing miracles for clients, very good at managing talented people, very good at communication. But by 1986 it was already obvious to everyone in the industry that the future was in size, Interpublic and Saatchi–style global ambition, acquisitions and mergers, partnerships, media buying power, and understanding the Japanese. Or pretending to. We had to change; at least I had to change. I had to start thinking the way our largest clients thought about the growth of their companies. The advertising business was clearly going to end up a handful of global giants. Either Wells Rich Greene began an aggressive acquisition program immediately or became an active partner in another agency's merger program or we should be pragmatic, focus on our creative reputation and shrink into a boutique designed to prove that small and personal was better than big when it comes to creative advertising. I had to get on my horse. Where was my will, I wondered. In my mind that day, leaning against the bulkhead of the plane, the horse and I looked at each other, it snorted, "Come on, let's go, let's run." I gave it a pat. "OK," I said, yawning, "soon."

Harding thought the time had come to have a dog in our life, so on one of my trips to our London office I drove out of the city to meet the Thomas Boardmans, head of the Cavalier King Charles Spaniel Club. The Boardmans had two puppies they planned to keep, to show and breed, but I sent flowers to Mrs. Boardman and candy, a Chanel handbag and scarf and she finally gave up, she loves her dogs and she decided that if we wanted the boys that much they would be getting good parents. Harding picked them up, two gorgeous fluffy little princes, and led them on little leads onto a private plane to take them to La Fiorentina. The stewardess fed them breast of chicken by hand and they never looked back. We called them Pasteque and Sandia, that's watermelon in French and Spanish—watermelon is Harding's favorite sweet. But there are no names in any language sweet enough for them, for what they meant to us.

We took them everywhere. We took them to Bermuda to have

Sandia and Pasteque, our beloved King Charles spaniels.

Thanksgiving with Ed and Sandy Acker and it was there that I had my first dream that was so dimensionally rich, so much realer than real, it made life seem to be the dream. In the dream I stood at the top of the steps of a medical amphitheater, there were viewers sitting here and there in the balcony, their attention was on two operating tables on the stage below, each of the tables held a motionless body covered with a sheet. I began taking firm, steady steps down to the stage and the operating tables, I was leaning on the arm of a faceless friend. The arm felt as real to me in every way as any human arm I have ever touched except that it was stronger, more supportive. It was, as they say, as firm as a rock. I was not frightened and in a curious way I was also awake to the dream and aware of the special experience. My friend on whom I leaned said as we got near the operating tables, "I wonder if we know anyone here." I sat up in my bed in Bermuda and wondered who it was that was going to die.

I guess the Lord must be in New York City

Returning from Bermuda, I took a long relaxing bath fragrant with lavender oil, not a thought in my head, when the 23rd Psalm scrolled up before my eyes. I wasn't absolutely certain it was the 23rd Psalm, but Harding assured me that what I repeated to him was in fact the 23rd. "He maketh me to lie down in green pastures; he leadeth me beside the still waters. He restoreth my soul."

Later, on the verge of falling asleep, I had a vision of a group of white kites soaring upwards in the sky. One, flying alone, was hurrying to join the group, and I was surprised by a clear cold certainty that I was going to die. I heard a voice say firmly, "Soon." I'd had enough visions in my everyday life to know they could be meaningful, so this nightmarish intuition terrified me, I forced it away from me, tried to ignore it, but I had a growing sense of something black and heavy in my air. I didn't say anything to Harding about it and he went off the next morning to Mustique to handle problems that had come up at the home we were building on the island.

I took Pasteque and Sandia for a walk before going to bed, it was bitter cold and ice was forming on the street, but on my way back to my building I was wrapped in a warm cloak of pale yellow glowing light and I had a vivid impression of being deeply loved. I lay in bed wondering about that light and then I had a terrible vision, I saw Harding alone in a bedroom like ours, he wore a robe and he was pacing. One of our daughters opened his door and brought him a tray. "Here's dinner, Dad," she said. I understood that I had died and Harding was being looked after by the children. That idea shocked me out of the fog I was settling into, the idea of abandoning Harding to the children in his older years seemed the worst possible betrayal, and as though I was drowning I fought my way up through something dark and primitive and powerful and screamed, "No!" And I heard, "You have the choice. Pray." I had no experience praying; I learned that night that when you need to pray, it comes naturally.

Kathie was having a mammogram the next morning. She had insisted that I have one, too, and it revealed I had a small, suspicious lump in my left breast and a shadow near the nodes under my left arm. "What do you think?" I asked the radiologist. I felt drunk. "Well, I'm not crazy about it," she said. "I'll send this X-ray to your doctor, you better find out about it right away." I told her to send it to Isadore Rosenfeld, who has been my doctor and great friend since he was introduced to me as a gift by Mary Lasker. Kathie and I staggered to the office, she leaned against my door all day, ready for anything. I called Harding, I could feel him, horrified, at the other end of the phone. We agreed I would make an appointment for us with Isadore the next morning and he would fly to New York immediately.

So I was going to die. It was over. My office was engulfed in bad-smelling doom. Everything in me turned off. I sat for hours there without moving, feeling nothing, thinking nothing, like a slug under heavy morphine, somewhere way past fear. Charlie and I were scheduled to go to the shoot of a commercial I had written later in the afternoon, but I couldn't raise a foot, a finger. I was paralyzed.

Then I experienced something that is indescribable, or at least I am not able to describe it, and after that I started to smile, I couldn't stop smiling, I couldn't control my mouth and my entire body started shaking, I couldn't control it, either. I knew that I was going to live and that my prayer was being answered by God.

Charlie and I went to the shoot, and on the way, in the dark of the car, I was still smiling and shaking, but he was talking and didn't notice. One of Procter & Gamble's advertising directors was at the shoot. I managed to discuss the commercial with him intelligently and then left for home to wait for Harding. I planned to tell him, first thing, about the experience I'd had, but when he arrived he was too worried, too frantic, so I waited.

Isadore Rosenfeld came to the apartment early in the morning to discuss the mammogram. He had met with friends at Memorial Hospital and had set up an appointment for me with the breast surgeon they thought was the best in the world, Dr. David Kinne. The mammogram was an excellent one, all the doctors agreed, there was no question about the tumor. The issue was whether to do a biopsy first and then make a decision or to go ahead and remove my breast immediately to be safer than safe. I could have a new breast constructed. Harding said to me, "What's the rush? Let's go slowly for Christ's sake, let's be careful, let's see the biopsy results." David Kinne agreed. "You may be a perfect candidate for a lumpectomy, Mrs. Lawrence, and we are seeing signs that for some women lumpectomy survival statistics are the best. I agree you should have a biopsy first and then we can make an informed decision."

Listening to so many smart, kind and concerned men talk about removing a part of my body made me very tired. I have never been wearier, but once again, on the cusp of sleep, I had a vision. I was in a room with all the doctors. I was busy closing all the windows and locking them, I suppose to keep death outside, when Dr. Kinne began doing one of those Greek dances that men do on Greek islands in movies. All the other doctors joined in and I did, too, and for a few minutes we were a Greek chorus line. It seemed clear that I was to get into step with Dr. Kinne and his crew at Memorial.

I wanted to pull the quilt over my head and sleep for days. I won-

dered where the Watcher in me had gone, I was going through this cancer experience with my brain and my emotions on panic alert, with my
heart in my mouth, tears threatening to flood any minute and in an
energy brownout. I was also hypersensitive to Wells Rich Greene, to
keeping my health private, so I had a bit of paranoia as well. We were
making a new business presentation to Rand Araskog at ITT that afternoon, the Araskogs were family friends, and at lunch one day Rand told
my daughter Katy he was looking for a new advertising agency. Katy,
very much her mother's girl, said, "You should talk to Mom about
Wells Rich Greene!" He did, and this was our day to make the presentation for his account. The presentation went well, Rand was making
radical changes in the company and we had a good feeling for them and
for him. Back in my office I called David Kinne's office and learned that
the biopsy was scheduled to be done at Memorial Hospital in a couple
of days.

I had my first night song that night. I was awakened at three, my
mind was filled with music, not Beethoven's Ninth, but a Frank Sinatra
kind of love song—it was insistent, I couldn't refuse, so I listened carefully and knew some of the words. Love songs arrived from time to time
for a few years, always waking me in the middle of the night, always
insistent. "We are communicating with music," my dream friend with
the strong arm told me in a later dream—I never saw his face. Sometimes I knew the words, other times I couldn't remember the exact
words so I bought the sheet music.

There were moments when I questioned whether I was having a
nervous breakdown. I certainly did feel that I had begun to live in two
worlds. I was enthralled with the unexpected possibility of a relationship with God, and it seemed to me that my life had changed fundamentally very suddenly. But it was the operations and the radiation
treatments that I dreaded. I was groggy when I awakened in my room
at Memorial after the biopsy, Linda Wachner was talking to Harding
near the window, they both looked haggard and they looked worse
when David Kinne came in with his report that the tumor was malignant. I was about to give up and just pass out but then I heard him say
that the tumor was even smaller than he had expected, it may have even

shrunk, he said with a smile, so the biopsy had become, in effect, a lumpectomy and I had had my operation. That was good news and I struggled to sit up. "You will have to have a few lymph nodes removed from under your arm for testing and a small series of radiation treatments to kill any cancer cells that could be left in the area—they're prophylactic treatments, to be safe," he said. "With cancer caught this early, if a lumpectomy is followed by radiation the survival rates are as good as if you had a modified radical mastectomy. You're lucky, Mrs. Lawrence." He was beaming, he was so pleased for me. I glanced in the mirror across from the bed, I looked exactly as if I'd had belladonna, the pupils of my eyes were gigantic. Oh my God, I was thinking, those machines.

We scheduled the operation to remove and test the lymph nodes for after the holidays, January 12. I had time to begin the agency's traditional holiday season. In those sweet innocent years nobody was politically correct, so we always had spectacular Christmas trees decorated as if the agency was filled with children, which it certainly was. We sent clients green baskets stuffed with red tulips. Every year the baskets were hand painted a different design. I don't think anyone ever threw away their baskets. Once, after we were dramatically divorced from a client, I got the saddest note from a wife who missed her basket of tulips. I put her back on the list and was rewarded with photographs she took of her family gathered around each year's basket of tulips. "You will never know how much I love these tulips," she wrote year after year after year.

Our Christmas parties were lush, we didn't think small, we dressed up all the rooms until they shimmered, we had music, sometimes bossa nova with caipirinhas on crushed ice with little red pestles to mash the juice out of the limes, as well as Christmas carols with hot toddies. We had presents for everybody and everybody's secretary, always something that was a minor thrill, the first year that Swatch watches appeared everybody received five and, to their amusement, one was bright orange. We had professional kitchens and a French chef and smart waiters and we served haute cuisine. We had 100 percent acceptances even from clients in Los Angeles and Seattle. Kathie and I were good at glamour, we had only three disasters in 30 years. Once, after a Chinese lunch we gave for P&G's top executives, we served fortune cookies that turned out to have raunchy dirty jokes in them. Our friends at Procter rolled on the floor laughing at our mortification. Once, idiotically, we gave Cartier pens to the secretaries at Bic; the secretaries were pleased but the Bic executives were not.

Executives from Japanese companies never knew what to make of a woman running a big, international advertising agency. They just blanked me out, didn't see me. When Toyota came to lunch with us I had mood rings on their plates. Mood rings had been around for about five minutes in America and you had to have a bookie to buy them, they were so hot. The Toyota executives were very polite and they examined their rings carefully, thanked me politely, rewrapped them and put them in their pockets—utterly mystified. It is impossible to explain a mood ring and keep your dignity. After that lunch I learned to discipline my enthusiasms with Japanese businessmen.

Kathie became so important in her friendships with our clients and in her PR role at the agency that she created a world of her own there, and Catherine Lebow, who had been my secretary, became my collaborator and will be, probably, until my last breath. She was born a can-do girl. Absolutely nothing is impossible. In one of my loving moments I got the idea of taping my favorite love songs and putting them into cassette holders labeled *The Love Collection* and sending them to clients. It was fun choosing the songs, a little Sinatra here and a little Carly Simon there—the headings throughout this book are songs from *The Love Collection.* We paid a small fortune to a disc jockey to group them onto cassettes. But when he delivered them I couldn't get them into my office—there were thousands of those cassettes that had to be assembled and placed into snazzy *Love Collection* holders. Catherine pulled all the women she could find at the agency into my office and set up a factory line, including Phyllis Wagner, who, although still the wife of the former mayor at the time, was not too grand to roll up her sleeves and fill cassette cases with love songs for clients. One of my fondest memories of Wells Rich Greene is the vision of those talented women stashing love songs into holders, all of them singing "Enough Is Enough" with Donna Summer and Barbra Streisand at the top of their lungs, directed energetically by Catherine Lebow.

We went to the hospital for the operation to remove my nodes in the predawn; the stars were shining. It felt as though the entire hospital was still on a holiday when Harding and I went from floor to floor carrying my little suitcase, looking for someone to have me, to take my nodes. My knees were jelly those days. Back-to-back operations, back-to-back anesthesia is a scourge on your nervous system and, no matter what you tell yourself, your subconscious makes your body jump up and down on the bed the second time they wheel you to the operating room. I knew the test results would be OK because the night before I entered the hospital I was awakened by a loud hissing noise in my ears, I thought something had gone wrong with the heating system in the apartment, and then I heard a ringing shout, "All systems go! All systems go!" "Are you trying to give me a nervous breakdown?" I yelled at whatever it was. Then I realized the meaning of "All systems go," an expression I had never heard anyone actually say before, and I was, again, profoundly grateful for the help I was receiving.

Still, that operation was not a piece of cake. Seven of us were parked in a hall without heating outside the operating rooms, there were six men who lay on their backs staring at the ceiling, not breathing, I thought maybe they were ghosts already, and me, cold and clammy, jumping up and down, chattering, circulation frozen to a halt, heart pounding like steel drums, rolling into the same operating room I'd seen a short time before with the same masked faces, the same pairs of eyes looking down into mine and then—out.

The nodes tested fine, but there is a period of healing, of therapy following an incision to remove nodes, when you must exercise your arm, which refuses to be raised above your shoulder. You must crawl with your fingers up a wall for days until, if you really truly persist, you can reach as high as you could before. I joined a group of other women in the hospital each day to practice the exercises. Under happier circumstances it would have been like taking a tai chi class, but most of the women were struggling with depression as well as their uncooperative arms. One young woman had had both breasts removed because breast cancer had killed her mother and sister. She radiated courage and leadership and she stimulated all the self-doubting, mournful women to reach higher, to exercise with enthusiasm, to smile back at her and to look forward to cheery days. She was gorgeous. But there was one quiet, colorless woman who worried me, she had given up on herself. I inquired about her and learned that she had nursed her husband who had cancer for years, he had died just a few days after she learned that she had breast cancer. "The awful part is that she was just fired from her job," the supervisor on my floor told me. "Her employer didn't give a damn. After all her husband's medical expenses and now hers, she's broke. She lives way out of town, I don't know how she'll get in here for radiation treatments, I'm afraid she won't have them." Harding and I made arrangements to help her and I've heard from her every year since then. After her treatments she moved to be near her daughter in California, she looks like a different person, cancer-free, radiantly alive, and having fun as a blonde.

Surviving cancer intensifies your awareness of other people's problems and makes you want to help everyone in the world who needs help. That is how Marie Williams came into my life, through a hospital in New York I visited that had an experimental program for children with AIDS. The women in charge of the program told me that Marie was the closest they had come to knowing a saint, she was acting as a foster parent for a few small children that she brought to the hospital each day to take part in the program. Marie is the kind of woman who, when given the responsibility for a newborn baby found in a toilet who has AIDS and was born drug-addicted, puts the baby on like a backpack and wears the baby next to her own skin for a year or two without pause and produces a miracle, HIV positive turns to HIV negative. She always has a passel of sick children, some that she has adopted; when I asked her what she needed most she told me she needed a home big enough to live in with all the children she could handle, so that's what she got. But Marie should have many mansions, and many children should have Marie.

Thirty radiation treatments were scheduled for me and nothing had changed, in early 1987 hospitals hadn't yet transformed cancer treatment centers with good psychology and smart decorating, they were still boiling the same green robes, the waiting rooms were still heartbreaking. I knew the ropes, I slipped in and out of the machine room and out the back door, I swam laps on the table, and discovered to my enormous relief, thanksgiving and joy that radiation of the breast did not give me nausea or diarrhea, I could work normally. Kathie went with Harding to Mustique to help him entertain clients and friends in our new house, they said I was caught up in a new business presentation and couldn't leave the agency, although we did tell a few very close friends about the radiation treatments.

Some cats know

A s though I had taken truth serum, I suddenly could not stop asking myself about the experiences I was having. "What is going on?" I would ask the air. "Tell me what is going on," I said to the ceiling. "What is this?" I didn't get an answer but I did get a direction. In a vivid dream, I appeared to myself, close-up, in the nightgown I was wearing, and eye to eye my dream self said to me, "You are a Gnostic seer. You *know.*" I got out of bed, went to Webster and looked under N. Then my brain connected "Gnostic," a new word to me, with "agnostic," as my father described himself the one and only time he and my mother talked about religion. My religious background was limited to a few years of Sunday school when I was five or six. There were no courses in religious theology at the Neighborhood Playhouse School of Theatre or at the drama school of Carnegie Tech, no courses in psychology, either. English, literature, history, dance, speech, yes, but nothing that informed me about the unconscious.

I had read the *Times,* the *Wall Street Journal* and the *Herald Tribune* every day of my business life, so I was broadly though scantily educated. I knew that American evangelical religions were growing. I'd read polls that reported 30 percent to 50 percent of Americans believed they had had a religio-mystical experience; 45 percent of them said they had felt as though they had become completely one with God and the universe. The Gallup Poll reported that one out of five described the "presence" as an inner voice, guidance, help from God, a guardian angel or conscience. Most of these people never spoke about their experiences to anyone for fear of being thought crazy. Equally large numbers believed that without any doubt they had seen an angel, and tales of near-death experiences, all strikingly similar, were being collected by Elisabeth Kübler-Ross and other doctors.

I'd read that Buddhism and the kabbalah were thriving on both coasts, LSD had its enthusiasts as a way to go up the mountain and intensify your senses, Catholics valued a pious life and good works more than miracles when making saints, William James was the rational man to read about religious experience, and that although Freud regarded religion as nonsense, Jung believed it to be authentic and had had religious experiences himself.

But then, I'd read that much and knew that little about Einstein's theory and his own unusually shaped inferior parietal lobules. I'd read about the human genome's biochemical code, the Andromeda galaxy and that we are all probably made of stardust, that Stephen Hawking's *Brief History of Time* was a best-seller so I could probably understand it if I would just give it a try. I read that although many books have been written about consciousness, no one knows what it is, and that biology offers a more dynamic, thrilling career in the future than technology, sociology, psychology or pharmacology.

So as a newspaper and magazine reader I had a skimmer's education about such things. I got the gist and had the gab but no meaningful understanding. In my world of advertising executives, lawyers and investment bankers, rock stars and movie executives, journalists and a sprinkling of European aristocracy nobody I knew had religious experiences. Nobody I knew discussed theology. Nobody I knew was politically philosophic, either; a person's identity had to do with what they did, not their religious or political views. Careers had become theological. A career was not about making money, unless you made it in truckloads, it was about following your bliss, expressing your creative self, and although what you bought said a lot about your style, there was an overriding morality that ran neck and neck with hard work and allowed you to feel casual about the money you made and spent. Our morality was semireligious. The people I knew talked about injustice and fraud and cruelty and how to help people—not God or the self or the spirit. No one was talking about the unconscious, either, in the eighties, when analysis was going out of style.

My Webster's dictionary was short and sweet about gnosis: "esoteric knowledge of spiritual truth held by the ancient Gnostics to be essential to salvation" was all I could find. That bit of information sent me out searching for more. I found *The Gnostic Religion* by Hans Jonas in a psychology bookstore and learned that Gnosticism was a religious movement of the earliest Christian times in which knowledge of God is a revelationary experience. Inner illumination replaces rational argument and theory. Its event in the soul transforms the knower by making him a participant in divine existence. The relation of knowing is mutual; being known occurs at the same time as knowing.

In Gnostic thinking God is alien to the universe which it did not create and does not govern. The universe is the work of archons. It is a vast prison, suspended within cosmic spheres, and its intent is to enslave us with appetites and passions that make up our psyche and prevent us from escaping and returning to God. However, hiding in our souls is the spirit, sparks of divine substance lost by a transcendent God. The sparks fell into the world and hid in our souls and bodies. They are unconscious of themselves, numb, asleep, ignorant. God sends a messenger to awaken them and give them knowledge of themselves. This transcendent God is unknown in the world and can't be discovered without such a revelation—gnosis. Equipped with gnosis, the souls after death travel upwards, leaving behind, at each cosmic sphere, their human appetites and passions. Once they manage to shed all of them and are no longer able to be enticed, they reach and reunite with the God beyond the world. This process of retrieving all the individual sparks is God's way of restoring its own lost wholeness.

In the mood I was in, that psychology bookstore was a candy store, and I loaded up with *Memories, Dreams, Reflections* and almost everything else Jung wrote, William James's *Varieties of Religious Experience,* Evelyn Underhill's *Mysticism,* Jacob Needleman's *Heart of Philosophy,* some Emerson, Augustine's *Confessions,* some Rumi, Huxley and a couple of books that attempted to make sense of Eastern religions in English.

"I need time off, I have to go away for a little while," I told Charlie and Ken. We were clutching the arms of our seats on a roller-coaster ride in a February storm on our way back from the P&G budget meetings in Cincinnati. I had just finished all the radiation and my nerves were threadbare, I winced at the La Brea tar pits we were bouncing through, and I must have looked really bad because Ken said gently, "That's great, you should go away and rest until you feel better, don't worry about anything, we'll handle things. I promise I'll send you detailed Marygrams every week." I packed up my books believing they would open the door to a new world for me and Harding and I went, first, to Mustique, and from there, to France.

Our first night in Mustique another vision arrived. I was on a miniature island, an old man appeared in a small boat and said to me, "He wants you to think about it." And so, at a mature age, beginning with my suitcase full of religious and psychology books, and with inner help, I began to educate myself, to think reflectively and to grow a little in some of the places where I had holes. Tom Stoppard says, in *The Real Thing,* that happiness is equilibrium. "Shift your weight," he says. I think he's right. I needed balancing, a leveling of the mind, to become as happy as I am. I don't mean to reduce spirituality to psychotherapy, although after the operation, after the experiences began, I thought I should discuss them with a few psychiatrists, so I had a meeting with a Freudian, a Jungian, an all-purpose modernist and with Dr. Lawrence LeShan, a research psychologist and psychotherapist. Dr. LeShan, in his earlier years, while a scientific skeptic, had been put to work with one of America's great psychics, Eileen Garrett. Working with Mrs. Garrett opened his mind and for years he investigated paranormal phenomena while studying consciousness. Recently he was honored with the Norman Cousins Award for his work with cancer patients in which he helps them mobilize their immune systems. Larry helped me to steady myself and to welcome the experiences. After hearing about them he mused, "Perhaps one side of you has developed as much as it can and the other side needs developing and it's erupting."

Cancer and the experiences it brought on gave me a precious inner life, opened my mind to all possibilities and taught me to think in a clearer way that has been strengthening. In one of my books I read that if you haven't died, you haven't lived. Cancer is horrific but it can also be an opportunity, a breakthrough to freedom, a door to a new life.

They can't take that away from me

Henry and Ed and Harding had never been to the running of the bulls in Pamplona, so that summer of 1987, Henry's last summer, we all reread Hemingway and boarded Henry's private 727 and flew off to Spain, where Ford matters and we were treated warmly. The festival itself is stunning. Everyone in town puts on white shirts with red scarves and then crowds into Pamplona's little squares moving like a single-cell organism—right hands up all together now, fly that red scarf, left hands up all together now, fly that red scarf and yell your lungs out! The Ford folk positioned us on balconies so that we would be in the beating heart of it all. Kate shot movies and got a Miró blur of red and white and black and then of maniacal bulls pounding down a skinny street tossing pretend matadors right and left to the crowd's hysterical delight. But those bulls were so pathetic in their tantrums, we were surprised at how upset we were for them and left the bullring almost immediately, wondering why we were surprised. Henry's executives were sympathetic and took us to an enchanting, old-fashioned Basque picnic and we returned to La Fiorentina clicking castanets like children, stamping our feet and howling those Spanish love wails—everyone but Henry. Henry was tired while we were in Spain, back at

La Fiorentina he took long naps; then things went wrong and in the fall, to everyone's horror, he died.

When people who are very dear to you die they don't leave. Henry never leaves Kate's heart or her mind for a second, of course, but some element of him moved into my mind, too, and into Harding's. He just moved in and made himself at home and appears in my memory when he wants to. When my father died he took up residence in my mind, too, he brought all his flowers with him, he comes front and center fairly often. And when Bob Six died he became part of Harding's mind gang and mine. That seems to be one of life's bittersweet blessings, having a head full of people you love who appear to have left the earth but who have taken up residence in your head and influence your decisions, give you ideas, color your emotions, enlarge your lovingness, expand your intelligence, give an edge to your sense of humor.

I went back to work. Wells Rich Greene was hustling the MCI account, one of the few thrilling Wild West accounts on the loose at the time, still small enough to have a sense of adventure. MCI was originally a microwave service for truckers. AT&T tried to rain on their parade, making a colossal mistake because the leader of MCI, Bill McGowan, had the nerve to sue them. Bill McGowan had the nerve of Darth Vader, the will of Teddy Roosevelt, the cool of Bill Gates and the strength of Hercules. He sued and sued AT&T and he won and was rewarded with immortality—look at MCI today. It developed into a serious competitor in the telephone business and the account, which had been at Benton & Bowles, was put up for review. Ken had hired a top-notch executive, Dick Hopple, who, before joining Wells Rich Greene, had worked on the MCI account at Benton & Bowles, and Dick got us into the playoffs.

MCI executives had a reputation for being a bunch of cowboy lawyers who rode antennas instead of horses—our kind of folks—and the advertising manager was a sizzling smartgirl who knew her way around teletechnology, Judy Ranzer. She put her arms around us and taught us the business. People told me she liked Dick Hopple's red suspenders, but they always say that about good-looking agency guys who wear lipstick-red suspenders. I thought Judy was a fervently ambitious lass, much too savvy to ever be silly; she had worked with Dick and she knew he would move heaven and earth to help her have a success and she was right.

MCI's old advertising had taken the position of the little guy in the business who attacks the big guy by biting his ankles. Its reputation started out iffy, it hadn't been too reliable, but it shaped up sharply and was offering strong, competitive service. We thought it was time for MCI to grow up and act real, like an aggressive and significant competitor in the telephone business. The problem was that nobody was shopping for new phone services when MCI came on, there was AT&T and Sprint, people were satisfied, nobody was hungry. We had to stretch for reasons why anyone should seriously shop for a new service. But we found some reasonably good reasons and then Charlie, Bob Wilvers and Charlie Carlson created a campaign of commercials that were like short takes from an avant-garde French movie—very intimate—in which people discussed telephone issues as intensely as the French would discuss a potential love affair. The style of those first commercials was oddly alluring for telephone advertising, and it was magnetic, it held you fast to your set, you didn't breathe, you wanted to hear every word those actors said about why MCI was superior to AT&T. The theme line was "Let us show you." MCI liked that positioning a lot but had trouble imagining the style, it was very new for advertising, so Paul Schulman, our production wonder man and creative manager, compressed a six-week production job into four days and the agency was able to present an Oscar-worthy movie as a sample commercial. After they saw it the MCI executives left the room to chat about us, and then Judy Ranzer returned and said, "Congratulations, partners!" We were in.

Bill McGowan loved those commercials and the agency. He was married to a sparkling woman who ran an airline catering business in Chicago, Sue Ling Gin, he brought her to La Fiorentina and mesmerized us with his *Star Wars* visions of MCI's future. Bert Roberts made many of MCI's dreams come true, but Bill was the rainmaker and he was a fearless man. He had somebody else's heart, one of the very first heart transplants, and he was very proud of it. He surprised me one

evening when he was running his hands over the many books I wa.
accumulating on religious experience, psychology, biology, theologies,
genetics, cognitive science, smart machines, physics—he'd read many
of them, he read everything that came his way, he was an information
gatherer. "You have a new heart, too, don't you, Mary?" he said. "Well,
you must never refuse an offer from yourself, you must always say yes."
I wasn't sure I understood him, I was dying to explore it, but others
joined us and we left for New York before we could talk again. We
made a lunch date to have that talk, but he became ill and soon he
pulled back at MCI and out of our sight.

"I can't bear it, I just can't bear it," I said to Charlie and then sat back
on the floor, where I'd been before the telephone call I had from Ed
Acker. "Ed's going to leave Pan Am, he's going to take early retirement." The whole agency mourned Ed's leaving. Pan Am had been such
a personal account, we'd felt like jugglers or as if we were all on the high
swings together—one step ahead of the sheriff sometimes, maybe, but
Pan Am and Wells Rich Greene had rung up a long string of successes,
producing a lot of revenue in a bad era for airlines. The pilots' union had
been taken over by a young, high-testosterone group who wanted to
find a buyer for Pan Am with deep enough pockets to guarantee their
salaries and pensions. They were feisty and they had made the other
unions nervous. Things had been higgledy-piggledy for a while. Ed
proposed to the board that Pan Am be split into two pieces, the share-
holders to get the Pan Am Shuttle and Pan Am World Services while
the airline itself was sold or merged. Jay Pritzker was ready to buy the
airline and merge it into Braniff subject to reasonable concessions from
the unions, but some of those unions were up to their ears in serendip-
ity, so nothing happened. The airline was getting to be like a dysfunc-
tional family; eventually the more serious unions agreed to agree but
they wanted prisoners, their deal specified that all the management had
to leave. Rebel employee groups make themselves feel good with ges-
tures like that. Ed thought the basic agreement was a good one for the
airline, so he left. Tom Plaskett became the new chairman.

I met with Tom Plaskett one evening at Pan Am. He didn't like me
before he walked into the room. I didn't like him after I walked out of

he room. There were ghosts of happy days in that room but I ignored them, I had salaries to pay, and I made a serious effort with him—even after he said, "Ed Acker made a lot of mistakes here," even after he said, "I haven't seen any great advertising thinking here." A few weeks later he offered Wells Rich Greene a new contract but with a financial agreement that the agency couldn't possibly afford, so we resigned the account.

We got up, shook ourselves off and started all over again. Ken had wisely kept the relationship he'd had with Jim O'Donnell at Continental Airlines. Jim was still at Continental, the senior vice-president of marketing programs, he and Ken liked each other. "What do you think, should I ask him to lunch to talk about the future?" Ken asked me. "Absolutely," I said. He did and they started meeting frequently, they developed a mutual philosophy and a friendship; then we all went to Houston and had a good meeting with Frank Lorenzo and we were given the Continental Airlines account.

Candy man

Ken was having a great success in the eighties. He had moved the Oil of Olay account smoothly through its acquisition by P&G and it was developing into a major piece of business at the agency. He was also keeping Procter convinced that Pringles was worth their time and resources and then, with tenacity, sensitivity, intelligence and good old-fashioned professional lust he won a big part of the enormous IBM account. I watched him do that from the sidelines with great admiration but also with a new awareness of the mutability of an agency's personality. I had not lifted a finger about IBM when it started an agency review, I thought IBM was deaf, dumb and blind and in a permanent state of denial and that it could not be given a new life by any advertising agency. Ken saw it as a magnificent global account that needed professional servicing, not a new life, and as Wells Rich Greene was capable of exquisite servicing, IBM would do well to choose us. "It's prestigious, it's profitable, everybody in town wants the account and so do I," he told me, his eyes glittering as they do when he's smitten.

At first he didn't know how to get into the running. IBM started out looking at Grey, Lintas, McCann, BBDO, JWT, Y&R, O&M and then, out of the blue, Ken received a call from Jim Reilly, the man in charge of IBM's advertising programs and its agency hunt. Ken made a leap onto some trapeze in his mind that gave him an IBM view of the agency and plucked a perfect cast of characters for Jim Reilly and then psyched himself up for him. There was no way Jim Reilly would not love Ken Olshan in the mood Ken was in, I guessed. From the minute Jim stepped out of the elevator to visit Wells Rich Greene Ken began taking notes, assiduously, of Jim's thoughts. He never lost one of those notes, either, and they were like flashlights finding a path through the jungles of our writers' minds so that Wells Rich Greene's creative work was always based firmly on Jim Reilly's thinking. Of course Jim liked it and us and especially Ken. When an IBM executive who was one of Jim's associates took a phone call in Ken's office and, upon seeing an Atari unit on his table, said to Ken quietly, "Get rid of that now," Ken told me about it and said, "I think I did it, I think I got us IBM." "You certainly did," I agreed.

With a little help from Charlie! A few months later I gave Charlie credit for winning the Hertz business—with a little help from Ken! Corralled, the two of them worked together seamlessly and powerfully. But I wasn't sure they had undying loyalty to one another. I didn't know, if I removed my eyes and hands, if they would bond in a way that would keep Wells Rich Greene's spaceship headed towards Mars and thrilling. That was the principal reason I met with Bill Weed, who was representing BDDP, a French agency that wanted to talk to us about some sort of working relationship. I liked what I knew about BDDP, I'd seen photographs of the principals, they had a cool, young, sophisticated style, and I'd heard that the agency's work was outstanding. There was something spicy about them, they gave off a new-wave-gunslinger confidence. I had the buoyant idea that they might be ideal international partners for Charlie and Ken and all the gifted people at Wells Rich Greene in a future, global agency if I continued to pull back as I had since my last operation. Or they might simply provide a better way for us to expand internationally.

So I accepted Bill Weed's suggestion of having coffee. Bill is a sincere, credible businessman. He persuaded me that BDDP was worth knowing more about, so I introduced him to Charlie and Ken and we decided that Ken was the right one to meet Jean-Claude Boulet, the president and chief executive officer of BDDP.

Ken took Jean-Claude to lunch at La Côte Basque and came back twinkling. "I like him. He's smart. I think we should learn more about the agency." He went to Paris and met the partners, Jean-Marie Dru and Marie-Catherine Dupuy, who had once been married and, as Ken said, "still have a nice warmth between them." He met Petit and Baum and Nolet, the other leading executives, and the heads of all the associate agencies, and he liked them all. He learned about the clients, the work, the creative awards, the philosophy, the energy, the ambitions. And he was impressed. "There are a couple of different relationships we can have with them," he reported to Charlie and me. "But what they really want to do now is to buy the controlling interest and merge the companies. They are ambitious, they're doing very well, but they know they need to have a major agency in the United States. The ball is in our court. What do we want to do? This is pretty sudden. Is this good for everybody here? How does it work for our clients? We need to study this deal client by client. My advice is to take this seriously now and decide one thing or another. We don't have time for schmoozing and games. What do you want to do, Mary?"

There had been a few times in the past when I had toyed with the idea of selling my interest in Wells Rich Greene and finding another life to live. But the investors who considered taking an interest in the agency would have been outside partners and they insisted that I run it. There was no point in selling my interest if I couldn't move on and do something new, and anyway, I think I was just stretching, getting a little fresh air, I wasn't serious.

I also had a long-running conversation with the Saatchis. It started in the early seventies when Wells Rich Greene needed an agency in London to handle TWA advertising in Europe. The day I approached Maurice about our acquiring his agency, Saatchi & Saatchi, it had practically no paying clients at all and Wells Rich Greene was roaring. Maurice was very young but he looked like a wise owl in his big glasses when he peered at me and said a tad theatrically, "Charles and I can't sell our agency to you, Mary, but we would consider a 50-50 merger and we would agree to your name being first." I laughed, but I understood the mystique right away and I thought Saatchi & Saatchi was marvelous.

Over the years we talked from time to time, and once, in the early eighties, we talked seriously when I believed that Charlie and Ken and I and Charles and Maurice and Martin Sorrell (who was still with them) could create an advertising DreamWorks. Maurice was always going around telling the press that "Saatchi & Saatchi could do the impossible." I thought that all of us together very likely could. We had a short, exciting negotiation, and while we were talking Maurice fell in love with Cap Ferrat, so he and his wife, fabulous Josephine Hart, bought a villa down the bay. The bubble burst, we never got together, but we are loving neighbors. Now when we sit over a long balmy dinner on an August night in the south of France, Maurice quotes T. S. Eliot to me:

> *Footfalls echo in the memory*
> *Down the passage which we did not take*
> *Towards the door we never opened*
> *Into the rose-garden . . .*

Josephine always snorts in her lovely Irish way and reminds us that "neither of you knows anything about poetry, I am the one who knows T. S. Eliot here." True. But Maurice and I know something about the loss of agencies and what might have been.

Ken had breakfast at the Park Lane with Jean-Claude Boulet to start a negotiation, to see where that took us. And I bored through my ambiguousness to face up to what I wanted to do. I loved the advertising business because everybody in it was always learning something, we learned in order to get clients and we learned in order to keep clients and we learned so that we would be ready for anything. We had to be totally alive, alert to everything everywhere, so that our marketing ideas and our advertising and our style were empathetic with consumers every second of every day. The slightest sloth, the slightest complacency and our empathy soured and we fell from grace. We knew that consciously but we also knew it in our bones and in our memories and in our spirits. We may not have been intellectuals but we were very smart. And we were a loving people, the most successful of us were passionate people, we loved our work, we loved our clients, we loved each other—some of the people I loved most on this earth were at Wells Rich Greene. Learning and loving was a heady way to live. Why would I ever leave such a business?

Rebus sic santibus. Circumstances have changed. That was the mantra my Latin teacher gave me in high school. She hated Latin, she taught it as if it was spelling, so it was never relevant, but she sneaked us the answers to her tests so we appeared to be good students and she appeared to be a great teacher. She wasn't stupid, she gave us Latin mantras so we could spout them when our parents visited us in class. We put on brilliant performances for parents. But all I retained from her class was *rebus sic santibus.*

And they *had* changed in the advertising business by 1990. Clients' businesses were getting vaster. They weren't just global, they were on their way to becoming universal. With all that reach they had to become more and more hierarchical, and top executives could no longer feel their fingers or their toes. CEOs weren't looking to their advertising agencies for salvation; clients didn't ask them for miracles, didn't expect any magic. They looked to their own financial resources, acquisitions, groups, systems, networks, to ever-increasing size to increase their value. If they looked to their agencies for outstanding talent, it was usually for symbolic advertising startling enough to get talked about for a week or two. More and more they were looking to their agencies for one-world marketing, one-stop shopping, intelligently integrated services and, above all, sophisticated, organizational expertise.

There were still smaller businesses, mostly retail and fashion companies, that relished a big idea and advertising profound enough to make an important difference to their bottom line. But in those cases advertising was becoming more of a hot art, and still is. As for the Internet, in 1990, looking down the long tunnel at the advertising possibilities in the Internet made scintillating chitchat, but broadband Webcasting and the Net's potential interactivity were dreams that are only now becoming opportunities for advertising—there was no leaping into the Internet to create an advertising world there in 1990.

Breaking up is hard to do

I drove out to the Hamptons for the air, it was out of season, lonesome, wonderful, it looked like a Barbra Streisand movie beach, those big grey waves, they helped because I think better on a stage. What was wrong with me that I was seriously considering giving up my interest in Wells Rich Greene, it was my baby! I had loved the agency so much when it was a tightrope with a possible big drop, when I could leap into the wild blue yonder with an idea that shattered expectations and traditions and sometimes, sensibilities. I had loved the birthing process of trying to produce an idea or advertising so magical it enlarged a client's business forever. I admitted to myself that I probably had the same kind of egomania that Formula One drivers driving for McLaren had, the same need to win over odds.

I threw some sand around the East Hampton beach and tried to love the idea of amassing a gargantuan Wells Rich Greene. It would think different, I would lure Steven Jobs and Shawn Fanning to help us with technology that would enable us to see and understand people from one corner of the universe to the other with an intimacy advertising had never known. I would lure Steven Spielberg to help us clone their needs with advertising that reached and hypnotized their true childlike inner selves. George Lucas would join Charlie and me and we would become the Einsteins of interactive advertising, offering experiential shopping that anticipated every desire so that by the time a shopper whispered, "Yes, yes, yes, I'll buy it," he or she would be exhausted, drenched with experience, sated, like after sex.

Ken and I would soar, transcending borders and cultures and politics. We would learn how to smell money, to feel where it was, we would attract bonds to our very selves so that we were always able to buy. We would be able to moneyspeak in every financial community from New York to Timbuktu and eventually we would acquire everybody and Wells Rich Greene would become the only agency in the world. It would operate in a thousand towers designed by Renzo Piano and Frank Gehry. Every one of them would have a 90-piece orchestra playing Bach in the lobby to keep our brains fit.

No. No. No. It was true that I was focused enough to be a field general, so I could take Wells Rich Greene to the summit if need be, but, unfortunately, my heart was in palpable advertising creation, the immediacy of it, the theatre in it, and I was lapidarian about every two-bit ad that came out of Wells Rich Greene. I was an old-fashioned girl, not a globalist. Anyway, the wind had come up, my nose was running and my feet were freezing in the dank sand, I was going to catch a cold. "Listen, kid," I said to myself, "there are infinite possibilities in life— let the people who love to globalize globalize, go out and find yourself a new thrill."

What pushed me over the edge, though, and made me sell and leave the agency was that I was getting in the way of people who couldn't fully develop their own selves as long as I was there, no matter what title or authority they had. I was too much of a symbol. Me in my big boots is the way I thought of it. I had started looking at Charlie and Ken and a fairly large tribe of exceptional Wells Rich Greeners, including my children, guiltily—they could not experience the freedom to be all I knew they could be at that agency as long as it was Mary's agency. Ultimately, the Mariology at Wells Rich Greene, which had created its success, would stifle the spirit of the place, and I didn't want to do that. Besides, whether I liked it or not, Wells Rich

Greene simply had to move on and globalize. So why not in a splendid marriage with the vivid talents of the French at BDDP?

C'est si bon

Ken and Jean-Pierre became the producers of a new show and the architects of a new agency and their meetings were exciting for them, they met in some rare stratosphere and returned all rosy and shining. I thought those two were made in heaven for one another, and Charlie and Jean-Marie were enthusiastic and supportive. Catherine Lebow is French and was our French connection. It was worrisome that the American executives didn't speak a word of French. However, the French executives spoke colloquial English. And it was worrisome that the French had a European business sensibility and a decidedly different view of life—there is nothing quite like the French view of life. But I thought the prize was so great and the people were so intelligent they would merge their different cultures come hell or high water.

The BDDP executives had no doubt they could afford what the merger would cost them. There was never a question in my mind about the financial values when we got to those discussions, but I felt strange defending my requirements, so I asked Harding to handle my case. It wasn't complicated, but, as in all negotiations, there were sticky moments, and a few times I suggested that the deal should be put off until another, later day. I was never 100 percent sure I was doing the right thing. I kept wanting to put my arms around Wells Rich Greene and squeeze and hug it, I could have forgotten all about that merger. Considering the monsoons, typhoons and hurricanes that blew in later, I know how infuriating that statement could be to people at BDDP, but it is the fact.

Ken and Charlie, Jean-Claude and his wife and Jean-Marie met with Harding and me at our home on Mustique, one of the ultimate private places, to consider each client of ours and theirs and how we would tell them of our plans. We talked in depth about the people who were vital to Wells Rich Greene, what we would say to each of them and how to create the necessary announcements. We were full of confidence, ambition and affection those days in Mustique. We returned to New York and on April 12, 1990, all together, smiles in our eyes, music in our voices, a dance in our step, we held a press conference at the agency and presented Wells BDDP to the advertising world.

I didn't hang around; that would have defeated everybody's purpose. When the elevator door closed I was left with the image of enough positive energy soaring among the executives of Wells BDDP to lift that agency to mega dimensions. Harding and I went to France, where we had blissful days in our pool, with our view. We had long lazy mornings on our Riva heading into glistening seas to St. Tropez and lunch in shacks on Pamploma beach, heading back after the sun dropped, staying far from shore so we could strip and sit high on the backs of the Riva seats like gulls, flying home through purple mist, not a thought between us, feeling freedom like medals for all those years on planes.

We went to our house in Mustique, a beautiful island, clean, safe, filled with interesting people who have interesting guests, and good friends like Jo and Brian Alexander, who direct things there. Mustique became the family home, the family would visit at the slightest hint and all of our friends came, even Edmond Safra, bless his heart, was persuaded to sail there with Lily, although he ambled through the sand with his cellular and his bank in his hand.

I so enjoyed spending more time with my family. I was there when Katy married a young Englishman, Lawrence Bryan, and when Pamela married a young Frenchman, Benoit Lombard. I was the supermom of weddings, planning roses and lilies and bridesmaids' bouquets and champagne feasts. I was there to buy bridal lingerie and to sit for hours as Hubert de Givenchy created ravishingly embellished white wedding dresses of frills and lace and rivulets of tulle, to walk proudly down the aisle and to cry when Harding gave our daughters' hands to those young men. When the babies arrived, I was there to greet Katy's Christina and Jonathan and Pamela's Olivia and Victoria. On occasion I had to be forcibly removed from the scene. I was there to help the family settle into their homes. Harding's son, Jim, and his son, Slater, moved to horse country in upper New York. State and his wife, Betsy, and their sons, Dylan and Wilson, moved to early-American Connecticut. Harding's daughter, Debbie, the family's chic New Yorker, moved into a glamorous, postmodern, Zen apartment in Manhattan. Katy's family moved to a horse farm on the New Jersey Shore, and Pam and her family chose the European life and moved to Geneva.

I was there when my mother, who had been losing her eyesight, could no longer read, and no matter what Pam or Katy or Catherine or Kathie or I came up with, we could never replace that absolute necessity in her life, so when she had heart fibrillations that dragged her in and out of hospitals and felt such a profound loss of hope, I was able to spend a lot of time with her, to hold her hand and squeeze it, and to say sweet nothings. One morning in France, very early, I heard a voice say, "She is ready to leave the world. She is dying. Go now." I got up and reached New York just in time for one last communication between us. We had promised each other that whoever died first would find a way to reassure the other that it was OK, all was well. Six months after Mother died she came to me in something bigger than a dream. She stood at the bottom of my bed, wearing a dress I knew, looking at me with great strength so that I would be alert and she said, "Mary, I thought you should know that Kass died." Kass was one of my friends when I was ten. I had not seen her or thought of her or mentioned her to my mother or anyone else in over 45 years. I read it as a fine code. So, I have absolutely no doubt at all that it is OK and all is well with my mother.

A few weeks later I fingered through the closet of memorabilia Mother and I kept and enjoyed together, mostly gowns I had worn through the years when I was dressing up so often, they delighted my mother. There was the Norman Norell mermaid dress of blue sequins I wore to the White House the evening I was seated next to President Marcos of the Philippines, who was the guest of honor at a dinner in the Rose Garden. Lady Bird Johnson had invited me to spend the night in the White House because I was working with Lyndon, trying to humanize his speeches. Harding introduced me to Lyndon, who looked on him as one of his family, and I spent weeks of afternoons on the Truman Balcony trying hard to produce more charisma in Lyndon's way of speaking. Lady Bird thought our efforts were funny as well as futile. We gave up, but by then we were friends. I called my mother from my bedroom in the White House but she was so certain the FBI was bugging the phones she wouldn't talk. "Shhhhh," she said, "shhhhh."

Lyndon once told me he thought I was so smart to have married Harding. So did Clare Boothe Luce. Another gown in the closet, a Halston chiffon, was the one I wore in Hawaii the evening Clare made a toast to me, saying, "I've always thought that Mary Wells was so smart—so smart to have married that man!" My mother's favorites, all the elegant Givenchys, were worn escorting Aileen Mehle ("Suzy"), who is like a sister, to costume galas at the Metropolitan. Aileen started writing in her column that I was the world's advertising genius the first day of Wells Rich Greene and never stopped—who knows how many clients of mine were brainwashed by Aileen! I wore those gowns to big parties like the ones Estée Lauder gave in her Manhattan town house. Estée always called me before her parties and said, "Now, darling, I know you don't have good jewelry, but this is an important evening so wear a nice dress." I wore them to receive a steady stream of awards, too, like the New Yorkers for New York Award, the Ohio Governor's Award and the Copywriters Hall of Fame Award. Mother was usually with me when I received an award. I still have the gowns. I'm told they are worth a pretty penny but they mean the world to me.

I didn't mourn the agency, partly because of the astonishing amount of detail that goes into domestic life but also because I didn't leave the advertising business with pallbearers. I moved on to live a new life, have new adventures, learn new tricks. But woven into the fabric of my daughters' marriages and the arrival of babies and exploring the world with Harding were telephone calls from almost everyone in New York, who wanted me to know that the honeymoon between Wells Rich Greene and BDDP, the promise to love, honor and endure, was in trouble.

The recession in the early nineties hurt the advertising industry on both sides of the Atlantic as clients cut their budgets, reducing agency income. When Continental Airlines filed for Chapter 11, leaving the agency an unsecured creditor with $7 million in media bills, Ken moved mountains to get the debt paid, but that scare and the reduced income all around changed the mood of the merger. The early confidence the principals had in each other began to unravel. I imagine BDDP and its investors had counted on Wells Rich Greene to pay for its own acquisition. It was close to a billion-dollar company with income and a profit that could be expected to carry the deal. No doubt everyone had the best intentions, but the executives in New York began to resent BDDP's relentless pursuit of income. "That's all they care about—they come in with their bags, fill them up and leave without a word about clients or the work or new business."

Jean-Marie Dru, in whom I had and have great faith, attended Pamela's wedding with his wife, and Jean-Claude Boulet made a pleasant house call. But that is all I saw of BDDP after I left the agency. I certainly didn't blame them, I was all too familiar with the fates of former chairmen and I assumed they had their own ideas about how to run the agency. Except that no one ever learned what those ideas were. When Wells BDDP began to lose clients and IBM pulled all of its advertising from the agency as well as from its other agencies around the world and put it all into one agency, Ogilvy, the executives of BDDP seemed to freeze. Some of them told the press they were intimidated by Ken Olshan and were afraid to upset him or his close relationships with clients. I asked myself why, if BDDP wasn't afraid to demand more from Ken in financial meetings, why would they be afraid to move in and claim the agency they had acquired? Considering the cost of the deal, the French government's kisses still warm on their cheeks, and their banker's support, they were expected to play a major role in New York. I had thought the deal was important enough to them that they would arrive at WRG in a full dress parade with elephants, tigers and all their big guns.

If they *had* moved in, if they had taken Ken and Charlie into their arms, bonded both sides' considerable talents, and gone to work seriously and with devotion on client problems, they would have learned quickly who was important to whom. They could have animated the agency with an exciting new culture, as originally planned, or at least helped reincarnate the old culture. Entitlement doesn't come automatically with a bank loan.

But they didn't come. To the employees of the former Wells Rich Greene the French principals appeared to be hirers, not doers. And as working hard is an act of love in America, they produced a mysterious vacuum at an agency used to high expectations of prodigious talented turn out. Jean-Marie and his wife spent a few months in New York. When they left, BDDP's Nick Baum, whose parents had been Americans, became what he called "the bridge," when what was needed was a new society, a new vision that was as French as it was American. That is what everyone had been expecting.

The French don't travel, of course. They are notorious as disinterested tourists. Why would anyone leave France? Even the *oiseaux* chirp prettier in France, they love to tell you. I heard that the BDDP executives could not persuade their families to move to America, and that's possible. I once read that French people go on Zoloft for separation anxiety when they leave the country. If you enjoy France as I do, you can sympathize. But, then, why make such an expensive and important acquisition in America?

Wells BDDP got some healthy new business, but the original accounts continued to leave. For a time the telephone calls I received seemed disoriented, the agency seemed to forget who it was—because it was *not* the reign of Mary, it was a history of groundbreaking television advertising created by pioneering thinkers with tremendous talent. Yet for a short time consultants and therapists were called in to find out *who it was.* God, it was impossible not to scream. In the privacy of my bedroom I screamed in my mind at a lot of people. However, I was fully aware that it would be churlish, to say the least, to sell your stock for a goodly sum, walk away and then complain. It was their agency, after all, and the total silence from Paris was chastening, it told me to be quiet. The Queen was dead.

Relationships finally got so feverish that Jean-Marie telephoned Ken in 1995 and fired him—unfortunately, on Rosh Hashana, a mistake in timing that suggested staggering insensitivity to Wells Rich Greene's clients and staff, a shame because Jean-Marie is not an insensitive man. But even at that pivotal moment the French did not move in to love and hold the remaining clients. Instead they hired a replacement for Ken, a mysterious choice, Frank Assumma, who had no previous relationships with the clients and had not demonstrated at any time in his career that he understood the particular creative culture of the agency.

Ron Moore, who was the chairman of Midas, said to the press, "After the agency was purchased we increasingly saw a highly driven service organization with a personal touch become a highly commercial financial concern."

Bob Wheling, the senior vice-president of market research for Procter & Gamble, said to the press, "We value long-term relationships but you have to have relationships with human beings."

After Ken was fired, Procter & Gamble executives called and asked to see Wells BDDP managers at eight a.m. the following Tuesday. Jean-Marie, Jean-Claude, Frank Assumma and Wells Rich Greene's illustrious Paula Forman attended the meeting. The P&G people put their arms around Paula and said, indicating the others, "Tell us, Paula, who *are* these people?"

It was downhill from there: $453 million in billings spiraled out the door between 1995 and 1998, and the agency closed its doors in May 1998. Procter & Gamble stood firm until January; what little was left in the final days was sold to Omnicom after a brief affair with an English group, GGT.

Charlie and Stan moved with their accounts to operate as a separate agency, Moss/Dragoti Advertising, under the banner of Doyle Dane Bernbach, which is under the banner of Omnicom. Ken is, among other things, on Saatchi & Saatchi's board of directors because Procter & Gamble wanted to continue to have his good advice. Kathie married Peter Weisman, and when she saw that the agency was going down she couldn't bear it and left, but Catherine, who married Seth Rosenberg, stayed until the bitter end hoping to help as the agency's French connection.

I kept thinking how fragile creative businesses are, especially advertising agencies—the names may stay on the door and the new talent may be good, but the spirit of place isn't the same. Wells Rich Greene was once an agency filled with exciting, talented people who were passionately in love with advertising, that was the spirit of place. It's gone; people have moved on and are forgetting. I am not haunted by the past, but I loved Wells Rich Greene; I thought I would write about it while it was still alive in my head, how it came to be, how it developed, how it was as seen through my eyes.

My collection of books has grown into a library. I continue to read and think about them, on some kind of pilgrim's journey in search of a grain of understanding. I also enjoy the luxury of having time to worry about everything I read in the *Herald Tribune* mornings. I read that some feminists are saying the revolution is over, we have won, women are accepted as congresswomen, chief executive officers, brain surgeons, pilots of 747s and soon, no doubt, as the President of the United States. So we are free, it seems, to watch *Sex and the City* and dress like Carmen Miranda in wedgies and sing "Yes We Have No Bananas" without guilt.

A bee buzzing in my brain that seems to be trapped there wonders that our women's movement stalled at our shores and has not moved on with the same power to such global women's issues as Indian women's dowries and their pyromaniacal mothers-in-law or to Arab and African clitorises or to veils and female priests and rabbis. Such issues are going to require movements as big and smart and muscled as the American women's rights movement.

I read with disappointment that polls report 60 percent or more of young single or married women in America prefer not to work outside the home, would choose smaller, more domestic lives. So now I'm worrying that women are born with bound feet in their brains. Was it Freud who said biology is destiny? I think young women who choose a smaller life are making a mistake. I believe that whether you are a woman or a man you are *supposed* to stretch everything that you are, you are *supposed* to love with all your might, you are *supposed* to have a big life, so that when all is said and done you can say to yourself, with feeling, "I loved my life so much."

These days my psyche is pushing me East. I have never been to India and it is beckoning to me. That bee is still buzzing in my brain about Indian mothers-in-law, so Harding searched and found the name of an agency in the backcountry of Bombay that helps women who are abused by their families when their dowries run out. Indian culture appears to be gentle and spiritual and oriented toward the feminine; I know there is a great deal to learn before I can understand those domestic tragedies. But Bombay is as good a place as any to begin to learn about a country as colorful and sensuous and complicated as India. So now my dreams are increasingly fiery orange and silken pink and fragrant with saffron. Recently the Italian painter Francesco Clemente, who spent much of his life in India, said to me, while painting my portrait, "Beware. India is dangerous. You will lose your heart there and you may never find a way back." Well, I'm not afraid of love, and I have always lived my life full tilt to the wind.

Page numbers in *italics* refer to illustrations.

A NOTE ON THE TYPE

The text of this book was set in Garamond No. 3. It is not a true copy of any of the designs of Claude Garamond (ca. 1480–1561), but an adaptation of his types, which set the European standard for two centuries. It probably owes as much to the designs of Jean Jannon, a Protestant printer working in Sedan in the early seventeenth century, who had worked with Garamond's romans earlier, in Paris, but who was denied their use because of Catholic censorship. Jannon's matrices came into the possession of the Imprimerie nationale, where they were thought to be by Garamond himself, and were so described when the Imprimerie revived the type in 1900. This particular version is based on an adaptation by Morris Fuller Benton.

Composed by North Market Street Graphics, Lancaster, Pennsylvania

Printed and bound by Quebecor Printing, Fairfield, Pennsylvania

Designed by Iris Weinstein

Printed in the United States
By Bookmasters